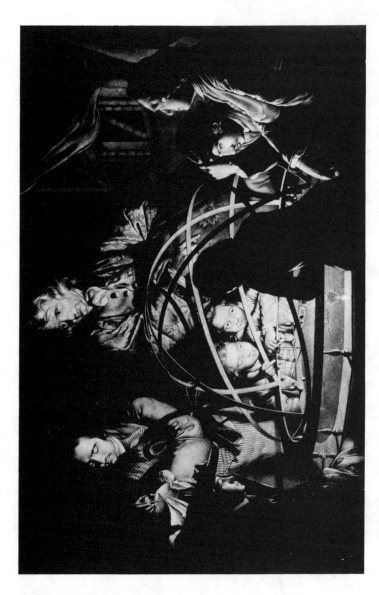

THE ORRERY, engraving by William Pether, after Joseph Wright of Derby, 1768 (Library of Congress).

THE
ENLIGHTENMENT
IN
AMERICA

Ernest Cassara
George Mason University

University Press of America

Lanham • New York • London

Copyright © **1988** by

University Press of America,® Inc.

4720 Boston Way
Lanham, MD 20706

3 Henrietta Street
London WC2E 8LU England

All rights reserved

Printed in the United States of America

British Cataloging in Publication Information Available

© 1975 by G. K. Hall & Co.

Library of Congress Cataloging-in-Publication Data

Cassara, Ernest, 1925–
The Enlightenment in America / Ernest Cassara.
p. cm.
Reprint. Originally published: New York : Twayne, ©1975.
(Twayne's world leaders series : TWLS 50).
Bibliography: p. Includes index.
1. United States—Intellectual life—18th century. 2. Enlightenment.
I. Title. II. Series: Twayne's world leaders series : TWLS 50.
E162.C34   1988   973—dc19   87–31699 CIP
ISBN 0–8191–6769–X (pbk. : alk. paper)

To
Richard O. Hathaway
and
John R. Turner,

Colleagues who have made
the study of history
an enjoyable task.

Contents

About the Author

Preface

Chronology

Introduction   15

1. The Life Style of the Enlightened American   25

2. The Pursuit of Science   49

3. The Rights of Man   68

4. The Science of Government   93

5. The Religion of Humanity   116

6. The Diffusion of Knowledge   145

   Conclusion   169

   Notes and References   173

   Selected Bibliography   191

   Index   201

About the Author

Ernest Cassara is currently professor of history at George Mason University, Fairfax, Virginia, and has served as chairman of the Department of History at that institution. He has previously taught at Tufts University, Albert Schweitzer College, Switzerland, where he also served as Director, and Goddard College, where he served as Dean. Dr. Cassara holds degrees from Tufts and Boston University and has done post-doctoral study at the University of Cambridge. He is presently at work on a research guide to American history which is scheduled for publication in 1975.

Preface

Books on life and thought in eighteenth-century America are plentiful. The Revolutionary period has come in for particular attention, although in recent years scholars have also turned their efforts to such areas as the history of science, the rise of liberal religion, and other topics which heretofore have been relatively neglected. No one to my knowledge, however, has attempted a synthesis of the various facets which made up the Enlightenment in America. This book is a modest effort to help fill this gap.

My dependence on the specialized works referred to above is made clear in the notes and bibliography. In addition, I would like to express my grateful appreciation to those institutions, and their helpful staffs, which have made their research facilities available to me: the American Philosophical Society (especially Dr. George Corner and Mr. Roy Goodman), the Library Company of Philadelphia, the Historical Society of Pennsylvania, the Van Pelt Library of the University of Pennsylvania, the New-York Historical Society, the New York Public Library, the Massachusetts Historical Society (especially Mrs. Fisher), the Houghton and Widener Libraries of Harvard University, the Boston Public Library, the Library of Dickinson College (especially Mrs. Martha C. Slotten), the Library of Congress (especially Milton Kaplan, Prints and Photographs Division), the Fenwick Library of George Mason University, and the Alderman Library of the University of Virginia.

Special words of thanks are due to the George Mason University Foundation which provided a generous grant, making it possible for me to visit the pleasant repositories listed above, and to Mrs. Betty Lockhart who typed the various drafts of this book with unfailing good humor.

ERNEST CASSARA

Chronology

1717	John Wise, *Vindication of the Government of the New-England Churches*, in opposing Presbyterian organization, places democracy of the Congregational churches on a basis of natural rights.
1723	Benjamin Franklin arrives in Philadelphia.
1727	Junto organized by Franklin.
1728	Botanical garden begun by John Bartram near Philadelphia.
1730	Mariner's quadrant invented by Thomas Godfrey.
1731	Pennsylvania Library Company organized by Franklin and Junto.
1732	First issue of *Poor Richard's Almanac* published by Franklin.
1734	Great Awakening begins in New England.
1742	"Pennsylvania Fireplace" (stove) invented by Franklin.
1743	American Philosophical Society formed. (Reorganized in 1769.)
1745	Cadwallader Colden, *An Explication of the First Causes of Action in Matter and of the Cause of Gravitation*.
1749	Academy for Youth established in Philadelphia.
1751	Benjamin Franklin, *Experiments and Observations on Electricity*.
	John Bartram, *Observations on . . . Travels from Pensilvania to Onandaga, Oswego and Lake Ontario in Canada*.
1754	French and Indian War (Seven Years' War) begins.
	Plan of Union [of colonies] by Franklin accepted at Albany Congress, but rejected by colonial legislatures and the British government.
1755	John Winthrop, *Lecture on Earthquakes*.

1761   Observation of the Transit of Venus across the face of the sun by John Winthrop in Newfoundland.

1764   Sugar Act by Parliament establishes principle of taxation of American colonies.

James Otis, *The Rights of the British Colonies Asserted and Proved*, on taxation without representation.

1765   Stamp Act passed by Parliament. American colonies respond with Nonimportation Agreements.

1766   Declaratory Act. Parliament repeals Stamp Act tax but asserts subordination of colonies to crown and Parliament.

1767   Parliament suspends New York Assembly for resisting Quartering Act.

Townshend Acts impose import duties on glass, lead, paint, and tea. Colonists respond with new Nonimportation Agreements.

1768   John Dickinson, *Farmer's Letters* declare Townshend Acts unconstitutional.

1769   Observation of the Transit of Venus across the face of the sun by David Rittenhouse in Norriton, Pennsylvania.

1770   Boston Massacre.

1772   Virginia Society for Promoting Useful Knowledge founded.

1773   Benjamin Rush, *Address . . . on Slave-Keeping*.

Tea Act by Parliament grants East India Company monopoly on trading of tea.

Boston Tea Party.

1774   Coercive ("Intolerable") Acts close port of Boston, abrogate Massachusetts Charter, etc.

Thomas Jefferson, *A Summary View of the Rights of British America*.

First Continental Congress gathers at Philadelphia.

1775   Battles of Lexington and Concord.

Battle of Bunker Hill.

1776   John Adams, *Thoughts on Government*.

Thomas Paine, *Common Sense*.

Virginia Declaration of Rights by George Mason adopted.

	Declaration of Independence.
	Thomas Paine, *The American Crisis*.
1777	Articles of Confederation adopted by Congress. (Finally ratified by states in 1781.)
1778	Franco-American Alliance becomes official and France enters the war against England.
1779	Bills for the More General Diffusion of Knowledge and Establishing Religious Freedom introduced by Jefferson in the Virginia legislature.
1780	French fleet and troops arrive to aid in American Revolution.
	American Academy of Arts and Sciences established in Boston.
	Slavery abolished by Pennsylvania and Massachusetts (followed by other states in following years).
1781	Surrender of Lord Cornwallis at Yorktown, Virginia.
1783	Treaty of Paris ends American Revolution.
1784	James Madison, *Memorial and Remonstrance on the Religious Rights of Man*.
	Ethan Allen, *Reason the Only Oracle of Man*.
	Charles Chauncy, *The Salvation of All Men*.
1785	Thomas Jefferson, *Notes on the State of Virginia*.
1786	Act for Establishing Religious Freedom passed in Virginia.
	Benjamin Rush, *A Plan for the Establishment of Public Schools . . . in Pennsylvania*.
	Shays' Rebellion begins in Massachusetts.
1787	Constitutional Convention at Philadelphia.
	Northwest Ordinance adopted by Congress.
	John Adams, *Defence of the Constitutions of Government of the United States*.
	Alexander Hamilton, James Madison, and John Jay, *The Federalist*.
1789	Benjamin Franklin, *On the Slave Trade*.
	Congress under the new Constitution assembles.
	George Washington inaugurated first President.
1791	Thomas Paine, *The Rights of Man*.
	The Bill of Rights, approved by the states, takes effect.

	William Bartram, *Travels through North & South Carolina, Georgia, East & West Florida, the Cherokee Country of the Chactaws*.
	Benjamin Franklin, *Autobiography* (in part) published posthumously in Paris.
1794	Thomas Paine, *The Age of Reason*.
	Whiskey Rebellion in Pennsylvania, over federal excise tax, suppressed by President Washington.
	Joseph Priestley arrives in America.
1796	John Adams elected President.
1798	Alien and Sedition Acts passed by Congress.
	Virginia and Kentucky Resolutions, written by Madison and Jefferson, declare Alien and Sedition Acts unconstitutional.
1800	Thomas Jefferson elected President.
1803	Louisiana Purchase arranged by Jefferson.
1805	Hosea Ballou, *A Treatise on Atonement*.
1807	Embargo Act passed by Congress at behest of President Jefferson in response to British and French wartime trade restrictions.
1808	African slave trade outlawed by Congress.
	James Madison elected President.
1812	Second war with Britain begins.
	Benjamin Rush, *Diseases of the Mind* (beginning of psychoanalysis).
1816	James Monroe elected President.
1817	American Colonization Society founded to support transportation of Negroes to Africa.
1819	University of Virginia chartered. (Begins operation in 1825.)
	William Ellery Channing, *Unitarian Christianity*, formulates liberal position.
1820	Missouri Compromise admits Maine and Missouri to the Union, maintaining balance of free and slave states.
1823	Monroe Doctrine proclaimed.
1824	John Quincy Adams elected President.
1826	Death of John Adams and Thomas Jefferson, 4 July.

Introduction

THE eighteenth century, notwithstanding all its errors and vices, has been, of all that are past, the most honorable to human nature. Knowledge and virtue were increased and diffused; arts, sciences, useful to men, ameliorating their condition, were improved more than in any former equal period.

—*John Adams*[1]

The men of the eighteenth century looked out on a very different world than that of their predecessors. The world view propounded by the Alexandrian astronomer Claudius Ptolemaeus (second century A.D.), which represented the earth as at the center of the universe, had dominated the Christian West for centuries. With the work of Copernicus, as refined by Kepler, Brahe, Galileo, and Newton in the seventeenth and early eighteenth centuries, the earth took its place as one of a number of planets revolving in space around the sun. The challenge faced by the men of the eighteenth century was to make sense of this heliocentric universe and to fit human beings and other creatures into a new intellectual context.

The Judeo-Christian interpretation of the meaning of life necessarily underwent reexamination, along with many other supposedly settled truths. Although relatively few men were inclined to abandon the concept of God, the traditional Christian interpretation of His nature and of His dealings with mankind underwent intense scrutiny. The orthodox Christian theology was more easy to accept in a Ptolemaic cosmos in which man was at the center of all things—after all, what was there to distract God from playing a continuing role on center stage of such a universe?—but it was much less easy to believe in a Copernican universe in which man inhabited one of many planets—and an infinitesimally tiny one at that—spinning through space. The God of this kind of cosmos surely had other things than the day-to-day strivings of the sons of Adam to preoccupy Him.

The thinking man of the eighteenth century might not have felt the same security as the man of what has been called the Age of Faith, but he did not shrink from the challenge of exploration. There were many pieces to fit into place in this great cosmic puzzle, and he went about the task with zest.

Empiricism became the new mode of investigation. Knowledge was to be gained by observation rather than received on the authority of past, nonempirical centuries. Theorizing, furthermore, must be based on observed fact only.

Fundamental to the empirical approach was the psychology of the English physician and philosopher, John Locke.[2] Locke stated that men gain their entire knowledge of the world through their senses. The mind of an infant coming into the world is a *tabula rasa*, and it is by impressions received through the senses and combined in the mind that ideas are formed.

No age can live without some presuppositions, however. Men of the Enlightenment believed firmly in the trustworthiness of nature. Nature was the handiwork of a deity who revealed Himself in the very orderliness of creation. Because God had endowed him with the instrument of reason, man was able to observe in the universe order, regularity, and predictability.

He did not live a life of pure reason, however. His emotions pulled him in various directions, so reason was not foolproof. If it were, he would be able to understand the total workings of the Creator. As optimistic as men of the Enlightenment may have been, they never presumed such a possibility. They were reasonable enough to distrust their own reason and were content to live within its limitations.

With all its limitations, however, reason held the key to a better understanding of the Master Craftsman Himself. They believed they could read in God's handiwork traces of His nature, which they pronounced to be benevolent. The less flattering characterizations of God as changeable and fickle, to be found in the Judeo-Christian Scriptures, were rejected as defamatory. Furthermore, they believed their benevolent deity was maligned by the Christian doctrines of original sin and atonement. It was unreasonable to believe that God would burden all men through the centuries with guilt resulting from the supposed transgression of Adam. They contemplated with horror the notion that God had sent His own son to earth to die in behalf of the transgressor. Such an immoral act, which would be roundly condemned if perpetrated by a human father, could not be attributed to a benevolent God.

This new vision of God had implications for their interpretation of the nature of man, as well. Contrary to Christian theology, they asserted that human nature is basically good. Man commits sins and must be held responsible for them, but these are genuine mistakes of judgment and cannot be linked to the alleged Fall of Adam. Man improves in his moral life, as he does in the other concerns of life: he learns from experience.

Life for these men of the eighteenth century was not lived in a medieval vale of tears but was buoyed by an optimism not to be found in previous centuries of Western history. This new optimism accounts for the growth of the idea of progress. Man was no longer conceived to be wallowing in a slough of despond but had the opportunity and ability to improve his own lot on earth and to make things better still for his children. Through the use of reason and through scientific advance the earth could be transformed into a very different place than it had been in previous, unenlightened ages.

Men's belief in the benevolence of the deity also influenced the development of the idea of the natural rights of man. The eighteenth century saw the almost complete erosion of the doctrine of the divine right of kings. The deity had not delegated authority to the crowned head of a nation—a king did not rule by "divine right"—but rather each person, by virtue of his humanity, possessed rights which were rooted in the nature of things. When man entered into a state of society, that is, when he became party to a "social contract," he surrendered some of his natural rights to government so that the rights of all could be protected. If and when a government was corrupted and became tyrannous, the people reserved the right to withdraw from the particular social contract and to enter into a new one. The classic expression of this proposition is found in the American Declaration of Independence. Jefferson proclaimed in glowing terms that "all men are created equal" and are endowed by nature's God with certain rights which, because they are rooted in the nature of things, cannot be denied them. When such an attempt is made, as the leaders of the American Revolutionary cause claimed was the case, revolution is justified.

Since the Creator endowed him with such rights, it is not unreasonable that He would expect man to strive to measure up to his responsibility. Where in previous Christian ages this might best be done by submission to the guidance of an authoritarian church and state, among the men of the Enlightenment it was assumed that the individual, with his reasoning ability, could live a life of virtue without such interference. Striving to achieve virtue becomes a central concern, for it is in such an effort that one can best express one's thanks to the benevolent deity.

The tenets briefly summarized above were held on both sides of the ocean, since the Enlightenment was a transatlantic intellectual movement. The question may arise as to whether we are justified in separating out for treatment the intellectual developments in America. Certainly the Americans were a colonial people with all that that designation implies. They were heavily dependent on Britain, the Mother Country of the dominant ethnic group. American manufactories were in a primitive state, where they existed at all. This was the result of British policy and the colonists did not think to question it during much of the period with which we are to deal. British mercantile policy further severely limited the possibility that the Americans would be able to open new markets for their raw materials beyond the borders of the empire.

Intellectually, too, the Americans were dependent to a great extent on the Old World, reading European books and periodicals and publishing relatively few of their own. Intellectual historians can point, also, to a lag in the movement of ideas from east to west. This is understandable purely in terms of the difficulty of communication, an ocean journey taking several months under favorable circumstances. But the historian implies more than a communications lag. The assumption is that the movement of ideas was from east to west and not, to any great extent, in the reverse direction.

Furthermore, the dramatis personae of the American Enlightenment were not always American in origin. For example, Dr. Cadwallader Colden, New York physician and politician, with diverse scientific interests, was born and educated in Scotland but established his career in America. We face a greater problem in a

person such as Dr. Joseph Priestley. That distinguished clergyman made his major contributions while in his native England.
But when English hysteria over his support of the French Revolution caused him to consider flight to Pennsylvania the better
part of valor in 1794, he brought his Nonconformist attitudes in
religion and politics with him. In America he continued writing
and publishing controversial historical works dealing with the rise
of the Christian church, which caused disquiet among the orthodox in religion. His outspoken support of the rising Jeffersonian Republican Party, however, threatened him more seriously.
He had it on no less an authority than President John Adams that
he would be in danger of being deported under the Alien Act of
1798, should he not refrain from further comment on American
political questions.[3] Priestley, although he never became a
naturalized citizen, escaped further harassment. Delighting in the
election of his appreciative friend Thomas Jefferson to the presidency in 1800, he continued his activities without fear of further
political repression until his death in 1804. An emigré such as
Priestley obviously complicates the task of isolating elements
which can be clearly labeled as belonging to an American Enlightenment.

One further example will suffice. After migrating to America
with the encouragement of Benjamin Franklin, Thomas Paine
gave unstinting service to the republican cause. His *Common
Sense* (1776) is said to have been responsible for converting many
to the cause of revolution, including respected figures such as
George Washington. The *Crisis Papers*, the first of which he
wrote in 1776 on a drumhead by the light of a campfire as
Washington's forces retreated across New Jersey and American
fortunes in war were at their lowest ebb, were responsible for
rousing a new burst of patriotic fervor and determination.

With the completion of the war, Paine turned his attention to
invention and traveled to Britain and France to promote his design of an iron bridge. In England he was caught up in the same
hysteria which engulfed Priestley; and in France, because of what
were considered too moderate views, he almost met his end on
the guillotine at the hands of the extremists. Paine returned to
the United States in 1802, no hero, however, because his vigorous attack on Christianity in the *Age of Reason* (1794) had
poisoned minds against him.

Should these men be considered Americans for the purposes of this study? Colden and Paine, yes, since they spent their most important years in America. Priestley, no, since his significant researches in science, history, and theology were made before he migrated. The movement of a large number of immigrants to the New World in this period obviously complicates the task of isolating elements that can be labeled distinctively American. Despite this difficulty, however, it can be shown that American contributions to this intellectual movement were significantly different enough from the European to warrant separate study.

There was a peculiar flavor to the American Enlightenment due to the natural environment in which it took place and due to the intellectual heritage of the Americans. When Thomas Jefferson acceded to the request of a French diplomat to supply information about his native land, he felt it best to begin his *Notes on the State of Virginia* with an extensive description of the natural environment. Compared to well-populated Europe, America was a wild, unsettled territory. Americans had much to learn about this vast new continent. It would have been impossible for Jefferson to write of the inhabitants, their economy, their social arrangements, without first explaining the lay of the land: the location of the rivers in relation to each other, the location of the mountains and valleys, the quality of the soil, and the nature of the climate. Only then could Jefferson's European readers comprehend the settlement pattern of the people and all that flowed from it.

Americans were anxious to share with each other and with Europeans news and information of discoveries they had made. The correspondence of Dr. Cadwallader Colden in New York and Dr. William Douglass in Boston is filled with details concerning the flora and fauna they had observed. This was equally true of the former's correspondence with Dr. Alexander Garden in Charleston. Up and down the continent, these men enjoyed a sense of discovery that was qualitatively different from the experience of long-settled Europeans. Although in the work of astronomy, physics, and chemistry Americans and Europeans had much to learn together, in geography, flora, and fauna the Americans discovered much that was unique. Colden in New York and John Bartram in Philadelphia supplied observations, sketches, and actual seeds and plants to their European correspondents. Carolus Linnaeus provided a new system of classification to the Western world. Colden, Bartram, and others applied the system in American botanical exploration, much to the satisfaction of the distinguished Swedish scientist. The travels of John Bartram and his son William into frontier areas of the United States were reported in widely read accounts.

The distinctiveness of America extended beyond the virgin nature of its territory to the psychological make-up of the Americans themselves. Although they were heavily dependent on the Old World, there grew in America, from the beginnings of colonial settlement, a seed which would eventually flower into the movement for independence. The seed was planted by the Puritans when they settled New England in the seventeenth century. In his sermon "The Model of Christian Charity," preached aboard the *Arabella* as it headed for the New World, Governor John Winthrop had called for the founding of a "city upon a hill" which, in its steadfast devotion to the word and ways of God, would serve as a model for the world to emulate.

The sense of mission which has ever since been a peculiar aspect of the American's mental make-up stems from these Puritan beginnings. It is to be observed, also, in a secularized form in the attitudes of Jefferson and his contemporaries toward the Old World. When they saw the corruption of political life and the misery of the poverty-stricken masses of the cities of Europe, they were convinced of the moral superiority of the inhabitants of the New World. As much as Jefferson may have been enthralled by the glories of Europe's cultural past, he was convinced that the future lay with America. The Old World was played out; the New was on the wave of the future. Not suffering from centuries of encrusted evils, America could offer the friend of liberty not only a haven but also the opportunity to participate in the building of a new, virtuous civilization. When J. Hector St. John de Crèvecoeur wrote of the American as a "new man,"[4] he was reflecting a widely held view.

Another of the distinctive contributions of the Americans to the Enlightenment was the political justification for the Revolution which broke out in 1775–76. The natural rights doctrine became the justification for the rebellion against George III and his ministers. The American Revolution was the word become flesh. But more important from the point of view of this volume was the apologia set forth by the erstwhile colonials in the many productions which flowed from the press both before and after that stirring event.

Equally important for Enlightenment thought was the frame of government which emerged from the Constitutional Convention at Philadelphia in 1787. The document produced by that assembly contained a skillful balancing of political theory with practical political fact. An intense campaign was waged to win acceptance for the form of government proposed. The *Federalist Papers* of Hamilton, Madison, and Jay spoke to the issues raised in New York and elsewhere by foes of the new Constitution, but they put these issues in a context which related them to the preoccupations of the political animal since the days of ancient Greece. The debate over a specific political situation called forth one of the great political documents of all time.

One of the unique features of the Constitution, as amended in the first few years of experience, was the Bill of Rights. Many of the rights described were the product of long Anglo-Saxon evolution. But to be noted among them was an innovation at that time exclusively American. Against all the experience of the Old World, but growing out of American events passed through the fires of enlightened thought, was the provision for separation of church and state. To many this was a hazardous experiment which was bound to fail. The experiment not only did not fail but it proved wrong the prevailing European view that the fabric of society could not be maintained without an intimate relationship between leaders spiritual and temporal.

In summary, then, it can be said that the thinkers of the Enlightenment in America made a distinctive contribution which is worthy of examination in and of itself. This is the justification for what follows in the various chapters of this book.

It is one of the assumptions of the historian that generalizations are vital if any sense is to be made of the past. This is especially true in the writing of intellectual history. In generalizing, however, we inevitably run the risk of distortion. The views summarized above as characteristic of the Enlightenment were not held by all thinking persons of the period. That all enlightened men and women, to take but one of several possible examples, were Deists is not true, as will emerge in chapter 5. But there was a common attitude toward the use of reason in religious matters shared by all who can be considered members of this movement. We will try to make the distinctions necessary to save us from distortions as we deal with each of our topics, but too many caveats along the way would make the writing of any history impossible.

It is also incumbent on the intellectual historian to relate movements of thought to movements of body. Ideas do not develop in a vacuum but grow out of the confrontation of an individual with other men and the events of his time. The effort will be made to relate thought to action but in such a way that this volume does not become a history of the times. However rewarding such an effort might be, the author is not prepared to undertake the task in the space assigned and doubts that if he did his editor and publisher would look on such an effort with complacency. Therefore, it will be necessary at times to hop, skip and jump over the period with which we are dealing. It may be that the chronological table included will become a more integral part of this book than is sometimes true in similar efforts.

It would be neat and compact if providence had provided that the American Enlightenment begin on 1 January 1700 and conclude on December 31, 1799. But such cooperation is more than the harried historian can expect. Thus, we confront the problem of providing reasonable terminal dates for this study. For reasons which will appear in the context of the story, a reasonable *terminus a quo* would be the second decade of the eighteenth century. The *terminus ad quem* adopted here is the year 1826—a date so late that it may seem odd to some. But enlightened ideas continued to have an impact in several areas of American life well into the nineteenth century. It is chosen, also, for sentimental reasons. On 4 July of that year, in one of the great coincidences of American history, John Adams, ninety-one, and Thomas Jefferson, eighty-three, died within a few hours of each other. Americans read great significance into this occurrence on the fiftieth anniversary of the Declaration of Independence. The Adams-Jefferson correspondence, one of the remarkable exchanges of history, had continued until April of that year. While these men —great minds of the Enlightenment—still were about the work of dissecting the accomplishments of the eighteenth century, who can say that the American Enlightenment was dead?

Something should be said about the method of treatment of the sources for this study. Whenever possible, printed sources are cited in the notes, since they are more readily available to the student. When manuscripts are cited, the repositories where they rest are given. At the risk of losing a certain amount of the charm of the eighteenth century, the capitalization and punctuation of the sources have been made consistent with present-day practice, although the eccentricities of spelling have been left as in the originals. In some manuscripts punctuation is nonexistent. In such cases it has quietly been supplied, without the use of *sic*.

What follows is not intended as an apologia for the Enlightenment in America. But lest it not become obvious due to his attempt to maintain a judicious stance above the battle, so to speak, the author should make it clear that he did not choose the words of John Adams—a man not noted for easy optimism —which head this introduction without some thought of their significance.

CHAPTER 1

The Life Style of the
Enlightened American

L IFE is of no value but as it brings us gratifications. Among the most
valuable of these is rational society. It informs the mind, sweetens
the temper, chears our spirits, and promotes health.

—*Thomas Jefferson*[1]

The British American colonies in the eighteenth century were
strung along the Atlantic seaboard. In the hundred or so years
since the earliest settlements the bulk of the inhabitants were still
within a few hundred miles of the coast. Inevitably the population was predominantly rural in composition, although several
cities, such as Boston, Newport, New York, Philadelphia, and
Charleston, were developing into significant economic and cultural centers. They, of course, were seaports in constant touch
with Britain and other parts of the world. Philadelphia—the city
which plays the most significant role in this history—was a
flourishing center of 10,000 by the end of the first quarter of the
eighteenth century. By midcentury it was second only to London
in size and importance in the empire. It claimed a population of
70,000 by the year 1800. Not until 1810 did it lose preeminence
in size to New York, which by then counted 96,000 inhabitants.

As these colonial cities became centers of world trade, the resultant wealth made possible the growth of a cultural life which
had not been feasible when they were concerned primarily with
survival. Growing wealth allowed time and leisure for the pursuit
of interests other than purely vocational ones and the surplus

necessary for the purchase of books, scientific apparatus, and other expressions of intellectual and cultural advance.

Most notable among the many who contributed to Philadelphia's growth and development was a young man from Boston who arrived in the city in 1723. The story of Benjamin Franklin's rise to wealth and fame as a printer, entrepreneur, and community leader is well known. A poor but ambitious lad, Franklin developed a happy facility for ingratiating himself with persons from all levels of society wherever he went. He was not long in Philadelphia when he cultivated a friendship with the most influential man in the Pennsylvania colony, James Logan, who had accompanied the founder William Penn to his new settlement as secretary and had remained to care for the interests of the proprietorship for the rest of his life. By the time the young Franklin met him, Logan's Quaker beliefs had undergone extensive liberalization. He had developed a passion for the Greek and Roman classics and also an intense interest in his natural surroundings in the New World. He encouraged Franklin and many other young men in their investigation of natural phenomena. He spent long hours with Franklin, discussing matters of philosophy. To his fellow Friend, the merchant Peter Collinson in London, he wrote that "Our Benjamin Franklin is certainly an extraordinary man, one of singular good judgment, but of equal modesty."[2] Franklin deferred to this most important of Philadelphia Quakers on all possible occasions. He made sure that in any civic project a space was left at the top of the list of sponsors for the name James Logan. He took particular pride when he was able to persuade Logan to allow him to publish the latter's translation of Cicero's *Cato Major* (1744).[3] Franklin lavished loving care on this production, which has been rated as the best ever to come from his press.

Logan encouraged many young men in their pursuit of knowledge and was generous in the lending of his books. Among them was fellow Quaker John Bartram, who was to make significant contributions to American botany. Logan was more than surprised when a young glazier, Thomas Godfrey, sought the loan of Newton's *Principia*. Godfrey was to develop the seaman's quadrant, although it was to become known as Hadley's after the Englishman who developed an instrument on the same principles some time later.

Many of Franklin's contributions to the life of Philadelphia grew out of his own attempts at personal development. His happy idea of forming a club of young men for "mutual improvement" resulted in what became known as the "Junto." Franklin got the idea from a venture of the Reverend Cotton Mather in his native Boston. Mather had promoted the formation of neighborhood societies which would meet regularly to discuss edifying religious topics. Given Franklin's worldly outlook, the mission of the Junto was defined differently. The twelve young men who participated were to bring to each meeting topics for discussion and each was required to present a paper to the group on a regular three-months rotation. To insure that the meetings did not degenerate into wrangling, it was specified that a fine would be levied on anyone who departed from the rules of civilized conversation. This rule probably insured the survival of the group, which otherwise easily could have fallen apart in dissension. Aside from the benefits derived from the necessity to organize ideas and present them persuasively at meetings, other advantages soon became obvious. The members were expected to look after each other's welfare in the community. At each weekly meeting the question was asked whether anyone needed help. The subtle and not so subtle promotion of fellow members had a positive effect on their fortunes and status in the community.

The Junto was a secret organization, its founders fearing that news of its existence would bring unwelcome applications for membership. But so successful was it that it was decided to form a series of subjuntos, each to be headed by a member of the original. The organization, which was in a position to work quietly and unobtrusively for common goals in the city, had its influence immeasurably extended when the subjuntos were formed and fanned out into the community.

Thomas Jefferson early learned the value of communication among bright, vital minds. Although reared in rural Virginia and introduced to intellectual pursuits by his father, his admission in 1760 to the College of William and Mary at Virginia's capital of Williamsburg brought him into contact with brilliant men who would serve him as models all of his life. Dr. William Small of Scotland, the only noncleric on the faculty, served as professor of mathematics but was, according to Jefferson, "a man profound in most of the useful branches of science, with a happy talent of communication, correct and gentlemanly manners, and an enlarged and liberal mind."[4] For a period of time Small also filled the chair of philosophy. He became attached to the young Jefferson and, in class and out, brought to all subjects of discussion the enlarged view of the Scottish Enlightenment. When Small returned to Britain he became part of the Birmingham scientific circle, which included James Watt, Erasmus Darwin, and Joseph Priestley.[5]

After his time at the college, Jefferson stayed on in Williamsburg to study law with George Wythe, who was to become a lifelong confidant and political ally. Himself steeped in the classics, he helped Jefferson see the law as part of a greater study of humanity.

Small and Wythe served as Jefferson's entrée to the social circle presided over by the colonial Governor Francis Fauquier, a man of wit and learning, whose father had served as secretary to Sir Isaac Newton. It was at the Governor's Palace that Jefferson may first have heard of Shaftesbury and Bolingbroke, leading figures of the English Enlightenment.[6] Fauquier ranked himself among their followers and no doubt referred often to them and their writings in the lively conversations of his circle of friends. Jefferson, who studied the violin in Williamsburg, played in the ensemble organized by the Governor. Music was to be one of his passions from this time forward.

From these gifted men Jefferson imbibed the inspiration to acquire many of the skills which combined to make him one of the more versatile men in a versatile age. As the editors of the most recent edition of his papers have written, "To catalogue the areas of his explorations is to list most of the principal categories of knowledge—law, government, history, mathematics, architecture, medicine, agriculture, languages and literature, education, music, philosophy, religion, and almost every branch of the natural sciences from astronomy through meteorology to zoology."[7]

Although the city offered innumerable advantages of social intercourse, eighteenth-century Americans were predominantly a rural folk. Without the immediate communication of the twentieth century, much of their lives was spent in relative isolation. The farmer was a central figure in America, and it is not incidental that some of the key writings of the period purported to be from men of the soil.[8] An informed farmer was apparently in a position to gain a serious hearing from his countrymen. So John Dickinson, a Philadelphia lawyer donning the garb of a tiller of the soil, could write in his *Farmer's Letters* of the advantages he had derived from his friendship with gentlemen of "abilities and learning" with whom he had discussed problems: "I have acquired, I believe, a greater knowledge in history, and the laws and constitution of my country, than is generally attained by men of my class, many of them not being so fortunate as I have been in the opportunities of getting information."[9]

Although romantic attitudes toward nature did not flower until the latter part of the eighteenth and the early nineteenth centuries, the eighteenth-century urban gentleman saw advantages in escape to the countryside. In the case of Cadwallader Colden it was to flee the political scene on Manhattan. He moved up the Hudson to a country seat he christened "Coldengham." "I hope I am now settled for some months," he wrote his medical friend William Douglass in Boston, "free from the troublesome broils which men's passions occasion in all public affairs. This gives me hopes of being able to amuse myself with more innocent and more agreeable speculations than usually attend the intrigues of state. The speculations that gave you and me the greatest pleasure in the pleasantest time of our life while we were in the Garden of Eden, before we knew good and evil, before we knew men." Country life provides a setting for such speculation away from "the unnatural pursuits of the busy part of mankind. A man that has sometime been tossed upon the dunghill of men's passions gratifies all his senses greedily with the quiet and innocent pleasures that nature freely offers in every step that he treds in the woods and fields."

But Colden laments that the one thing that is missing in the country is the opportunity to share ideas. It was this lack that led him to suggest to Douglass the establishment of a learned society, based in Boston, which would require that each member contribute a paper on some aspect of the arts and sciences. The secretary of the society would be charged with circulating the papers among members in the Boston area for comment and correction and then they would be published for the members at a distance.[10] A variation of this idea was to take hold later and produce significant learned societies in eighteenth-century America.

Benjamin Franklin took to a farm in the country for a period but missed the stimulus of the city and moved right back again. But the idea of the country seat as a refuge from the embroilments of the political world continued to be an appealing one. John Adams and Thomas Jefferson, through their long years of political service, often claimed to want to get away from it all and return to the soil, Adams to his farm in Braintree, Massachusetts, Jefferson to his plantation home on Monticello. Whether they would actually have been content in such self-exile is doubtful. But this oft-expressed desire was fostered by the fact that they were steeped in classical lore. The idealized figure of Cincinnatus was constantly in the mind's eye. That citizen of Rome in the sixth and fifth centuries B.C. had left his plow when summoned by the Senate to serve the state and then, when duty was done, had quietly returned to his furrows.

Jefferson, writing to his younger friend, James Madison, tried without success to lure him into purchasing land in the neighborhood of Charlottesville so that he would be near his seat at Monticello. He was also greatly disappointed when he learned that Joseph Priestley, on his migration to the United States, had chosen to live in Northumberland, Pennsylvania. He had hoped to attract the Doctor to the environs of Monticello. It was in Philadelphia that Priestley had planned to settle when he arrived in 1794. That he did not was due to financial considerations, since it was a more expensive place to live than he could afford. So he contented himself with occasional forays into the city to visit or to preach.

The Virginia planter forever fought off the loneliness caused by extensive plantations and the resultant geographical separation from his friends and neighbors. Jefferson did not have the advantages enjoyed by his intellectual sympathizers in the towns and cities of the New England and middle Atlantic settlements or of the few towns of any significance in the South. He no doubt missed the intellectual stimulation of Williamsburg. Since he was not notably successful in bringing a circle of intellectuals for permanent residence near his mountain, he had to depend on his well-developed library and his extensive correspondence for stimulation. There were those occasions, of course, when Jefferson played host to visitors who came especially to see him, and when he became famous his house was often filled with the curious who were passing through the area.

Important in the development of Jefferson's interests were the years he spent away from Monticello in various political responsibilities. His years in France as minister plenipotentiary in the 1780s brought him into contact with many of the finest minds of the Old World and into the presence of the art and culture of the

Western tradition. Jefferson drank deeply at this spring, but nonetheless he preferred to be at home in the company of American intellectuals. He was to comment that one evening at Dr. Franklin's in Philadelphia in the company of David Rittenhouse, the astronomer, and Francis Hopkinson, wit and musician as well as lawyer and politician, was worth a whole week in Paris. It was possible to gather in Philadelphia on several hour's notice a group of like minds, something which Jefferson was seldom able to do with months of planning at Monticello.

Good company, meaning intellectually stimulating conversation, was one of the supreme gratifications of life for men of the Enlightenment. They loved to talk about literary, scientific, and other developments, to share ideas and new information on the ever-expanding exploration of their still virgin continent. The gentleman, advised Cadwallader Colden, "While he reads and thinks by turns . . . should, in the intervals, cultivate his intellectual faculties by general conversation, where he may obtain more useful knowledge than can be learned from books." Confrontation of vital minds with various interests was beneficial to all concerned. Sole pursuit of one's professional interest narrowed an individual's outlook on life. Colden concluded: "The mere scholar, the mere physician, the mere lawyer, musician or painter, take them out of their own way, and they are often more insipid than the mere plowman."[11]

The civilized discourse which played so great a part in the Enlightenment was based on a firm conviction that men are reasonable creatures who are capable of discovering truth. Ideas and beliefs, solely because they had been handed on with the authority of the past, were not to be accepted. Previous ages had made the mistake of believing that truth could be established by fiat of government or the church. But, in the long run, such an approach was bound to fail. Jefferson pointed out that "in France the emetic was once forbidden as a medicine, and the potatoe as an article of food. Government is just as infallible too when it fixes systems in physics. Galileo was sent to the inquisition for affirming that the earth was a sphere: the government had declared it to be as flat as a trencher, and Galileo was obliged to abjure his error. This error however at length prevailed, the earth became a globe. . . ."[12]

Cadwallader Colden, in a philosophical discourse written for the guidance of his grandson, blamed the attempt to control

men's minds on "priestcraft." From ancient times down to the
Reformation the church deliberately kept men in ignorance.
Since the priests dominated education, they could stifle ideas
they considered dangerous. So it was that they attempted to suppress the ideas of Copernicus, who published his work when near
death so they could not touch him. Galileo was forced to recant
what was plainly visible through his telescope.[13] "Nothing was so
effectual in establishing the dominion of the priests as the education of youth, which they assumed solely to themselves. They
know well how easy it is to instill strong prejudices into young
minds, and of what force these prejudices are during the whole
course of life," Colden declared. Son of a Protestant minister and
once headed for the ministry himself, Colden included the Protestant "priests" in this condemnation.[14] He ridiculed what he
considered the trivia dwelt on by the church. The priests spent
much time on useless terminology, with definitions of terms such
as "substance," "quality," "mode," and "accident," theological definitions which really explain nothing because they are not related
to real life experience. These stand in the way of true learning,
that is, of physics and the modern sciences. Colden encouraged
his grandson to think for himself and not to hesitate to express his
own ideas: "Young men it is true ought to be diffident of their
own judgement because they want that knowledge which others
have and they want likewise their experience, but it is not of so
bad consequence to make a rash judgement as to form your
judgement merely on the judgement of others. Never receive
anything as truth till you are fully convinced; till then receive
your master's dictates as probable and with no farther submission
to his opinion."[15]

The men of the Enlightenment stressed the importance of resisting all encroachments of "authority" on the free mind. It was
in the context of an attempt by clerical leaders to create a national religion—and thus national control—that Jefferson made his
famous pronouncement: "I have sworn upon the altar of God, eternal hostility against every form of tyranny over the mind of
man."[16] Nonetheless, the enlightened man maintained a healthy
skepticism concerning the capacity of reason. It had its definite
limits and these had to be recognized. In answer to a proposition
expressed in a letter from Colden, James Logan attempted to
draw some boundaries: "I can say nothing to thy hypothesis, not
fully understanding it as yet, besides that for some time past I

have been very dull to such inquiries, being persuaded that they are but guesses and that the truth in those cases is placed designedly without our reach; that is, that we have no organs fitted for ye discovery and that all that remains for us is to make ye most advantageous uses of what certainly discovers itself to us."[17]

As one might expect, it was the hardheaded Benjamin Franklin who best put the use of reason in perspective, basing his conclusion on an experience which had occurred on his first voyage from Boston to Philadelphia. For some time Franklin had been practicing a vegetarian diet, both because he believed it better for health and because he was disquieted by man's penchant for devouring living creatures. While the boat on which he was traveling was becalmed off Block Island, the crew took advantage of the opportunity to get in some fishing. They caught quite a few large cod and proceeded to clean and fry them. When the beguiling odors reached Franklin's vegetarian nostrils, he was torn between his principle and his desire to join in the feast. Franklin could not help but notice that when the sailors had cut open the cod, their stomachs contained many smaller fish. ". . . Then thought I, 'If you eat one another, I don't see why we mayn't eat you.'" From then on he ate meat, "returning only now and then occasionally to a vegetable diet." From this experience, Franklin drew a compelling moral: "So convenient a thing is it to be a *reasonable creature*, since it enables one to find or make a reason for everything one has a mind to do."[18]

Thus enlightened men exercised reason in examining its limitations. Whatever its shortcomings, however, reason was to the man of the Enlightenment as central as faith had been to Christians of previous ages. Or, as the great French *Encyclopédie* put it, "Reason is to the *philosophe* what grace is to the Christian."[19] It offered him the best opportunity to understand the world around him, to put in an orderly scheme the bits and pieces of information which he accumulated by the empirical method.

Having said this, however, it is important to note that the men of the American Enlightenment were men of action rather than systematic thinkers. The New World was not yet prepared to support professional philosophers or literary men and would not be until well into the nineteenth century. The thought of the period emerged from the crucible of action.

The first responsibility of these men was to make their way in the world. They were less introspective than the men of the preceding age and more concerned with their daily routine and the society around them. Their diaries, journals, and letters are concerned more with public affairs than with the state of their souls. The diary of John Adams, for instance, displays the result of much inward searching. He constantly questions his own abilities and performance and expresses determination to do better in the future. The soul-searching is of a very different kind, however, than that of an earlier period. Gone is the intense conviction of sin so striking in the diaries of his Puritan forebears.

Benjamin Franklin is an excellent exemplification of the man of thought in action. He often has been cited as the prototype of the rising bourgeoisie in America. This honor has been bestowed on him by historians in large part because of the *Autobiography* in which he set forth the story of his rise from humble beginnings to a position of eminence on both sides of the Atlantic.

Because he was born in Boston, he received a basic education in the school system established by the Puritan founders. Although slated by his father for a career in the ministry, and thus a Harvard education, he missed out on this when his father changed his mind and apprenticed him instead to his printer brother. From this point, whatever education Franklin received was self-education. He went about the business with great zest. He was voracious in his consumption of books, spending every possible moment with those he was able to buy or borrow.

Franklin had an immense curiosity to know what was going on around him. He used his learning to advance himself in Boston, and then in Philadelphia to which he moved in rebellion against his brother when he was seventeen. But, as he himself indicates, there was strong motivation in him to improve the lot of his fellow beings. This was no doubt his inheritance of the Puritan imperative to right the wrongs of society.

Franklin, in writing of his childhood, remembered the influence on him of Cotton Mather's *Essays to Do Good*.[20] In this homily that latter-day Puritan divine appealed one by one to the magistracy and professions to help improve the tone of society, an obligation to be performed in the hope that God would continue to look with favor on His New England. Whatever ethical influence this tract had on Franklin, the theology of Mather's *Essays* was lost on him. He had already begun the process of divesting himself of the various layers of Puritan belief, a process which began when he read what was designed as an attack on Deism.

Franklin found that the ideas impugned were more convincing, a result obviously not intended by the author. For the rest of his life Franklin was not a believer in Christian theology. His public infidelity became less pronounced as he matured, since he realized one does not make one's way in the world by offending others, but, also, because he was to share the tolerance for difference of opinion which was to be one of the more pronounced distinctions between Christians and free thinkers in the eighteenth century.

Franklin placed his faith in action rather than in ideology. He spent his energies in attempts to ameliorate the harshness of life in the city around him. To accomplish his ends, he did not hesitate to manipulate persons and conditions. He honestly reported many instances of this in the *Autobiography*. One example should suffice. He was particularly proud of the ploy he devised for raising money to establish a hospital in Philadelphia. When the subscription drive began to flag, he lobbied for a promise of a matching grant from the Pennsylvania legislature on condition that the private effort first raise a certain amount. Many members of the Assembly opposed the venture, but, since they were convinced the private fund-raising would not be successful, they were willing to "have the credit of being charitable without the expense. . . ." Franklin then used the promise of the legislative grant as a means of convincing citizens that their donations, in effect, would be doubled. This insured success of the fund drive. As Franklin wrote, "I do not remember any of my political maneuvers the success of which gave me at the time more pleasure, or wherein after thinking of it I more easily excused myself for having made some use of cunning."[21]

Franklin was particularly happy when the situation allowed him to accomplish his public end and, at the same time, receive credit for engineering it, if not among the populace which had been manipulated and was unaware of it, then among those influential ones in the community with whom he was anxious to stand in good stead. If one concentrated on the goal to be achieved and was not overly concerned to receive credit, one could be much more effective. But he found that bread cast upon the water would certainly return. If someone else tried to take credit for his activity behind the scenes, he was usually found out and discredited and Franklin was doubly rewarded—for the original achievement and for his seeming unconcern to receive credit.

Franklin, a master of psychology, applied the same technique of indirection in his personal dealings. Rather than a frontal attack in discussion, he allowed the other person credit for ideas he himself was attempting to promote. In addition, instead of a direct expression of opinion, he laced his conversation with expressions such as "I conceive," "I apprehend," "I imagine," or it "so appears to me at present."[22] He successfully turned away wrath by asking favors of the opposition. When as clerk of the Pennsylvania Assembly he encountered determined opposition from a member, he made it a point to borrow a book from the gentleman (making sure to return it promptly) and found from then on his erstwhile opponent was very cordial, kind and considerate.

It would be misleading, however, to give the impression that Franklin was capable of insinuating himself into the affections of all. Some disliked his evasiveness and slyness and distrusted him because of it. Inevitably, once he became active in the political arena, he was bound to become an object of opprobrium in the eyes of at least some of the opposition.

Having concluded that argument was counterproductive, Franklin disciplined himself to appear diffident and reticent. He used this technique quite effectively in his years of public service. When as an agent in England of various American colonies, it was revealed that he had received intercepted letters of Lieutenant Governor Thomas Hutchinson of Massachusetts and had sent them to Boston where they were published in 1772 (against his instructions), he was excoriated by Alexander Wedderburn at a meeting of the Privy Council. Because he was successful in self-discipline, he restrained himself and said nothing in reply. What appeared to be a humiliation at the time worked to his advantage in the long run. His public stance remained one of reluctance to speak and a modesty of demeanor.[23] Franklin, however, was not at all backward in expressing himself in private either with gentlemen or the ladies and gained a reputation as a great raconteur.

Whether in the company of kings or *philosophes*, Franklin never forgot his humble beginnings. Even long after his business success had released him from monetary care and allowed him freedom to pursue scientific projects and to become enmeshed in politics, he claimed that he was a printer.

Although many of the figures who play a part in the American Enlightenment received extensive formal education, it was assumed that life was a long process in which education never came to an end. The more one studied, the better prepared one was to play an intelligent, constructive role in human affairs. When James Madison was designated a delegate to the Constitutional Convention held in Philadelphia in 1787, he considered it perfectly natural to prepare for his role there by making a thorough study of the history of constitutional development. He must learn as much as he could of earlier federations: their formations, their successes, and their fatal flaws. When John Adams in the same year set for himself the task of writing an apology for the constitutions of the American states, as they had been written during and following the Revolution, he did the same. His *Defence of the Constitutions of Government of the United States* drew on as much historical precedent as he was able to muster.

When all was said and done, the leaders of the American Enlightenment expected a person to take charge of his own education. One could entreat and cajole, but the young were expected to learn what a later generation would call inner-directedness. When his father, who was away in Philadelphia attending the Continental Congress, wrote him advising him on his studies, ten-year-old John Quincy Adams replied apologetically that "I love to receive letters very well, much better than I love to write them, but I make a poor figure at composition; my head is much too fickle; my thoughts are running after birds' eggs, play and trifles, till I get vexed with myself." Admitting that he had only gotten through the third volume of Smollet, when he should have finished the set by then, he had put together a daily schedule for himself; but still he hoped his father would give him "some instructions with regard to my time and advise me how to proportion my studies and my play, in writing, and I will keep them by me and endeavor to follow them. I am, dear sir, with a present determination of growing better, Yours. . . ."[24] By age eleven, John Quincy felt qualified to give the younger Charles some brotherly advice, since he said their goals were the same: "to qualify ourselves to be useful members of society and to get a living in the world." "We are sent into the world for some end," he added; "it is our duty to discover by close study what this end is and when we once discover it to pursue it with unconquerable perseverance."[25]

The demands made on the young individual to shape his future in conformity with the ideal held up to him by society, were just as great in the age of Enlightenment as they were in the preceding Puritan age. The ultimate justification had changed, of course. One might no longer explain his actions by reference to demands made on him by a jealous deity who expected him to live as though he were among the elect—those predestined for eternal life in the future world. Like little John Quincy, one looked forward to being a useful member of society, at the same time that he went about the business of getting a living.

Both of these aims would be helped along immeasurably by the reading of good books. Whether it be the hard-working and ambitious Franklin in the printshop, Jefferson on his plantation, or the young John Quincy Adams seeking to make his way in the old Puritan commonwealth, he placed great faith in what could be learned from literature.

We can gain a good impression of what the enlightened man considered a well-stocked library from personal book inventories which have survived. More useful, however, are the justifications for reading certain works which emerge in letters of the period. Jefferson's thoughts on what constituted a basic library are revealed in a response to an inquiry made by a prospective brother-in-law.[26] It is our luck that Jefferson did not restrict himself to the thirty pounds sterling that Robert Skipwith had to spend but looked beyond that limitation in the hope that the library would be expanded as his finances made it possible.

The ideal library is a mix of the ancients and the moderns. Jefferson does not limit himself to "the learned lumber of Greek and Roman reading," but rather holds the view that "every thing is useful which contributes to fix us in the principles and practice of virtue." His list ranges over belle-lettres and the fine arts, criticism, politics and economics, religion, law, ancient and modern history, and science. In the first category, along with Homer and Vergil, he lists the greats of his own and the preceding ages in English, French, and Spanish literature. Chaucer, Shakespeare, Dryden, Milton, Pope, Swift, Moliere, Cervantes, Rousseau are all there. Addison, Steele, Goldsmith, Richardson, Smollett, and Fielding give the list a contemporary flavor.

Possibly in fear that he would bring a frown to Skipwith's face, he believes it necessary to apologize for the inclusion of fiction in the catalogue. He defends his choice on moral grounds: "When any signal act of charity or of gratitude, for instance, is presented either to our sight or imagination, we are deeply impressed with

its beauty and feel a strong desire in ourselves of doing charitable
and grateful acts also. On the contrary when we see or read of
any atrocious deed, we are disgusted with its deformity and conceive an abhorrence of vice. Now every emotion of this kind is an
exercise of our virtuous dispositions; and dispositions of the mind,
like limbs of the body, acquire strength by exercise. But exercise
produces habit; and in the instance of which we speak, the exercise being of moral feelings, produces a habit of thinking and acting virtuously." So, in perusing *A Sentimental Journey* the reader
neither knows nor cares "whether Lawrence Sterne really went to
France, whether he was there accosted by the poor Franciscan,
at first rebuked him unkindly, and then gave him a peace offer-
ing; or whether the whole be not a fiction. In either case we are
equally sorrowful at the rebuke, and secretly resolve *we* will
never do so: we are pleased with the subsequent atonement, and
view with emulation a soul candidly acknowledging its fault, and
making a just reparation."

As one would expect, under politics we find the staples of
eighteenth-century thought: Montesquieu, Locke, Sidney,
Bolingbroke.

The list on religion is heavily spiced with the Stoics, whom Jefferson found so compatible: Epictetus, Marcus Aurelius, Seneca,
and Cicero, along with Xenophon's *Memorabilia* of Socrates, since
Jefferson could not stand Plato. On other occasions he disparaged
his "foggy mind"[27] and insisted that Plato used Socrates as a
mouthpiece for the "whimsies of his own brain."[28] The questioning, the doubts, and the skepticism of the eighteenth century are
represented by Locke, Kames, Bolingbroke, and Hume.

Blackstone is inevitably listed under law, as is Lord Kames.

Classical history is also predictable with Livy, Sallust, Tacitus,
Caesar, and Plutarch, among others. Modern history has its share
of rationalist historians with Robertson and Hume there, along
with histories of Virginia by Sir William Keith and William Stith,
the latter work including less than a filiopietistic approach to the
worthies who settled the Old Dominion. The five volumes of
Bayle's skeptical *Dictionary* are included under ancient history.

His scientific section is a mix of narratives of travel and observation with theory and experiment. Buffon is there, of course, in
the realm of natural history, and Jefferson was no doubt happy to
be able to list an American, Benjamin Franklin being represented
by his *Experiments and Observations on Electricity*. It need

hardly be said that, given the experience of the American colonists up to the date of this letter, 1771, it is not surprising that so few should appear in such a catalogue.

Although Jefferson lists the works of the leading *philosophe* under "miscellaneous," Gilbert Chinard, who made an intensive study of Jefferson's literary preferences, could find little or no influence of Voltaire's ideas on the American, at least as far as this can be measured by explicit references in Jefferson's writings.[29]

Whether this list is fairly reflective of Jefferson's own reading could be tested if time were devoted to such a project. Tentatively the answer can be in the affirmative. To take one example, Professor Chinard, in his study of Jefferson's *Commonplace Book*, counted many references to the Scottish jurist Henry Home, Lord Kames, who, it is clear, Jefferson greatly admired. In this list of books, the works of Kames appear under criticism, religion, law, and science.

Jefferson gave this advice when he was twenty-eight years old. When he was forty-two he had the occasion to advise his nephew Peter Carr on a regimen of reading which the young man should undertake now that he was in Williamsburg preparing to enter the college.[30] This list is partial, since he intends at this point merely to get the young man started. Still, it is revealing of Jefferson's thoughts on education. He would have Peter begin with history, ancient and modern. Although he recommends a volume by a modern writer to provide an overview, he would have Peter concentrate on the original Greek and Latin historians.

This historical diet is to be followed by Greek and Latin poetry and then by past and contemporary greats in English—Milton, Pope, and—"in order to form your style in your own language"—Swift.

For moral works, Peter is to turn to the Stoics, Epictetus and Cicero. Xenophon's *Memorabilia* will introduce him to Socrates. Overcoming personal distaste, Jefferson adds "Plato's Socratic dialogues. . . ."

Jefferson promised to suggest later a course in mathematics, natural philosophy (i.e., science), and natural history. But Peter must prepare for this by pushing his study of French, in which most of these books are written. After French, Spanish is the most important language for him to learn because of "our future connection with Spain. . . ."[31]

Jefferson is just as concerned with his nephew's body as with his mind. He warns against staying up late at night, a practice which he believes injurious both to physical and mental health. Horseback riding also should be avoided. The young man should use his legs. The Europeans are proud of their development of the horse, but not so Jefferson: "An Indian goes on foot nearly as far in a day, for a long journey, as an enfeebled white does on his horse, and he will tire the best horses. There is no habit you will value so much as that of walking far without fatigue. I would advise you to take your exercise in the afternoon. Not because it is the best time for exercise for certainly it is not: but because it is the best time to spare from your studies; and habit will soon reconcile it to health and render it nearly as useful as if you gave to that the more precious hours of the day. A little walk of half an hour in the morning when you first rise is adviseable also. It shakes off sleep, and produces other good effects in the animal oeconomy."

This Jeffersonian correspondence demonstrates that classical learning was as important to the American Enlightenment as to the European. Jefferson, despite his strong interest in modern ideas, remarked to Adams that the thing he prized most highly was the classical education his father had insisted he pursue: "I would not exchange this attainment for anything which I would then have acquired and have since acquired."[32] He, in his turn, insisted that his children enjoy the same benefit. Adams agreed that the classics were indispensable, "in spight of our friend Rush. . . ."[33]

Dr. Benjamin Rush questioned the value of a classical education, although he himself had acquired a thorough one at Princeton and his own writings are studded with allusions to the literature and events of antiquity. Rush did concede, however, that in the case of professions such as law, medicine, and teaching, a knowledge of the classics was necessary.[34] But in other cases, such as that of the astronomer David Rittenhouse, persons accomplished more because they were ignorant of, and therefore not hampered by, classical thinking.

The more extreme position was taken by Thomas Paine who saw no advantage in reading books in the "dead languages." Ideas were the important things and the great books, after all, were available in translation.

This debate on the value of the classics for modern life was relatively new. America was still steeped in them. Classical influences were found everywhere: in poetry and prose, in speeches, conversation, and correspondence, in common almanacs, in political debate (the newspapers were filled with classical noms de plume), in place names and in the architecture that graced such locales, and even in the names conferred on slaves throughout the American colonies.

To some extent, of course, this influence was superficial, but in men such as Adams and Jefferson it was profound. As the noted classicist Richard Gummere has written, these men displayed in their correspondence "a mastery of the classics and a practical application of ancient ideas to modern situations. They were at home in Latin, and Jefferson's Greek was actively kept up."[35]

The Americans were not to throw their lot to the side of the moderns as yet. Classical learning was held in high esteem because it was still "practical." When it became "impractical," because it was not seen as contributing to the solution of modern problems, it was to be shunted aside.

Jefferson also points to the utility of learning the French and Spanish languages. The most practical of these men, Benjamin Franklin, had missed an education in the classical languages, since he only attended the Boston Latin School for one year. But curiosity and natural inclination motivated him later in life to study languages on his own. He discovered, much to his delight, that his learning of French, Italian, and Spanish made it possible for him to turn to Latin and learn it with much greater facility than would have been the case otherwise. Thus, he recommended that the order of learning the languages be reversed. He believed that this change would overcome the drop-out rate; students, he said, usually abandoned Latin after a few years of study.

One of the most important vehicles for self-improvement was the *Spectator*. On establishing that remarkable periodical in London in 1711, Joseph Addison and Richard Steele had announced that it was their purpose "to banish vice and ignorance out of the territories of Great Britain." Said Mr. Spectator, "I shall endeavour to enliven morality with wit and to temper wit with morality. . . ."[36] Along with its predecessor, the *Tatler* (1709–1711), and its successor, the *Guardian* (1713), the *Spectator* (1711–1712) had a profound effect on the life style of the English-speaking Enlightenment. Bound volumes of the periodicals were to be found everywhere. Addison and Steele, using the vehicle of the "Spectator Club," and the "de Coverley papers," commented in gentle satire on the attitudes and morality of their time and set the tone of manners and morals for innumerable readers late into the eighteenth century. In addition, they did much to popularize new scientific discoveries.[37]

Franklin and Madison, among others, explicitly comment on the influence of the *Spectator* in their development. Madison, in his brief autobiography, referring to himself in the third person, pointed out that "One of the earliest books which engaged his attention was the 'Spectator,' which from his own experience he inferred to be peculiarly adapted to inculcate in youthful minds just sentiments, an appetite for knowledge, and a taste for the improvement of the mind and manners. . . ."[38] Madison recommended it to his nephew, since it encouraged "a lively sense of the duties, the virtues and the proprieties of life."[39] Jefferson recognized that a good library could not be without it when he included it, along with the *Tatler* and the *Guardian*, in his catalogue for the library of Robert Skipwith.

The young Franklin used the *Spectator* as a model for his own writing. He would read an essay and hours later attempt to reproduce its sentiments in his own words. He would then compare his effort with the original, seeking hints for improvement. The influence of the *Spectator* stood him in good stead when he attempted to break into the world of newspaper writers. With the *Spectator* clearly in mind, in terms of both style and content, he created the figure of Silence Dogood, who commented on the foibles of her life and friends in Boston. These papers, written secretly, Franklin slipped under the door of his brother James's printing shop. James decided to make use of them, so they appeared in his *New England Courant*, bringing much favorable comment.[40]

So impressed was Franklin with the utility of using the *Spectator* as a model that years later (1751) he advocated that it be included in the curriculum of the Academy at Philadelphia. Franklin said the "scholars" should render the ideas from the *Spectator* papers in their own words. He thought the famous publication could be used efficaciously in other ways as well. Students should be required to read aloud from the papers to improve their facility in that art and to help them master the parts of speech.[41]

One of the most skillful emulators of Addison and Steele was Francis Hopkinson, a man of many abilities: poet, composer and performer, as well as attorney, merchant, politician, and statesman. He was a Signer from New Jersey, where he resided for awhile, although most of his productive years were spent in Philadelphia. His three volumes of collected works[42] include political satires, some quite sharp, not to say biting; poems and songs, some quite impressive, such as "Over the hills far away," and light pieces written in *Spectator* style for the newspapers of the day.

The virtue which the *Spectator* sought to promote in its satirical manner was one of the primary concerns of the enlightened man. The classical ideal of virtue took the place of Christian piety. As we shall see in a later chapter, Franklin and his contemporaries discarded belief in the fall of man, believing the story of Adam to be a myth. As rational creatures of God's making, it was incumbent on them to strive to live virtuous lives. This attempt became their form of worship.

We can best define the meaning of virtue by examining the most striking of attempts to achieve it, that of Benjamin Franklin. He first resolved to reorder his life on a definite "plan of conduct" on board ship as he returned from two years in London in 1726. Because he felt a definite dissatisfaction with the "confused variety" of events and experiences which had made up his first twenty years, he drew up a series of resolutions so that in the future he might "live in all respects like a rational creature. . . ."[43]

The list called first for a life of "extreme frugality. . . ." This characteristic, of course, is usually associated with Franklin, so it should be noted that he looked on this as a temporary expedient since he had debts that he wanted to pay off. The injunctions to frugality found in his *Poor Richard's Almanac* over the years he did not observe himself, once it became possible to ignore them. Franklin was not an ascetic, and asceticism was not an ideal of the Enlightenment. Like the others of his time, Franklin enjoyed the fruits of his labor to the fullest extent. He did believe in industry, however—both its appearance and its reality. He concluded early in his career that he must establish a reputation for industriousness, even if he must use techniques of public relations. As he frankly told posterity in his *Autobiography*: "In order to secure my credit and character as a tradesman, I took care not only to be in *reality* industrious and frugal, but to avoid all appearances to the contrary. I dressed plainly; I was seen at no places of idle diversion. I never went out a fishing or shooting; a book, indeed, sometimes debauched me from my work, but that was seldom, snug, and gave no scandal; and to show that I was not above my business, I sometimes brought home the paper I purchased at the store through the streets on a wheelbarrow. Thus being esteemed an industrious, thriving young man and paying duly for what I bought, the merchants who imported stationery solicited my custom, others proposed supplying me with books, and I went on swimmingly."[44] Franklin's Plan of Conduct eschewed any schemes to get rich quick and called for patient, hard work.

It also called for speaking the truth "in every instance" and to avoid giving people false expectations. He would "aim at sincerity in every word and action—the most amiable excellence in a rational being."[45] On the other hand, Franklin vowed that he would not go to extremes for the sake of truth. He attempted to strike the golden mean. He would not speak ill of any man and, "by some means," find it possible to speak well even of a person in whom he found fault.[46]

Franklin's famous regimen for achieving virtue was conceived some time later. He labeled it a "bold and arduous project. . . ." His goal: "moral perfection"! Since he thought he knew the difference between right and wrong, he saw no reason why he might not live "without committing any fault at any time. . . ." He discovered, however, that the scheme was more easily conceived than executed. Apparently "natural inclination," his habits, and his friends continued to get in his way. He must devise a method. First he drew up a list of virtues, thirteen in all, a list worth reproducing *in toto* because it reveals as much of the attitudes of the Enlightenment as it does of Franklin's particular problems of behavior.

1. TEMPERANCE
Eat not to dullness; drink not to elevation.
2. SILENCE
Speak not but what may benefit others or yourself; avoid trifling conversation.
3. ORDER
Let all your things have their places; let each part of your business have its time.

4. RESOLUTION
Resolve to perform what you ought; perform without fail what you resolve.

5. FRUGALITY
Make no expense but to do good to others or yourself; *i.e.*, waste nothing.

6. INDUSTRY
Lose no time; be always employed in something useful; cut off all unnecessary actions.

7. SINCERITY
Use no hurtful deceit; think innocently and justly, and, if you speak, speak accordingly.

8. JUSTICE
Wrong none by doing injuries or omitting the benefits that are your duty.

9. MODERATION
Avoid extremes; forbear resenting injuries so much as you think they deserve.

10. CLEANLINESS
Tolerate no uncleanliness in body, clothes, or habitation.

11. TRANQUILITY
Be not disturbed at trifles, or at accidents common or unavoidable.

12. CHASTITY
Rarely use venery but for health or offspring, never to dullness, weakness, or the injury of your own or another's peace or reputation.

13. HUMILITY
Imitate Jesus and Socrates.[47]

Realizing that he would have difficulty in reaching these ideals if he attempted them all at once, Franklin decided to master them one at a time. He devoted a week to each, at the end of each day reckoning up his lapses. To help in the task, he made up a table with the days of the week across the top and the thirteen virtues down the side. Drawing lines across and down, he created boxes. When he did not live up to the standard set, he would put a mark in the relevant box. This allowed him to keep score on his progress at the end of each day.

With the passage of time Franklin became less rigorous in his score-keeping and then put it aside, although he would return to it from time to time, putting himself through a refresher course.

It has been remarked that Franklin was a theoretical rather than a practicing moralist.[48] Certainly, questions can be raised concerning various aspects of his life. His oft-repeated manipulation of the community—even if in behalf of ventures he considered for its own good—raises questions about his basic integrity. He fathered a child by a woman unknown to us. Yet he was honest to the point of bringing this bastard into his home and raising him as if he were a legitimate son. If accounts which have come down to us are correct, Franklin had trouble observing his rule twelve, "Chastity," right into his old age, but, then, one does not include in a list of rules or resolutions items which are not at issue.

It is clear from other men of the age that they sought to live by a rigorous code. It is instructive to read the correspondence of Jefferson with the young people for whom he felt a special responsibility. The injunctions regarding the importance of industry, for instance, are as strong from this Southern planter as they are in the bourgeois Franklin. The complaints of his young daughter, Martha, that she could not read the type in Livy, provided Jefferson with the occasion to lecture her on industry and the importance of self-reliance. The Europeans, he observed, were incapable of doing anything for themselves. They had shops and specialists for everything. But this was not true in America. Americans—in this case Martha—had to do most things for themselves. They could not plead helplessness. In a pioneer land, the American had to shift for himself, to be self-sufficient.[49]

The code Jefferson advocated was, like Franklin's, closely related to the necessity to get on in the world. He recommended that his grandson, Thomas Jefferson Randolph,[50] remember the method of Dr. Franklin and not argue with others but rather ask questions, suggest doubts. Jefferson saw no inconsistency in this indirect approach to disagreement and a conviction that one must do what is right: "A determination never to do what is wrong, prudence and good humor, will go far towards securing to you the estimation of the world."[51] Dumas Malone has suggested that Jefferson displayed the Southern aristocratic bent not to offend anyone.[52] But, in this attitude, he certainly was little different from Franklin, who obviously had not been influenced by Southern ways.

However gracious one might be in expressing disagreement, Jefferson was nevertheless insistent on honesty as basic to the good life. He advised his nephew Peter Carr that he should place honesty above all things: ". . . Give the earth itself and all it contains rather than do an immoral act." Dishonesty with the tongue eventually leads to dishonesty of the heart. "An honest heart being the first blessing, a knowing head is the second."[53] One may give the young all the advice in the world, but Jefferson believed that virtue was innate in man. He told Peter that there was really nothing that a professor could tell him about moral philosophy. The Creator has built virtue into the nature of man.[54] Jefferson disagreed with enlightened thinkers, such as Helvetius, who believed morality stems from self-interest: "The Creator would indeed have been a bungling artist had he intended man for a social animal, without planting in him social dispositions."[55]

Yet the honesty that Jefferson advocated forced him to face certain realities. It was clear that some individuals were not born with a strong moral sense. Society had attempted to compensate by subjecting children to an education which sought to supply this lack.

Ideally, the individual should take control of his own life, as was attempted by Franklin when he drew up the list of virtues which he should strive to attain. When his friend Joseph Priestley in 1772 was weighing an invitation to become Lord Shelburne's librarian and literary companion, he turned to Franklin for advice. The latter explained to him the method he used to help him make decisions. He would arrange two columns on a piece of paper in which to write the pros and cons of a question as they occurred to him over several days. The process should take at least that long so that no salient points would be overlooked. Then Franklin would compare the strength of the various points, running lines through those which seemed to cancel each other out. The column with the most remaining considerations he judged to be the most weighty. On the basis of this "moral or prudential algebra," he would make his decision.[56]

Franklin's regimen is the most striking example of the systematic manner in which men of the American Enlightenment sought to govern their lives. If it seems overly systematic to us, we should remember that the approach did not seem so restrictive to them, for it was quite consistent with the mechanistic world view of the age. It was a reasonable application to human affairs of the methodical approach which was proving so fruitful in the pursuit of science.

CHAPTER 2

The Pursuit of Science

I T is evident that all our valuable attainments depend upon a diligent and close application in our pursuit after facts, which are painfully and laboriously acquired, that discoveries have succeeded each other by a flow and gradual advancement, and that one invention is linked in with and leads to many others which are remote and unforeseen.

—*Owen Biddle*[1]

As I. Bernard Cohen, the noted historian of science, has pointed out, "the men of the eighteenth century were no less credulous than men had been in any previous period."[2] Many learned men, including Voltaire, believed in the existence of the "jumar," a cross between a horse and a cow. The distinguished Swedish scientist Carolus Linnaeus, among others, believed "that swallows hibernate under water."[3] Despite the persistence of old beliefs, the man of the eighteenth century was to adapt to a fundamental change of world view. He lived to see the replacement of the Ptolemaic cosmology with its geocentric view of the earth by the Copernican cosmology in which the sun became the center of our universe with the earth taking its place among the planets revolving around it.

With the demotion of the earth from the center of creation, there began a reordering of the universe and the "parts" that make it up. This proceeded, as Professor Cohen has noted, in a "genuine empirical" manner. Modern science surrendered the interest of an earlier age in ultimate causes and explanations and settled instead for the partial understanding that was pieced out as a result of exploration and experimentation. The new explanation of the nature of lightning, for example, had a profound effect on man's basic belief. If, as Franklin demonstrated, lightning struck because of atmospheric conditions, and not, as theologians claimed, because of the direct intervention of an angry God, the deity took up an existence at least once removed from the workings of His universe. John Winthrop, descendant of the Puritan Governor of the same name and professor of science at Harvard, would lead a campaign to convince people that earthquakes also are natural phenomena and are not to be interpreted as signs of God's displeasure. Although God may have established the rules for the operations of nature—that is, natural law—nature in effect becomes an independent entity. It is to be understood on its own terms and is not to be seen as an instrument through which God rewards and punishes man.

Benjamin Franklin, former denizen of the Puritan stronghold of Boston, best expressed how far thought had moved from the days of the original John Winthrop, a mere hundred years before, when he wrote: "Nor is it of much importance to us to know the manner in which nature executes her laws: 'tis enough if we know the laws themselves. 'Tis of real use to know that china left in the air unsupported will fall and break; but how it comes to fall, and why it breaks, are matters of speculation. 'Tis a pleasure indeed to know them, but we can preserve our china without it."[4]

The removal of God from immediate concern with the details of the working of the universe did not necessarily lead to atheism. As we shall see in chapter 5, few men of the Enlightenment went to that extreme position. Rather, they maintained their belief in the deity by considering nature as an expression of His handiwork. John Bartram, the Quaker farmer from Pennsylvania who made notable contributions to scientific knowledge, best expressed the new view when he exclaimed, "Through the telescope I see God in his glory."

The men of the American Enlightenment were eager to explore their natural surroundings. Europeans made great strides in the study of astronomy and the related problems of space; they contributed to a new understanding of physics, chemistry, and biology; but the Americans, in addition to contributions in these areas, had a whole new continent to explore. They were encouraged in this exploration by friends in the Old World, particularly the members of the Royal Society of London for Improving Natural Knowledge. The Society, which had been chartered a century before by Charles II, was the most respected learned organization in the English-speaking world. Its journal, the *Philosophical Transactions*, carried summaries of its meetings and the papers presented before it and, therefore, was an important vehicle for the spread of new scientific ideas. Americans who were deemed worthy of honor for their accomplishments were elected members of the Society. But whether members or no, many were inspired to contribute their findings to the Society in the hope of eventual admission to its ranks and for the sheer love of deepening man's knowledge of his world.

Particularly encouraging to the Americans in their explorations and in gaining recognition for their accomplishments before the Royal Society was Peter Collinson. A Quaker merchant in London, Collinson carried on an extensive correspondence with the colonists, a correspondence which combined business with the pleasures of natural history and philosophy. Furthermore, Collinson was responsible for putting in touch with each other several Americans who played an influential role in establishing the foundations of science in America.

The influence on the Americans was not solely British. The Swedish biologist Carolus Linnaeus also carried on an extensive American correspondence and sought out a number of knowledgeable colonists who could collect botanical and zoological specimens to send him. In addition, he instructed them in the effort to fit newly discovered American genera into his new Linnaean system of classification. This link with the New World was appreciably strengthened when Linnaeus's colleague Peter Kalm, under the sponsorship of the Swedish Royal Academy of Science, visited the American colonies and made an extensive tour from 1748 to 1751, observing and collecting specimens and incidentally endearing himself to many of the Americans who found him a warm, congenial person.[5]

Among themselves Americans with scientific interests carried on an extensive correspondence in which they exchanged information and ideas and stimulated further research and exploration. Incomplete though it must be, an examination of the emergence of this scientific circle will provide an insight into the problems its members faced in piecing together an understanding of their American surroundings. Particularly instructive in this regard was the exchange begun in the 1720s between the physician William Douglass, who a few years before had arrived in Boston, with his fellow Scotsman Dr. Cadwallader Colden, who settled in New York after a brief period in Philadelphia. One would expect that a physician would be interested in the "endemial, epidemical and incident diseases" of the area but in his first few years in New England Douglass also made a collection of more than seven hundred varieties of plants found within five miles of Boston. He then enlarged the radius of his explorations, also examining animals and minerals as he went. He sent Colden a copy of his record of "winds and weather in Boston. . . ." To illustrate the obstacles facing Americans in scientific research at that period, it must be pointed out that it was made on the basis of "naked eye, pen, ink, and paper," for he had no thermometer or barometer and was not aware of any in the area!

The enlightened mind's empirical interest is well displayed in Douglass' request for reciprocity from Colden. He wants information about New York, "but pray send nothing but what is exactly true and fact; take nothing from credulous people."[6]

Colden and Douglass were also in touch with Franklin in Philadelphia and exchanged many reports of experiments and observations with him. Franklin may well have met Douglass before he migrated from Boston to Philadelphia, for the latter was a contributor to his brother James's *New England Courant*.[7] Franklin's esteemed Philadelphian elder James Logan was the cousin of Colden's wife, but they were brought together through their scientific exchanges, Logan increasingly putting aside his lucrative land speculation and fur trade with the Indians to devote himself to optics, astronomy, botany (his contributions were recognized by Linnaeus), and especially mathematics.[8] It was Logan who helped John Bartram get his study of botany underway. To this list should be added Dr. Alexander Garden, another Scottish emigré, who established a medical practice in Charles Town, South Carolina, but soon began the investigations of plant and animal life which brought him into this scientific circle.

This catalogue of individuals is very far from complete, but it illustrates that there was much scientific activity across colonial lines.

It would be impossible to include in this review of scientific contributions made by enlightened Americans all of the figures who justifiably could be mentioned. We shall restrict ourselves to a few individuals who made particularly notable contributions and who played a significant role in achieving recognition for American science in international circles.

J. Hector St. John de Crèvecoeur in his *Letters from an American Farmer* has preserved an account of how John Bartram became captivated by botany. Bartram, who had received barely the rudiments of an education, basic reading and writing, labored on a small farm near Philadelphia. ". . . One day I was very busy in holding my plough (for thee see'st that I am but a ploughman), and being weary I ran under the shade of a tree to repose myself. I cast my eyes on a daisy; I plucked it mechanically and viewed it with more curiosity than common country farmers are wont to do, and observed therein very many distinct parts, some perpendicular, some horizontal. 'What a shame,' said my mind, or something that inspired my mind, 'that thee shouldest have employed so many years in tilling the earth and destroying so many flowers and plants without being acquainted with their structures and their uses!' This seeming inspiration suddenly awakened my curiosity, for these were not thoughts to which I had been accustomed."[9]

Bartram got hold of a Latin grammar and persuaded a neighboring schoolmaster to tutor him in the language. In three months he felt prepared well enough to tackle Linnaeus. He borrowed books on botany from James Logan, who explained to him the Linnaean sexual system of plant classification. Logan also encouraged Bartram to go beyond the plants of the immediate Philadelphia area. Since Logan was in constant negotiation with the Indians, he made it possible in 1743 for Bartram to accompany the Indian agent Conrad Weiser on a trip to New York to confer with the Onondaga. Along with the surveyor and cartographer, Lewis Evans, one of Franklin's circle, Bartram made what was to be one of the longest of his many botanizing journeys.[10]

He kept a simple day-by-day account of what he observed along the way. When he later sent it to Peter Collinson, the latter thought it worthy of publication (1751). This book of *Observations*,[11] so unpretentious and lacking in literary merit in the eyes of a later century, helped bring Bartram international recognition. Also contributing to his fame was the botanical garden he developed at Kingsessing, near Philadelphia, where he gathered exotica from around the world and planted them in the

same kind of settings from which they came. Just as Bartram
supplied Linnaeus, Queen Ulrica of Sweden, and other Europeans with specimens of American plants, so he received the
benefit of reciprocation.

Linnaeus called Bartram the greatest natural botanist in the
world; and in 1765 Peter Collinson and Benjamin Franklin prevailed on George III to appoint him Royal Botanist, a position
which brought with it a modest yearly stipend which allowed him
to continue his scientific pursuits.[12]

Bartram trained two sons, John and William, to carry on his
work. The former took over the botanical garden on his death
while the latter gained fame almost equal to his father's from his
botanizing journeys. His book of *Travels*[13] through the southeast-
ern part of the United States, published in 1791, was widely
read. It is written in an ornamented, romantic style and supposedly inspired the setting of Samuel Taylor Coleridge's "Kubla
Khan" and influenced Wordsworth's nature poetry.[14]

On a trip to New York in 1742 John Bartram had met Cadwallader Colden at his country seat "Coldengham," at the foot of the
Catskills on the Hudson, west of Newburgh. He was much impressed with this politician who preferred scientific endeavor to
public life. Bartram wrote that Colden "received and entertained
me with all the demonstrations of civility and respect that were
convenient. He is one of the most facetious, agreeable gentlemen, ever met with."[15] The Quaker farmer apparently enjoyed a
good Scottish sense of humor. Colden found Bartram equally
pleasant.

In the following year, 1743, Colden received international rec-
ognition for the botanical work he had done in Linnaeus's *Acta
Societates Regiae Scientiarum Upsaliensis*, which contained "Plan-
tae Coldenhamiae in provincia Novaboracensi Americanes sponte
Crescentes."[16] Linnaeus also was to name a genus of plants,
"Coldenia."

It was Colden's established reputation which, among other
things, impelled a young Scottish migrant to visit him. Dr. Alexander Garden had arrived in Charles Town to practice medicine
in 1752.[17] Two years later, on a trip to escape the South Caroli-
nian heat, which was affecting his health, he traveled north and
sought out Colden.[18] While he was at Coldengham John Bartram
arrived unexpectedly. Garden exclaimed: "How grateful was such
a meeting to me! and how unusual in this part of the world! What

congratulations and salutations passed between us!"[19] On his trip back to the South, Garden spent some time with Bartram at the botanical garden at Kingsessing.

By the time Bartram and Garden came together at Colden's, he had begun to leave botany behind and to give his attention to other scientific endeavors. But not until he had trained a substitute in his daughter Jane. Jane Colden, rather unusual in that time, did not marry until she was thirty-five, so she had time to learn botany from her father. He put her to work collecting specimens for his far-flung correspondents. She learned to make sketches of plants and using printer's ink with "a simple kind of rolling press" was able to take impressions of the leaves of plants.[20]

Jane Colden learned enough to utilize the Linnaean system. According to Peter Collinson she was the only woman on either side of the Atlantic to do so.[21] To Johann Friederich Gronovius at Leiden, Colden explained why he sought to interest Jane in botany in the first place: "I thought that botany is an amusement which may be made agreable for the ladies who are often at a loss to fill up their time. . . . Their natural curiosity & the pleasure they take in the beauty & variety of dress seems to fit them for it. The chief reason that few or none of them have hitherto applied themselves to this study, I believe, is because all the books of any value are wrote in Latin & so filled with technical words that the obtaining the necessary previous knowledge is so tiresome & disagreable that they are discouraged at the first setting out & give it over before they can receive any pleasure in the pursuit."[22] Although Jane Colden became an accomplished botanist, her father's thought that it was a useful way to while away female time proved to be the case. When a few years after this letter she married, she apparently lost interest in botany.[23] In so doing she lived up to family and societal expectation.

Like other botanists, Jane Colden occasionally made mistakes in classification. As one result of his acquaintance with her, Alexander Garden's name was to be attached to the *Hypericum virginicum*, L. in 1755. The "Gardenia," as it turned out, was not the newly discovered genus Jane Colden thought it was. Flattered as he was, Garden had suspected it all along.[24] The delicate flower which is now called the "Gardenia" was named by Linnaeus, who conferred the honor in 1762 in recognition of Garden's various accomplishments both in botany and zoology.[25]

The latter involvement was the result of the urging of Linnaeus that he utilize his trips for the collection of animal specimens as well as botanical.

One result was Garden's discovery of the mud iguana, a feat which enhanced his fame in Europe. He went on to discover a freshwater soft-shelled turtle (an edible delicacy).[26]

Certain European influences which can be labeled negative paradoxically had a positive effect on the development of American science. Most notable of these was the work of the famous French scholar, Count Georges Louis Leclerc de Buffon, who, in his *Natural History*, derided the animal life of America, which he pictured as dwarfed and stunted compared to that found in Europe. Buffon's view was widely accepted in Europe and enraged Americans who had reason to believe that the reverse was true, that America produced large, more healthy specimens than did Europe.

Although Thomas Jefferson's book, *Notes on the State of Virginia*[27] was written in response to a request of Francois Marbois, secretary of the French legation at Philadelphia, for information on the characteristics of the American landscape and its inhabitants, in a sense it was inspired by Buffon. Jefferson sought to refute his perverse views. Beyond the pages of his book, he also attempted to refute Buffon with actual specimens. While serving as American minister to France, Jefferson urged a friend at home to send the horns, skin, and skeleton of a moose to him so that he could once and for all lay to rest Buffon's misrepresentations. Jefferson was sorely disappointed with the specimen when it arrived, knowing that indeed it was not the largest obtainable; still it was large enough to challenge the great Buffon and make him wonder if he had been wrong on this score.

Jefferson's *Notes* are just that. In response to Marbois's inquiry, he assembled the jottings on observations he had made over the years of various aspects of his native land. It should be recalled that the Virginia with which he dealt included within its borders present-day West Virginia and Kentucky and much more. He began with the lay of the land, discussing the tidewater area, the piedmont and the mountains, and the great Shenandoah Valley. He described the location of the rivers and discussed their navigability and their potential. But Jefferson went beyond the physical features of the land and dealt with the inhabitants, beast and human. True philosopher that he was, he could not merely describe the lot of the black man as slave and the destructive relationship with the white master, but spoke of his own hopes for emancipation. He could not deal with the religion of the inhabitants without recording the effort to separate church and state in Virginia and to establish freedom of belief in perpetuity. The book, with its rich discussion of the manifold aspects of human experience in a particular American context, was the only one that Jefferson deliberately set out to write. Intended for Marbois, and then in a very limited edition for his friends, Jefferson finally decided to issue an official edition (1785) to compete with a corrupted version of a Parisian printer. From the perspective of the twentieth century many of the publications of the period have proved ephemeral. His *Notes*, however, because they are set in a large philosophic framework, and written in the inimitably lucid Jeffersonian prose, provide a stimulating revelation of the mind of the American Enlightenment.

The members of the natural history circle, as it has been called, made significant contributions in botany and zoology. Although many of the same flora and fauna appeared on both sides of the ocean, the genera and species of the new continent had to be demonstrated to be the same as those in Europe. In addition, the Americans had the thrill of discovering "new," that is, unknown, genera and species and adding them to the catalogue of Western man's knowledge. Colden and Bartram among others published catalogues of their own work and through their extensive correspondence and exchanges of specimens with men like Linnaeus and Gronovius made an international contribution.

Americans made contributions in fields other than the biological that immediately surrounded them. Like the Europeans, they were drawn to an observation of the heavens, through Copernican-Newtonian eyes. Two figures emerged most prominently in astronomy during the eighteenth century: David Rittenhouse and John Winthrop. They came from very different social and educational backgrounds.

Rittenhouse was born on a farm in Norriton, twenty miles northwest of Philadelphia. His father was a second-generation Pennsylvania German, his mother of English Quaker background. Little is known of David Rittenhouse's educational experience, but he apparently had meager formal schooling and was largely self-taught, especially in the sciences. Although he took up the family business of farming, his interest in mechanics led him into a career of clock and instrument making. He produced telescopes and surveyor's instruments. Several striking examples of his work have been preserved. The most impressive of these, the instrument for which he was highly praised in his day, was the Orrery.[28] Rittenhouse built several clocks which included planetaria as part of their mechanisms, but the two full-scale Orreries he created called for a complete knowledge of the Newtonian solar system and the ability to design and build a mechanical representation of that system. By the turning of a handle the Orrery was to reproduce—backwards as well as forwards—the movement of the planets in relation to each other over a period of five thousand years. Unlike other Orreries which were constructed on a flat surface, Rittenhouse chose a vertical surface and installed the works in a cabinet patterned after a Chippendale bookcase.[29] He spent several years working through the mathematics involved. In 1768 he projected his work in a description written for the American Philosophical Society: "This machine is intended to have three faces, standing perpendicular to the horizon: . . . From the centre arises an axis to support a gilded brass ball intended to represent the sun. Round this ball move others, made of brass or ivory, to represent the planets. . . . When the machine is put in motion, by the turning of a winch, there are three indexes which point out the hour of the day, the day of the month, and the year (according to the Julian account), answering to that situation of the heavenly bodies which is then represented; and so continually for a period of 5000 years either forward or backward. . . . The two lesser faces are to be four feet in height. . . . One of them will represent and exhibit all the appearances of Jupiter and his satellites—their eclipses, transits, and inclinations; likewise, all the appearances of Saturn. . . . And the other will represent all the phenomena of the moon. . . ."[30]

The Orrery is symbolic of the age in which it was built. The universe was believed to be a mechanical contrivance, predictable in its workings. This great machine was popularly likened to the works of a clock. The Infinite Clockmaker—that is what Rittenhouse was in a finite frame—designed the machine, wound it up, and started it on its predictable course.

The second accomplishment which established Rittenhouse's fame as an astronomer was his planning and building of the equipment for the observation of the transit of the planet Venus across the face of the sun predicted for the year 1769. The Royal Society in London promoted observation by various groups across the American colonies. Although Benjamin Franklin, then American agent in London and active participant in the proceedings of the Society, believed Boston the most likely American center to support such a scientific venture with money and talent, he was pleasantly surprised to find that his adopted city was eager and able to perform the task. Philadelphia had indeed developed further in his long absence.

One of the prime movers of the effort was the Reverend William Smith, Provost of the College of Philadelphia which had grown out of the Academy established by Franklin and his associates. Smith, one of the most controversial, partisan, and objectionable personalities of his time, had the drive and organizational talent to promote and execute the observation. He consistently sustained the scientific efforts of Rittenhouse and had the requisite knowledge to take an active part in the observation himself.

Rittenhouse set about the task of building an observatory and all of the equipment needed at his farm at Norriton. When the great day came he, Smith, and several others were placed strategically in the environs of Philadelphia while Owen Biddle made an observation from Cape Henlopen on Delaware Bay. It is understandable that, after months of preparation, Rittenhouse's expectation was so great that when Venus hit the rim of the sun he momentarily fainted. This made it impossible for him to check with Smith as to the exact time of contact and obviously detracted from the results of their observation. On the other hand, the main purpose of the observation was to determine the sun's parallax and thus the distance of the sun from the earth. Despite this drawback, Rittenhouse's estimate was very close to that reckoned with the use of present-day instruments.

The second colonial astronomer of particular note, John Winthrop, also took part in the observation of the transit of Venus in 1769. Winthrop was elected Hollis professor of mathematics and of natural and experimental philosophy at Harvard in 1738, when he was just twenty-three years old, and held the post till his death in 1779. He obviously was suspected of liberal views; for, when he was nominated for the position, an attempt was made to examine him on his religion, an attempt that was voted down by the Board of Overseers of the College.[31] That the suspicion was justified is clear from Winthrop's close association with his student Jonathan Mayhew, who was to be classed as a flaming liberal during his career as minister of the West Church in Boston, and with Mayhew's friend, Charles Chauncy, another leading rationalist clergyman of the day.[32]

Winthrop had observed the earlier transit of Venus from Newfoundland in 1761, thus taking part in the two observations of this particular cosmic phenomenon possible in the lifetime of him and his contemporaries. That expedition was made with the support of the royal government of Massachusetts. The leading capitalist and politician, James Bowdoin, a man of many scientific interests, had prevailed on Governor Francis Bernard and his fellow members of the Governor's Council to support the venture. Bernard, understanding the fiscal concerns of the House of Representatives in a day when the subject of taxation was of vital interest, explained that since the province's sloop was making a trip north to Penobscot anyway that that was "the best and least expensive method" of getting the professor and his equipment to the site.[33]

If the results were to be valid, it was necessary that the observation be made at several widely separated positions on the earth and timed precisely. Since the transit of 1761 was not to be visible from the settled colonies, Winthrop led the expedition north.

By 1769 Winthrop's health was not good enough to allow him to consider a trip to Lake Superior, considered the ideal spot for the observation on the North American continent. His attempt to organize provincial financial support for such an expedition, although like the earlier one supported by James Bowdoin, ran afoul of the political problems slowly building toward the American Revolution.

Among Winthrop's more important contributions toward the establishment of an enlightened intellectual climate was his public exchange in 1755 with the Reverend Thomas Prince of Boston on the subject of earthquakes. On 1 November of that year the great earthquake had killed tens of thousands and had destroyed Lisbon and its treasures. Several tremors were also felt later that month in New England, terrifying many persons. Prince chose to bolster the old Puritan theological view by dusting off and republishing his sermonic effort of 1727 entitled *Earthquakes the Works of God and Tokens of His Just Displeasure*. In an appendix he added a new twist, implying that the new-fangled invention of the lightning rod and the fad to install them in Boston was probably responsible for such earthly disruption. This was more than Professor Winthrop could abide. He went after the Reverend Mr. Prince in a series of publications which, as a contemporary put it, "laid Mr. Prince flat on [his] back."[34]

Winthrop pointed out that "philosophy, like everything else, has had its fashions, and the reigning mode of late has been to explain everything by electricity." Therefore, attempts had been made to use electricity in the cure of "gout, blindness, deafness, dumbness, and what not!"[35]

Winthrop did not deny that theology had a just concern in such matters, but he shifted the accent in the discussion to natural causes. He attacked Prince more on scientific grounds for his fallacious speculation on the cause of earthquakes than on theological grounds. However, he sought to educate the public via the newspapers, complaining that Prince saw divinity rather than natural philosophy as the discipline which dealt with the deity behind material things. He made greater claims for the province of natural philosophy (science) than his friend Franklin would have been willing to concede. He hinged his argument on that favorite idea of the eighteenth century that there existed a chain of being of which man and other living creatures were parts. ". . . The main business of natural philosophy is to trace the chain of natural causes from one link to another, till we come to the First Cause who in philosophy is considered as presiding over and continuously actuating this whole chain and every link of it. . . ."[36]

Old theological attitudes persist and are not easily overcome. Within a few years of Winthrop's public campaign for a new understanding of earthquakes, he found it necessary to counter superstitious views on comets. When an anonymous gentleman warned of potential disaster to mankind in a pamphlet entitled *Blazing Stars Messengers of God's Wrath* (1759), Winthrop countered by delivering two lectures on the subject to students at Harvard and making sure they were published.[37]

Winthrop had much to do with popular interest in electricity, for he had supported the theories of Benjamin Franklin. Franklin was inspired to begin dabbling in electricity at a time when he was planning early retirement from business so that he could devote the balance of his life to the promotion of causes in which he was interested. His earlier regimen of self-discipline had paid off. His partnerships with apprentices whom he had helped set up in

various American cities and his other investments gave him influence far beyond Philadelphia, while his position as deputy postmaster under the royal government allowed him to use the mails
gratis and thus to act as a conduit for the exchange of scientific
and other beneficial ideas among the colonial thinkers.

Franklin became interested in pursuing electrical experiments
as a result of the lectures on science of a peripatetic Scottish clergyman who made a tour through the American colonies. Franklin
managed to purchase some of the electrical equipment from Dr.
Archibald Spencer, and, as he became more intrigued with the
subject, he was to get Peter Collinson to send more sophisticated
apparatus from London.

Franklin approached electricity with a fresh view. Not only was
it a new, relatively undeveloped field, but he had little
mathematical knowledge and little theoretical knowledge. His accomplishment has raised the question in some minds as to
whether his naiveté was not a benefit.[38] Not knowing what had
been done previously in the field, he did not hesitate to try all
kinds of experimentation with as close to a completely open mind
as one is likely to have.

Franklin encouraged Colden in New York, Winthrop and Bowdoin in Boston, and others to experiment with electricity. His
correspondence with them gives a step-by-step account of his various experiments—his successes and failures clearly and openly
noted. There is no attempt to cover up failure; rather, it is looked
upon as part of the experimental process. It is important, believed Franklin, to know what does not work as well as what
does.

Franklin's correspondence with Peter Collinson gained him international fame. Collinson read Franklin's successive letters describing his experiments before the meetings of the Royal Society, and they were published in the *Philosophical Transactions*.
Collinson then collected them and arranged for their publication
as a volume with the title *Experiments and Observations on
Electricity* (1751). This volume was republished in Europe at least
eleven times down to the American Revolution. Not until 1941
did an American edition appear, a fact which attests the high
place which Franklin has held in science in European eyes.[39]

It is clear from Franklin's letters that his efforts were carried
out with the help of a number of Philadelphia friends. Indeed,
electricity became all the rage, and Franklin found his house

crowded by the curious day after day—so much so that he repli-
cated his apparatus and encouraged others to carry on demonstrations to help draw off the crowds which were probably getting in
his way.

Franklin's contributions were both theoretical and practical. He
developed the categories in which electrical thinking still pro-
ceeds. The distinction between positive and negative electricity is
household terminology today. It is unnecessary to repeat the
story of the kite experiment—an American success story perpetuated in each succeeding generation—by which Franklin demonstrated his claim that lightning was the same "fluid" as the
electricity generated on earth.

Lightning rods, the use of which the Reverend Thomas Prince
decried, were among the more practical applications of Franklin's
electrical discoveries. But their introduction and acceptance did
not come without a struggle. The implications were theological as
well as physical. As we have seen, it was believed, probably by
most people, that lightning was a sign of God's displeasure; in
other words that God hurled bolts at those who were wayward.
To install lightning rods to ground the electrical charge was in the
eyes of believers obviously impious. But the campaign in behalf
of the use of lightning rods, although it had various humorous aspects, was profoundly significant. It is clear that when churches,
after much debate and dissension, began to install them yet
another important aspect of the eighteenth-century world view
had been altered.

Given his personality and outlook on life, one would expect
that Franklin's experimentation would take a practical bent. Looking back over his life in his *Autobiography*, he takes time and
space to discourse on such things as how to keep the streets of a
city clean (a technique still not mastered in many places). This
discourse sets the mood for a generalization which provides an insight into not only Franklin but the mode of thinking of his age:
"Human felicity is produced not so much by great pieces of good
fortune that seldom happen as by little advantages that occur
every day. Thus if you teach a poor young man to shave himself
and keep his razor in order, you may contribute more to the
happiness of his life than in giving him a thousand guineas. The
money may be soon spent, the regret only remaining of having
foolishly consumed it; but in the other case he escapes the fre-
quent vexation of waiting for barbers and of their sometimes dirty

fingers, offensive breaths, and dull razors; he shaves when most convenient to him and enjoys daily the pleasure of its being done with a good instrument."[40]

Following the principle of promoting human felicity, Franklin was ever on the lookout for ways to make the load of living a little lighter. The development of the lightning rod obviously grew out of experimentation and the application of theory. But, just as felicitous, were his other inventions which stemmed from his propensity to tinker. Franklin's idea of joining in the bifocal part of a distance lens with part of one which helps a person to read material up close, allows the author of these pages to avoid the constant changing of eyeglasses. His observation that street lights in London consisted of globes which were entirely shattered when struck led him to promote a foursided frame for such lights—only part of which was likely to be broken at a time by a blow. He also observed that London street lights in just a few hours of operation became sooty and relatively ineffective. How much better to allow air in at the bottom which would carry exhaust out through the top, thus keeping the glass clean much longer.

Aside from the lightning rod, Franklin's contemporaries in the northern clime probably thanked him most for the development in 1742 of the "open stove," or "Pennsylvania Fireplace." It was obvious that most of the warmth produced by a standard fireplace went up the chimney and Franklin was not the first to bring the fire "out into the room" in a stove. But, although stoves were an improvement over the fireplace, they still allowed too much heat to escape through the chimney. His great discovery was the result of the application of physical principles to the improvement of the product. If, as in the case of the street lamp, one allowed air in at the bottom, it would emerge from the top. In this case, air passed through a chamber that was separate from the firebox of the stove; it entered at the bottom as cool air and came out the top thoroughly warmed and circulated around the room.

Not only was this stove much more effective in producing heat, but, just as important, it cut down on the consumption of wood—a crucial feature in the city where wood was much less accessible than in the countryside and so much more expensive. In the pamphlet describing the working of the Pennsylvania fireplace, Franklin claimed a saving of three-quarters on the amount of wood consumed. Certainly a significant contribution to human felicity. This pamphlet is fascinating reading. His writing style was so winning that, as a contemporary remarked, he could even make reading about stoves interesting.[41]

According to Franklin, Governor George Thomas of Pennsylvania offered him a patent for the exclusive selling of his stove, but he refused it: ". . . I declined it from a principle which has ever weighed with me on such occasions, viz., that, as we enjoy great advantages from the inventions of others, we should be glad of an opportunity to serve others by any invention of ours; and this we should do freely and generously."[42]

As we have seen, Cadwallader Colden grew increasingly impatient with the detail of botanical classification. Having turned over that chore to his daughter Jane, he began to indulge in cosmic speculation. He sought to improve on the work of Sir Isaac Newton, in itself an amazing breach of filiopiety when one considers that in eighteenth-century philosophical homes Sir Isaac was venerated as a household god. Colden's *Explication of the First Causes of Action in Matter, and of the Cause of Gravitation*, published in 1745, and the expanded edition published in 1751, caused consternation among his friends; none of them could understand it.

Franklin's New York printing partner had published the book. For this reason alone he might have an interest in the success of the venture. But, more important, was his great friendship with Colden. But friendship did not make it any the easier to understand what he had written. Franklin wrote him to say that he was making notes as he read and that he would send his reactions later. He promised "without reserve, [to] give you my thoughts as they rose, knowing by experience that you make candid allowances to your friends."

Franklin had delivered copies of the book, as Colden had asked him, to Lewis Evans and John Bartram. "The former declares he cannot understand it," Franklin wrote; "the latter told me the other day that he could not read it with the necessary attention till after harvest, but he apprehended he should find it out of his reach."[43] Franklin could not use a harvest as an excuse, but four months later he complained to Colden in a letter that he did not have time for the steady concentration needed. He mentioned several friends who had read the book and had given up on it! ". . . I am almost ready to join with the rest and give it up as beyond my reach."[44]

Whether anyone in America ever understood the book is not on record, but it is doubtful. Colden became so discouraged that he sent it and related papers to the library of the University of Edinburgh for safekeeping, apparently with the confident expectation that someone in a future generation would understand his exposition and that posterity would appreciate the depth of his thought even if his contemporaries did not.

His book was apparently understood by some Europeans, however, but they were no more receptive than the Americans had been. The distinguished Swiss mathematician and physicist Leonhard Euler of the Berlin Academy analyzed the book in a communication read to the Royal Society in London and, although he thought it contained "many ingenious reflections," complained, among other things, that Colden's ignorance of mechanics undermined his attempt to challenge "the best established propositions of the late Sir Isaac Newton. . . ."[45]

As befits people in a virgin territory, American scientific concerns were practical. The case of Colden's cosmic speculation is the most notable departure from this principle, and the result was a great disappointment to him and his scientific circle. The pragmatic, utilitarian approach continued as the basic component in the American's outlook down to the twentieth century.

Science in eighteenth-century America was the pursuit of amateurs. In few if any instances did individuals earn a living by scientific endeavor. It was considered the duty of the enlightened person to add to man's store of knowledge without thought of personal gain. The reward was the thrill of discovery and the recognition gained among other philosophers for one's contribution.

The exchange of ideas and the trading of specimens makes it apparent that there was an international community of science in which the Americans worked in partnership with their European brethren. The American Revolution did not disrupt this unity. The pursuit of scientific knowledge was a common venture which transcended political divisions. This position was affirmed in the midst of hostilities by the American Philosophical Society, which put the interests of mankind above those of nationalism.

The divisions between loyalists and patriots in the new United States were another matter, however. Cadwallader Colden who served as Lieutenant Governor of New York in the stormy period before the outbreak of war remained loyal to the crown, but he mercifully passed away in 1776. The bitterness in many cases divided families. William Franklin remained loyal while his father reluctantly became a leading revolutionary. Alexander Garden, unhappy with the idea of independence but keeping his own counsel, was banished from Charles Town in the year of American victory and, like many other loyalists, saw his property confiscated, even though his son served in the Revolutionary army. He spent his final years in England, where he continued his contributions to scientific knowledge.

The accomplishments of the Americans in science accrued to their benefit in other areas as well. Their claims to maturity as a people were taken much more seriously than otherwise would have been the case. Although some such as Colden and Garden remained loyal to the crown, the greater number of American scientists supported the patriot cause. Franklin's discoveries in electricity established him in the eyes of Europe as the leading American scientist. By the time he journeyed to England in 1757 as agent for a number of American colonies, his reputation as a natural philosopher was more firm there than in the colonies. This reputation added immeasurably to his influence as a diplomat. When in 1776 he arrived in Paris to negotiate a treaty of assistance, he was received by adoring Frenchmen as the exemplification of the best of enlightened America. With the possible exception of George III, few would take issue with the tribute paid Franklin by the French statesman Turgot:

Eripuit caelo fulmen, sceptrumque tyrannis.

He snatched from heaven the lightning,
the sceptre from tyrants' hands.

CHAPTER 3

The Rights of Man

A LL eyes are opened, or opening, to the rights of man. The general spread of the light of science has already laid open to every view the palpable truth that the mass of mankind has not been born with saddles on their backs, nor a favored few booted and spurred ready to ride them legitimately, by the grace of God.

—*Thomas Jefferson*[1]

Revolution doth powerfully concentrate the mind. The "Glorious Revolution" which replaced James II with William and Mary on the English throne in 1688 stimulated a great reexamination of the nature of society and the dynamics which hold men together in governments. The physician and philosopher John Locke provided propositions concerning these questions which were useful in his time and later in America as events propelled the colonists to consider breaking the ties which had bound them to Britain. In disputing Stuart pretensions and justifying the installation of William and Mary, Locke refuted the idea of absolute monarchy, of the divine right of kings to rule a subservient people. He insisted that power flows from the people and that the state should be their agent not their oppressor. Society is composed of free individuals who have contracted together to form a government which will be beneficial to all. When the cause is just, the people, as was true when they drove James from the throne, have a natural right to dissolve or alter the social contract that they have previously made.[2]

Locke and several other English thinkers, such as Harrington and Sidney, provided many of the elements which were to figure prominently in American thinking. Particularly important was the belief in the natural rights of man. The concept of natural law can be traced back to Greek and Roman philosophy. It was adapted to the needs of each subsequent age. In the eighteenth century it was believed to be central to the design of the universe. Newton demonstrated in mathematical terms what the Creator had provided in the physical laws by which His universe was governed. Natural law was not merely an abstraction but "the observed harmonious behavior of material objects"[3]—observed, that is, by the reason which was so great a component of the mind of man. Man was an intimate part of this mechanistic, natural world, the exploration of which consumed so much of the attention of men of the Enlightenment.

The same laws which were inherent in the universe ideally could be observed in man's behavior and in his institutions. If they were not so easily discovered in contemporary world governments, it was because men had departed from the natural state that was in complete harmony with nature. That men had earlier lived in a pure state of nature became a firm conviction, and much effort went into the attempt to reform present society so that it would conform to the image of the earlier condition.

Since they were not systematic philosophers, the enlightened Americans did not worry how natural rights related to natural law; but they made the connection in the belief that both were basic to the order which the deity had built into the universe. Of these natural rights, John Dickinson wrote, "We claim them from a higher source—from the King of kings, and Lord of all the earth." They were not the gifts or grants of rulers but rather were to be recognized as innate to the human condition: "They are not annexed to us by parchments and seals. They are created in us by the decrees of Providence which establish the laws of our nature. They are born with us; exist with us; and cannot be taken from us by any human power without taking our lives. In short, they are founded on the immutable maxims of reason and justice."[4]

The argument connecting natural law and the rights of man was first used in America in a most unlikely context, within the Congregational churches. At the turn of the eighteenth century these descendants of the Puritans became embroiled in a dispute over reorganization. From the beginning of the New England settlements the churches had been self-governing—thus the term congregational—although, for the promotion of amity and cooperation across town lines, they had joined in district associations. In 1705 it was proposed that these associations be vested with a certain measure of control over the churches and the ministry. One of the strongest opponents of this attempt to presbyterianize the Congregational churches was the Reverend John Wise, who in successive publications defended the democratic procedures of the Congregational churches. His *Vindication of the Government of the New-England Churches* in 1717 places democracy on a foundation of the natural rights of man. It is significant that Wise cites the work of a leading thinker of the European Enlightenment, Samuel Pufendorf's *De Jure Natural et Gentium* (1672; English trans. 1703 and 1710), as having great influence on his thought concerning the law of nature.

Wise helped ward off the spector of Presbyterianism. So effective was his argument concerning the natural rights of man that his *Vindication* was republished in 1772, when the dispute between the colonists and Great Britain was building to a climax.

Belief in natural rights became firmly implanted in American thinking in succeeding years and is the basis for much of the thought of the Revolutionary generation. When the brilliant, but erratic attorney, James Otis, sought to state the case of Massachusetts against the encroachments of the British Parliament in 1764, he insisted that man has "natural liberty" and has the "law of nature for his rule." This is the gift of God and cannot be "annihilated."[5] Although Otis at this stage of the argument did not doubt that Parliament had the right to tax the Americans, he stated that there is a higher law than Parliament can legislate —the deity's "natural laws"—and that Parliament's enactments ideally should conform to it. Should Parliament fail in this, Otis is sure that the British courts will override it. In this provision he sees the British constitution's system of checks and balances. This argument had its effect on his younger contemporary John Adams, who spent his long life constantly affirming the importance of this feature.

Otis also ties his theories to the workings of the Newtonian universe. Government, he says, is founded in the "unchangeable will of God, the author of nature, whose laws never vary." It is founded in the necessities of man's nature and is not "an arbitrary thing, depending merely on compact or human will for its existence." Government comes as naturally to man as does sex. He continues: "The same omniscient, omnipotent, infinitely good and gracious Creator of the universe, who has been pleased to make it necessary that what we call matter should gravitate, for the celestial bodies to roll round their axes, dance their orbits and perform their various revolutions in that beautiful order and concert, which we all admire, has made it equally necessary that from Adam and Eve to these degenerate days, the different sexes should sweetly attract each other, form societies of single families, of which larger bodies and communities are as naturally, mechanically, and necessarily combined, as the dew of Heaven and the soft distilling rain is collected by the all enliv'ning heat of the sun."[6]

The same philosophical basis underlay Jefferson's *Summary View of the Rights of British America* (1774), written as a position paper addressed to the Assembly of Virginia but published for all to read, a publication which brought Jefferson to the attention of a continental audience. He, like Otis, speaks of the "rights of human nature." Like Locke, he denies that they are derived from the king: ". . . Kings are the servants, not the proprietors of the people."[7] But where Otis concedes the right of Parliament to legislate for America, Jefferson takes a radically different position. He claims that Parliament has no rights in the matter. The original Americans had exercised what he called their right of emigration, a right "which nature has given to all men. . . ." It is not choice but chance which governs the birthplace of an individual. The British American colonists had chosen, however, to change their place of abode and migrate from the mother country to the New World. Jefferson likened this emigration to that of the Saxons who in ancient times had chosen to leave "their native wilds and woods in the North of Europe"[8] and move across the English Channel to sparsely populated Britain. As did many of his contemporaries, he accepted the claim of the Whig historians that the Saxons embodied in their way of life the virtues of a natural society, with a king elected by all of the people and a democratic witenagemot, the original of Parliaments.

In this golden age, the mother country of the Saxons had not attempted to control their destiny when they moved to the British Isles. It followed that Great Britain should have "too firm a feeling of the rights derived to them from their ancestors" to attempt to control the Americans. The colonists, Jefferson asserted, had migrated to America at their own expense, not at the expense of the British nation: "Their own blood was spilt in acquiring lands for their settlement, their own fortunes expended in making that settlement effectual. For themselves they fought, for themselves they conquered, and for themselves alone they have right to hold."[9]

Jefferson insisted that the only thing that tied the American colonists to England was their allegiance, freely given, to the British throne. George was king of America, as he was Prince of Hanover, the German state from which his family came to the British throne. He stands in relation to the various American legislatures as he does to the British Parliament or the legislature of Hanover. The British Parliament by its actions has violated the rights of the Americans. To Jefferson it is preposterous that a legislature representing 160,000 electors in Britain should be telling 4,000,000 Americans what to do. When it suspends the New York legislature, closes the port of Boston—to break the will of Massachusetts—and when it insists that trials for murder in America be held in England, it is acting the role of usurper.

Although he affirms America's allegiance to the crown, Jefferson's remarks concerning George III are stern and hardly civil. He condemns a number of actions by the king, some of the indictments to appear again later in his draft of the Declaration of Independence. Jefferson justifies his use of free language with the king on the ground that flattery is not an American art![10]

Jefferson found few in Virginia who were yet prepared to take such a radical position. He was supported by his old mentor and friend, George Wythe, but hardly anyone else. Americans, on the whole, still conceded the right of Parliament to control their destiny. John Adams, who had become acquainted with Jefferson in the Continental Congress at Philadelphia, argued the same proposition in the North. His letters to a Boston newspaper, signed "Novanglus," claimed that Parliament lacked authority over the colonies. America owed its allegiance to the king. Adams insisted that Massachusetts stood in the same relation to George as did Britain. There was a revolution in Massachusetts at the same time that the Glorious Revolution brought William and Mary to the throne of England. At the conclusion of that upheaval, Massachusetts made a contract with William of Orange as did Britain. Adams was referring to the new Massachusetts charter of 1691.[11]

Americans had good cause to take seriously the idea of the social contract. Their colonial governments, such as that of Virginia, had been based on charters granted by the crown. The

Separatists, or Pilgrims, at Plymouth had formed a compact designed to hold the community together when it was clear that the
Mayflower had landed well beyond the bounds of Virginia, its
original destination. In the case of Massachusetts Bay, the company charter had been transformed by the Puritans in the 1630s
into an instrument of government, in one of the first acts of quiet
rebellion on the American shore. When later in that decade immigrants from Massachusetts moved south to Connecticut, they
had devised a frame of government in the first conscious act of
constitution-writing in American history. These few examples illustrate that the social contract was more than a theoretical concept for the Americans; it was part of the reality of their experience in the New World.

From the beginning, the legislatures of the colonies enjoyed a
large measure of autonomy and often pitted their strength against
royal governors appointed by the government in London. The
British empire was so loosely organized that the colonials ran
their own affairs with relatively little interference. When the
home government finally attempted to exert more energetic
supervision, the Americans did not take it kindly. What at first
was ineptness on the part of succeeding British ministries came to
be interpreted by the colonials as a conspiracy to enslave them,
to deprive them of their ancient rights as Englishmen.[12] Once
their suspicion grew into conviction, it was just a matter of time
before the Americans, some much more reluctantly than others,
would be driven to decisive action.

The most persuasive of the champions of the American cause
was Thomas Paine. When his *Common Sense* appeared in January
of 1776, the battles of Lexington and Concord and of Bunker Hill
had occurred, and the Americans now had to make a choice between an accommodation with an angry king or independence.
Paine's pamphlet was described by contemporaries, and by historians since, as one of the most effective pieces ever put into
print. George Washington, who had continued to toast the king's
health nightly while encamped with American troops in Cambridge, was convinced by Paine's "sound doctrine and unanswer-
able reasoning. . . ." He was sure that if the British squadrons
continued such outrages as the shelling of Falmouth and Norfolk,
these "flaming arguments," along with *Common Sense*, would
leave few in doubt concerning "the propriety of a separation."[13]
Paine's diatribe, indeed, did rally a hesitating continent to make

the break and declare independence. Dr. Benjamin Rush of Philadelphia, a member of the Continental Congress, had inspired Paine to write the pamphlet, since he, an established physician, could not do it himself for fear of offending friends and clients who were opposed to separation from Britain.[14] Paine, who had recently migrated to America with letters of introduction from Franklin, whom he had met in London, had little to lose. This journalistic effort, along with the *Crisis Papers* written at the point of lowest fortune of the American cause, established Paine as a hard-hitting proponent of revolution. One of the secrets of the success of *Common Sense* was Paine's common touch. He was capable of embodying great philosophical questions in memorable phrases which everyone could understand. Paine's practical arguments were equally incisive. The line which Dr. Rush found particularly fetching is a good example of the author's striking ability to reduce complicated arguments to their simplest terms: "Nothing can be conceived of more absurd than three millions of people flocking to the American shore, every time a vessel arrives from England, to know what portion of liberty they shall enjoy."[15] After he had finished each section of *Common Sense*, Paine showed it to Rush, Franklin, Rittenhouse, and the archrevolutionary agitator from Boston, Sam Adams.

Paine includes in his argument references to natural rights and the social compact[16] but he obviously takes them for granted. ("A government of our own is our natural right. . . .") The principle, after all, had had a thorough airing before his arrival in America. He is more concerned to undercut the British monarchy and monarchs generally. For Paine, kings and their courtiers are ruffians. The particular king, George III, is a "royal brute." The British line of sovereigns is the result of usurpation by William of Normandy who crossed the channel from France in 1066 and seized power in England. William, to boot, was a bastard: "A French bastard landing with an armed banditti and establishing himself king of England against the consent of the natives, is in plain terms a very paltry rascally original."[17] So much for the pretensions of the British throne.

But Paine's message is not wholly negative; he also summons Americans to a noble vision. With the fervor of a convert, he sees America as an asylum for freedom.[18] It has an opportunity which is unique: "to begin the world over again."[19] Americans, then, should not hesitate. They have the resources, if they will only summon the will, to expel the British from their shores. After Lexington and Concord and Bunker Hill, there can be no talk of reconciliation. George and his banditti have shown themselves for what they are. Paine claims that he has never met a thinking person on either side of the water who does not believe that an eventual separation of Britain and America will take place. So why wait?

He provided Americans with advice as to what form a declaration of independence should take. His outline for a proposed "manifesto" can be compared profitably with Jefferson's formulation later in that crucial year.[20] Whether Jefferson and the other members of the committee chosen by Congress to present a draft for its consideration remembered Paine's outline has not been noted. There is no doubt, however, that Jefferson was influenced by the work of his friend George Mason who had drafted "The Virginia Declaration of Rights" several weeks before Jefferson set to work. Certainly the similarity of sentiment and phrasing is striking.

Mason was probably the most reluctant of the participants in Virginia's new General Assembly. An intensely private man, with great problems of health, he much preferred to superintend the affairs of his plantation on the shores of the Potomac. On the other hand, the expectation of Virginia that her gentry would serve when called upon necessarily superseded all personal objections. Mason was a logical choice to formulate the Declaration, since he was deeply learned on the subject of the rights of Englishmen. His statement, which was a preface to the new state constitution, had a profound influence on the bills of rights written into the other state constitutions; and a good case can be made for the idea that it served as a model thirteen years later for the drafters of the French revolutionary Declaration of the Rights of Man.[21]

The striking similarity between the Virginia Declaration and Jefferson's is obvious on the reading of section 1 of the former: "That all men are by nature equally free and independent and have certain inherent rights, of which, when they enter into a state of society, they cannot, by any compact, deprive or divest their posterity; namely, the enjoyment of life and liberty, with the means of acquiring and possessing property, and pursuing and obtaining happiness and safety."

Jefferson's more taut phrasing, of course, read as follows: "We hold these truths to be self-evident, that all men are created equal, that they are endowed by their Creator with certain un-alienable rights, that among these are life, liberty, and the pursuit of happiness."[22] Inevitably both Mason and Jefferson were heavily dependent on the ideas, and the formulation, of John Locke in his *Second Treatise on Civil Government*.

Where Jefferson was writing for the new nation and the world, Mason had a different audience. Jefferson had to prove that George III indeed was a royal brute and encumbered his document with a lengthy indictment of the king. Mason dealt with the natural rights of the people and the first principles and proper bounds of government. Many of the points which appear later in the national Bill of Rights are outlined in the Virginia Declaration: a speedy trial by a jury of one's peers; bans on "excessive fines," and "cruel and unusual punishments," and on "general warrants"; provision for a "well regulated militia," civilian control of the military, and against "standing armies, in time of peace"; and statements of the rights of freedom of the press and freedom of religion. It is obvious to a later age that many of these rights had been achieved through long centuries of struggle against authoritarian rulers. Some of them were asserted as the result of bitter colonial experience with the British crown and Parliament. But in the heat of the struggle, the Americans tended not to make these distinctions and to cast the mantle of natural rights over all of them.

The doctrine of the natural rights of man played an important part in both declarations. Jefferson invoked the "Laws of Nature and of Nature's God" as the justification for the desire of the colonies for an existence separate from that of Britain. It is to "secure" these natural rights that "governments are instituted among men"; but if "government becomes destructive of these ends," the people have the right, indeed the duty, to dissolve the social contract, "to alter or to abolish it," and to establish a new one: "to institute new government, laying its foundation on such principles and organizing its powers in such form as to them shall seem most likely to effect their safety and happiness." In a later generation these principles were labeled "glittering generalities," but the fifty-five men who at Philadelphia subscribed to them with their "lives . . . fortunes and . . . sacred honor" knew that if the Revolution failed they were, in effect, putting their necks in a noose.

The rights of man became the great ideological rallying cry of the last quarter of the eighteenth century. The effect of the Mason and Jefferson declarations was not to stop at water's edge but leap over the Atlantic. Where the cause of the Revolutionary Americans was bolstered by the philosophy of enlightened Europeans, the cause of French revolutionaries was bolstered by the philosophy and accomplishments of the enlightened Americans.

Paine's aversion to monarchy and his belief that independence is a natural right evidence themselves in the *Crisis*,[23] as they had in *Common Sense*. But his most sustained argument on behalf of the rights of man was to be embodied in his book by that title written in response to Edmund Burke's eloquent attack on the French Revolution. Paine was in England promoting his design for an iron bridge; for, like other leaders of the American Enlightenment, he had his own interest in scientific development. He observed the developing revolution in France from across the Channel and cheered the revolutionaries on. Paine saw the revolution as another evidence of the progress made in establishing man's rights against tyranny. Burke, on the other hand, saw the revolution in France as a threat to all he held dear. He, like Paine, believed in rights—he had been a supporter of the American cause in the House of Commons—but he believed them to be based on a very different foundation, a foundation which could be easily undermined by what he considered madness in France. Paine was in constant touch with Burke while the latter was drafting his *Reflections on the Revolution in France* and impatiently awaited publication so he could answer him in a diatribe of his own. Burke's book was published in November, 1790; Paine's *Rights of Man* in February, 1791; and the issue was joined.

Paine's response is one of his longer works. Where in his American writings he took the natural rights argument for granted, here he developed it in full detail. In the case of his American writings it was unnecessary, as has been pointed out, because earlier writers had asserted the principle time and again, but also because the American colonies were, on the whole, not subject to the encrusted traditions which had grown up over the centuries of European experience. In America Paine was not contending against an aristocracy and all of the practices that that word connotes.

The *Rights of Man* was a work of international significance. It not only justified the turmoil which was occurring in France, but

it also justified the Americans in their Revolution. It celebrated
their accomplishments, but, more importantly, it lent support to
those who were working for the further democratization of
American society. Even though we shall return to the events of
1776 shortly, it will be useful at this point to examine Paine's
apologia for the light it casts on revolutionary thinking on both
sides of the Atlantic.

The fundamental difference between Burke and Paine can be
briefly stated. Burke believed that Englishmen enjoyed rights by
prescription, that is, rights that had been achieved in a process of
organic evolution over the centuries of British experience. Their
civil rights were recognized as legitimate by long usage. He
feared the position taken by a priori theorists such as Dr. Richard
Price, whose preaching was one of the provocations for his
Reflections. That Nonconformist (Unitarian) clergyman had defended the goings-on in France on the ground of doctrinaire
natural rights. To say, as Price had, that the English king owed
his throne to the Revolution of 1688 was to misread history.
Burke insisted that the legitimacy of the English throne be traced
back to the landing of William the Conqueror in 1066. Paine
agreed with Burke in this, saying the Revolution of 1688 was a
mere change in government. The English monarchy should be
traced back to William of Normandy; we have already seen what
Paine thought of the actions of that "French bastard."

He rejected Burke's theory of prescription; for if the rights of
the people were wrung from, or granted by, a king, a shift in the
balance of power in a government might lead to their being taken
away. Just as nature is unchanging and unchangeable, so are the
natural rights of man. They can be traced back to the beginning
of the world, for they stem from man's creation by God: "Every
generation is equal in rights to the generations which preceded
it, by the same rule that every individual is born equal in rights
with his contemporary."[24]

Although men may be self-sufficient as individuals, they join in
a social contract to assume a mutual aid and a happiness[25] which
would otherwise be missing in life. Paine believed Burke wrong
in his fears that civilized life would unravel with the overthrow of
the French government. He points to America an an example of
what actually happens. Americans in their states demonstrated
they could live without government, society being sufficient, for
several years after the beginning of the Revolution: "The old gov-

ernments had been abolished, and the country was too much oc-
cupied in defense to employ its attention in establishing new
governments; yet, during this interval, order and harmony were
preserved as inviolate as in any country in Europe."[26]

Paine was a minimalist when it came to government. He did
not think it took much to keep society going: "It is but few general laws that civilized life requires, and those of such common
usefulness, that whether they are enforced by forms of government or not, the effect will be nearly the same."[27] As he had
written at another time, government is the badge of lost inno-
cence, so obviously the less of it impinging on man in society the
better.

Having accounted for man's natural rights, Paine attempted to
show that civil rights flowed from them. As men in a state of nature had agreed to form a social contract, so they agreed to place
in a common stock some of their natural rights for the good of the
whole: "Natural rights are those which appertain to man in right
of his existence. Of this kind are all the intellectual rights, or
rights of the mind, and also all those rights of acting as an individual for his own comfort and happiness which are not injurious
to the natural rights of others. Civil rights are those which appertain to man in right of his being a member of society." Natural
rights, such as freedom of religious belief, can be exercised by
the individual in a state of society, but his civil rights he has not
the power to exercise alone, declared Paine. "Society *grants* him
nothing. Every man is proprietor in society, and draws on capital
as a matter of right." In effect, man exchanges a natural right for
a civil right when he becomes a member of society. Using this
principle as a guide, Paine says it is not difficult to tell which
governments of his day originated in a social compact and which
did not.[28]

Although Burke was upset with what was occurring in France,
his greater concern was the threat these events posed to England. He takes great umbrage at the treatment of the French
queen by the mob, and other events equally distasteful; but his
real concern is to ward off the specter of revolution in England
by discrediting Dr. Price, and then Paine, and others who celebrated the events in France and threatened the same for England.
He sought to convince Englishmen that they had surrendered
their rights to revolution in the settlement of 1688. He argued
that Parliament at that time had bound the English nation and its

posterity to the monarchy. Paine scoffed at the proposition that
any generation can abdicate the rights of a future generation:
"Every age and generation must be as free to act for itself, *in all
cases*, as the ages and generation which preceded it. The vanity
and presumption of governing beyond the grave is the most
ridiculous and insolent of all tyrannies."[29]

Had Paine's book dealt wholly with abstract natural rights, it
might not have gained much attention. But, as he had in America
in *Common Sense*, he called for the abolition of the monarchy
and the nobility and the institution of a republic in which individuals would be judged on their worth rather than on their
wealth or birth. The British government under Pitt charged him
with sedition. Paine fled to France, barely escaping arrest as he
left England.

Burke saw to it that the publication of the second part of
Paine's *Rights of Man* was outlawed. His rhetoric directly fed the
emotion which resulted in an English reign of terror, with mobs
in Birmingham destroying Noncomformist meetinghouses and the
homes of Dr. Joseph Priestley and other liberals. Burke himself,
afraid revolution would break out in England, ordered that his
body be buried secretly lest the revolutionaries dig it up and des-
ecrate his remains.

It is not necessarily true that Burke was suffering paranoia. In
the second part of the *Rights of Man* Paine painted a glowing picture of American progress and condemned the corruption which
had overtaken the old regimes of Europe. He speculated that the
revolutionary movement was moving from America to Europe.
Revolution was "the order of the day."[30]

Let us turn our attention again to America in the crucial year
1776. With the Declaration of Independence drafted and submitted to Congress, Jefferson had to undergo the editorial process
which is always painful to an author who thinks highly of the language, and this by a committee of over fifty members (the Congress in committee of the whole). The pain was alleviated some-
what by Dr. Franklin who, in his inimitable way, sought to con-
sole the younger man with some advice. "I have made it a
rule, . . . whenever in my power, to avoid becoming the
draughtsman of papers to be reviewed by a public body. I took
my lesson from an incident which I will relate to you. When I
was a journeyman printer, one of my companions, an apprentice
hatter, having served out his time, was about to open shop for

himself. His first concern was to have a handsome sign-board with a proper inscription. He composed it in these words, 'John Thompson, Hatter, makes and sells hats for ready money,' with a figure of a hat subjoined. But he thought he would submit it to his friends for their amendments. The first he showed it to thought the word 'hatter' tautologous, because followed by the words 'makes hats,' which show he was a hatter. It was struck out. The next observed that the word 'makes' might as well be omitted, because his customers would not care who made the hats. If good and to their mind, they would buy, by whomsoever made. He struck it out. A third said he thought the words 'for ready money' were useless, as it was not the custom of the place to sell on credit. Everyone who purchased expected to pay. They were parted with, and the inscription now stood, 'John Thompson sells hats.' 'Sells hats!' says his next friend. 'Why nobody will expect you to give them away. What then is the use of that word?' It was stricken out, and 'hats' followed it, the rather as there was one painted on the board. So his inscription was reduced ultimately to 'John Thompson' with the figure of a hat subjoined."[31]

Jefferson left Philadelphia shortly after the adoption of the Declaration, for he was anxious to be part of the quickening political events in his native state. He had many ideas for change which he hoped to accomplish via legislation and legal reform. His work in behalf of separation of church and state and education will be dealt with in other chapters, but his efforts to establish legal equality of the entire citizenry is particularly relevant under the rubric of the rights of man.

Jefferson arranged to be appointed to a committee of the House of Delegates which was commissioned to recodify Virginia law. He wanted to excise what he considered "many very vicious points" from regal days[32] and bring it into line with the principles of a republic. With him on this committee on recodification served George Mason, George Wythe, Edmund Pendleton, and Thomas L. Lee. Mason soon withdrew, pleading that he was no lawyer and would be of very little use in such a project. Lee withdrew for the same reason.

The original pattern of settlement in Virginia had led to the desire to maintain such feudal practices of the Old World as primogeniture and entail. The first stipulated that if a man died intestate his lands and other property would pass to his eldest son. Entail, which forbade the division of estates, insured the maintenance intact of the extensive plantations. Although there was much land to be claimed to the west, these laws insured in the settled areas the perpetuation of the aristocratic aspirations of the gentry. Jefferson's effort to overturn these provisions, therefore, was more than symbolic.

Pendleton attempted to temper these moves toward liberalization. "Mr. Pendleton wished to preserve the right of primogeniture," wrote Jefferson, "but seeing at once that that could not prevail, he proposed we should adopt the Hebrew principle and give a double portion to the elder son. I observed that if the eldest son could eat twice as much or do double work, it might be a natural evidence of his right to a double portion; but being on a par in his powers and wants with his brothers and sisters, he should be on a par also in the partition of the patrimony; and such was the decision of the other members."[33]

Jefferson, who in the Continental Congress, according to John Adams, hardly spoke a word in debate (although he was an excellent committeeman), in the Virginia House of Delegates found himself taking a leading role, so intent was he in overthrowing the vestiges of aristocracy. He was aided by various persons, depending on the question at issue; but it was George Mason, as Jefferson wrote, who was the "most steadfast, able and zealous; who was himself a host."[34] These men, aristocrats themselves by any measure which can be applied, led the way to the democratization of the Old Dominion.

Jefferson was convinced that every man must have a stake in society and this could only be accomplished by giving all a stake in the land. He even went so far as to include in a proposed constitution for Virginia, which he drafted while serving his term in Congress in 1776 and sent home for consideration, a stipulation that each man who was landless would be given fifty acres by the commonwealth. This would assure that each man could be entrusted with the franchise. The proposal proved too radical for his fellow Virginians who chose to ignore it.

In abolishing primogeniture and entail and making it possible for the land to be distributed among all the children of a family in each generation, Jefferson was promoting the replacement of an "artificial" aristocracy with an "aristocracy of virtue and talent, which nature has wisely provided for the direction of the interests of society, and scattered with equal hand through all its conditions. . . ." Since such an aristocracy of virtue and talent was "essential to a well-ordered republic,"[35] Jefferson spent much of his energy in this period creating conditions which would facilitate its emergence. In the eyes of some this amounted to a dangerous "leveling" of society, but Jefferson's intent was just the opposite. Although all men were created equal, they did not necessarily remain so. Certain persons could obviously contribute more to society than others; but for the sake of themselves as individuals and for the sake of the republic their virtues and talents must be nourished and allowed to emerge, no matter what their economic level. One of Jefferson's great concerns was to set up an educational system to help accomplish this.[36] (See chapter 6.)

The problems of equality and inequality in American life consumed much of the attention of men of the Enlightenment in the Revolutionary generation. John Adams had to deal with the subject when, in England as American minister, in 1787–88 he published a defense of the constitutions of the American states. He pointed out that there is "a moral and political equality of rights and duties" among Americans. Distinctions created by hereditary titles have not developed in the new states. On the other hand, there are inequalities from other causes. Wealth creates distinctions. The possession by some of much wealth in money and lands creates dependency on the part of workmen, the professionals, men of literature, and others. Children of such wealthy families have advantages of better education and exposure to "public characters," something less fortunate children obviously were deprived of. Although not a man of wealth himself, Adams may have been thinking of his elder son, John Quincy, who gained a wide exposure to public figures in his years abroad with his father.

These facts had great implications, thought Adams, for the arrangements of government. He would set the representatives of this level of society off into a senate, for fear that if they were included in a "popular assembly," they would gradually gain all power into their own hands. But, segregated in a senate, they could be kept in check by an executive, on the one hand, and a popular assembly, on the other. Thus, the talents of such a "natural aristocracy" would be harnessed for the good of the state.[37]

Adams and Jefferson continued to debate the question of the composition of this "natural aristocracy" into their old age. Jefferson, writing Adams in 1813, made the distinction between an "artificial aristocracy" which is "founded on wealth and birth" and one founded on "virtue or talents": "May we not even say that that form of government is the best which provides the most effectually for a pure selection of these natural aristoi into the offices of government? The artificial aristocracy is a mischievous ingredient in government, and provision should be made to prevent its ascendency."[38]

Adams, in his response, was not sure that Jefferson was using the words in the same sense as he: "Fashion has introduced an indeterminate use of the word talents. Education, wealth, strength, beauty, stature, birth, marriage, graceful attitudes and motions, gait, air, complexion, physiognomy, are talents, as well as genius, science, and learning." These qualities, thought Adams, after all, influence votes in a republic and have to be taken into account: "Every man will have an equal vote; but when deliberations and discussions are opened, it will be found that twenty-five, by their talents, virtues being equal, will be able to carry fifty votes. Every one of these twenty-five is an aristocrat in my sense of the word; whether he obtains one vote in addition to his own, by his birth, fortune, figure, eloquence, science, learning, craft, cunning, or even his character for good fellowship and a *bon vivant*."[39]

Adams felt he had to correct other Jeffersonians, in addition to their leader, on this point. In a letter the following year to the philosopher of Jeffersonian agrarian democracy, John Taylor of Caroline County, Virginia, he vented his rage at the distortions of the issue due to the hopelessly optimistic preachments of the French *philosophes* Helvetius and Rousseau: "That all men are born to equal rights is true. . . . But to teach that all men are born with equal powers and faculties, to equal influence in society, to equal property and advantages through life, is as gross a fraud, as glaring an imposition on the credulity of the people as ever was practiced by monks, by Druids, by Brahmins, by priests of the immortal Lama, or by the self-styled philosophers of the French Revolution. For honor's sake, Mr. Taylor, for truth and virtue's sake, let American philosophers and politicians despise it."[40]

Closely related to the question of aristocracy was that of the use of titles in a democratic republic. Tom Paine saw the desire for titles as an expression of a certain unfortunate "foppery" in the human character. Men like to show off titles as a little girl shows off a "riband" or a child shows off a new garter. In the revolution, France was right in dispensing with such childish practices. By abolishing titles, thought Paine, France had not "leveled" all but rather it had "exalted" all. The French had discovered that society must have new standards for judging a person's worth: "It must now take the substantial ground of character, instead of the chimerical ground of titles; and they have brought their titles to the altar and made of them a burnt-offering to reason."[41]

The impatience of the democratically inclined of the Enlightenment with honorific titles was expressed early by the printer's apprentice, Benjamin Franklin, in his brother's *New England Courant* in 1723, when he poked fun at the whole idea: "In old time it was no disrespect for men and women to be called by their own names. Adam was never called Master Adam; we never read of Noah Esquire, Lot Knight and Baronet, nor the Right Honourable Abraham, Viscount Mesopotamia, Baron of Canaan."[42]

Americans, on the whole, had resisted such "fopperies," but with the close of the Revolution, a new—and some thought very serious—threat loomed. A project was set on foot to create an hereditary order of officers who had served in the war with General Washington at their head. Membership in the Society of the Cincinnati was to pass to the eldest son. The fearful saw this society as the sprouts of a plant which could grow to serious proportions. For the first time in the continent's experience there was an excuse to nurture a homegrown aristocracy. Washington had several reservations about the society and sought the advice of Jefferson who apparently persuaded the general that there were inherent dangers in such an organization. Washington found the members too devoted to the idea of such a society to abandon it, but he did persuade them to alter some of its features.[43] Jefferson, soon after in France as American minister, continued in correspondence with the general to express his fears and those of his European acquaintances (who certainly had firsthand experience in these matters). A Society of the Cincinnati, he wrote the general, may spawn an aristocracy in America and bring with it all the burdens that such an aristocracy had brought to France.[44] All the more frightening to the friends of liberty was the fact that the Society of the Cincinnati was to carry on its affairs in secret. Secret military organizations bode ill for the future of the republic.[45]

Probably the most effective weapon against such a development was ridicule. Franklin, who had always enjoyed playing with numbers, figured that "A man's son, for instance, is but half of his family, the other half belonging to the family of his wife. His son, too, marrying into another family, his share in the grandson is but a fourth. . . . In nine generations, which would not require more than three hundred years (no very great antiquity for a family), our present Chevalier of the Order of Cincinnatus's share in the then existing knight will be but a 512th part. . . ." Franklin thought the Chinese system of honors superior: ". . . Among the Chinese, the most ancient, and from long experience the wisest of nations, honour does not *descend*, but *ascends*. If a man . . . is promoted . . . to the rank of Mandarin, his parents are immediately entitled to all the same ceremonies of respect . . . as due to the Mandarin himself, on the supposition that it must have been owing to the education, instruction, and good example afforded him by his parents, that he was rendered capable of serving the publick.

"This *ascending* honour is therefore useful to the state, as it encourages parents to give their children a good and virtuous education. But the *descending honour*, to posterity who could have no share in obtaining it, is not only groundless and absurd, but often hurtful to that posterity. . . ."[46]

Growing concern over titles and inherited honors was fed by the campaign of John Adams and others to introduce high-flown terms of address for the president and other officers of government under the Constitution of 1787 when it was organized two years later. "His Highness" or "His Most Benign Highness," Adams recommended as possible forms of address for General Washington as the first President, in the conviction that such terms of respect and a certain formality were necessary if the new government was to succeed. The democratically inclined did not believe America had fought a Revolution to free itself of monarchical government only to run the risk of creating an atmosphere that would bring in a new monarchy at home. William Maclay, a practical—and Adams would have said "leveling"—politician from the Pennsylvania frontier and others fought Vice President Adams every step of the way. Ultimately Adams had to accept defeat. The proper form of address for the chief magistrate of the United States of America became "Mr. President."[47]

The highest hurdle in the way of successful accomplishment of the campaign on behalf of the rights of man was slavery. Concern over the lot of the Negro, both slave and freedman, emerges in the thought of practically all of the men of the Enlightenment. Most made efforts to ameliorate the degraded condition of the blacks.

The most consistent efforts to eradicate the evil were carried on among the Friends, led by the remarkable tailor John Woolman and the equally dedicated schoolmaster Anthony Benezet. It was Benezet who first turned the attention of Dr. Benjamin Rush, the owner of a slave himself, to the question of abolition. Benezet was hoping that Rush would spur a drive among the Presbyterians, who by 1773 shared power in the Pennsylvania legislature with the Quakers, to support legislation which would so increase the tax on the importation of slaves that the practice would become prohibitive.[48] In a hard-hitting pamphlet entitled *Address to the Inhabitants of the British Settlements in America, upon Slave-Keeping*, Rush argued that the practice was "so foreign to the human mind that the moral faculties, as well as those of the understanding, are debased and rendered torpid by it."[49] Rush believed that if the black man were removed from the degrading condition of slavery, he would be shown to be equal to the white. The usual charges of vice against the Negro—that he is idle, a thief, and treacherous—stem from his condition, not from his nature, said Rush. He advocated that importation of slaves be halted and that, although present slaves may not be prepared for freedom, young blacks be educated in preparation for taking their place as free men in society.[50]

The following year (1774), Jefferson took up the question of slavery in his *Summary View of the Rights of British America*. Jefferson blamed George III for vetoing American legislative acts which would have eliminated the slave trade, claiming that he put the financial interests of "a few British corsairs" before those of the colonies.[51] He returned to this theme in his draft of the Declaration of Independence two years later. In biting tones, the Virginian accused King George of waging "cruel war against human nature itself, violating its most sacred rights of life and liberty in the persons of a distant people who never offended him, captivating and carrying them into slavery in another hemisphere, or to incur miserable death in their transportation hither." George III had blocked efforts to abolish or put limits to "this execrable commerce." If this were not bad enough, the king was now encouraging the slaves, with the promise of freedom, to rise and take vengeance on their owners, "thus paying off former crimes committed against the liberties of one people with crimes which he urges them to commit against the lives of another."[52] This inflammatory passage did not survive the editing of the Continental Congress which decided to strike all references to slavery from the Declaration at the insistence of such colonies as South Carolina and Georgia which desired to continue to import slaves. To achieve unity of the colonies to declare independence was its overriding concern. Jefferson's glowing proclamation that all men are created equal was left to stand while his condemnation of the slave trade, which would have bolstered that assertion, was stricken.

But he had better luck in Virginia. Among the reforms he hurried back to his home state to promote was this one. In 1778 he introduced a bill in the General Assembly to stop importation of slaves. It passed without opposition. Jefferson and his friends had planned that an amendment to the bill would be offered from the floor calling for emancipation, but it was not done when it became clear that public opinion was not ready for it.[53]

Just as the British hoped to utilize slaves in subduing the rebellious Americans, some Americans thought it proper to do the same on the other side. Alexander Hamilton advocated this course, believing the blacks would perform well in the Revolutionary forces if put under good commanders, since they were more used to taking orders than were the whites. He said that blacks were misjudged to be stupid because of their lack of cultivation but "their natural faculties are probably as good as ours. . . ." As Washington's *aide-de-camp*, Hamilton promoted the project. He hoped that giving the slaves their "freedom with their muskets" would be an inducement to them and encourage other blacks as well. He expressed the fervent desire that the project succeed, "for the dictates of humanity and true policy equally interest me in favour of this unfortunate class of men."[54]

With the presence of several outstanding figures of the Enlightenment at the Constitutional Convention of 1787, it was inevitable that the problem of slavery would be fully aired. George Mason was a leader in the effort to rid the projected new government of the evil. He insisted that the Constitution could not allow for such a practice, for slavery led to the corruption of the people: "Every master of slaves is born a petty tyrant." He pointed out that the British government had many times checked Virginia's attempt to end the slave trade. Since independence, however, Virginia, as well as Maryland and, in substance, North Carolina, had succeeded in doing so. It was incumbent on the new government to impose a universal ban. If South Carolina and Georgia were allowed to continue importation, the West would be flooded with slaves.[55]

The opponents of the institution won one victory at the Convention. Under provisions of the Constitution, importation of slaves would be prohibited at the end of twenty years, starting in 1808. But slavery itself was not touched. The issue arose again when the subject of representation was before the group. The deep South, in order to balance the greater population of the North, would have preferred that slaves be reckoned in for the purpose of proportioning members in the House of Representatives. Mason, among others, fought this kind of hypocrisy, which would have slaves counted for this purpose but their existence denied when it came to rights of citizenship. The famous compromise which devised the rule that slaves would be counted as three-fifths in relation to the white population, questionable as it was, allowed Mason to assuage his conscience to the extent that he did not walk out of the Convention as he was sorely tempted to do.[56] As it was, Mason refused to sign the document and returned to Virginia to oppose its adoption by that state on the ground that, in addition to its sufferance of slavery, it granted too much power to the central government.

While the Convention was in progress in Philadelphia, the Congress under the Articles of Confederation was taking a very significant step. On 13 July 1787, it adopted the Northwest Ordinance, which included a prohibition against the spread of slavery into the states to be created in the northwestern territories (present-day Midwest). Whatever criticisms may have been made of the Articles for their ineffectiveness, this provision demonstrated the ability of the government as then constituted to take enlightened action which would have profound consequences for the future development of the United States.[57]

Under the new government formed in 1789 the Congress was almost immediately confronted with the issue of slavery, thanks to the efforts of Benjamin Franklin. The venerable sage interested himself in his last years in a campaign to eliminate that evil. In 1787 he revived the first abolitionist society which had been formed by the Friends in 1775, becoming President of this Pennsylvania Society for Promoting the Abolition of Slavery and the Relief of Free Negroes Unlawfully Held in Bondage.[58] The Society presented a memorial to the first Congress in February, 1789. That body was not at all anxious to take up such a divisive issue so early in its career and decided that since slavery was an internal matter in the various states, it had no jurisdiction over it.[59] As Van Doren has written, "Franklin on the 23rd [of March], with less than a month still to live, wrote *On the Slave Trade*, a hoax and a parody worthy of his liveliest years."[60] Using as a springboard the speech of James Jackson of Georgia in Congress to the effect that that body could not meddle in state affairs and legislate concerning slavery, Franklin said he was reminded of a speech one hundred years ago by "Sidi Mehemet Ibrahim, a member of the Divan of Algiers. . . . It was against granting the petition of the sect called Erika, or Purists, who prayed for the abolition of piracy and slavery, as being unjust. Mr. Jackson does not quote it; perhaps he has not seen it. If, therefore, some of its reasonings are to be found in his eloquent speech, it may only show that men's interests and intellects operate and are operated on with surprising similarity in all countries and climates, when under similar circumstances." Franklin put many of Jackson's arguments in the mouth of Sidi Mehemet Ibrahim in his defense of the right of the Algerines to keep Christian slaves: "The Divan came to this resolution: 'The doctrine that plundering and enslaving the Christians is unjust is at best problematical; but that it is the interest of this state to continue the practice is clear; therefore let the petition be rejected.' And it was rejected accordingly." As Van Doren has pointed out, "At a time when the Algerine pirates were detested by all Americans, and their taking of Christian slaves abominated, Franklin compared the American and the Algerine policies and satirically proved that there was nothing to choose between them."[61]

The concern over slavery was more than a concern for an oppressed race. In the debate of the Constitutional Convention, George Mason had spoken of the pernicious effect the institution had on the manners of the white man, aside from all of the questions of state policy concerned. Jefferson had done the same in his *Notes on the State of Virginia*. The whole relationship between the master and the slave was one "of the most boisterous passions, the most unremitting despotism on the one part, and

degrading submissions on the other." And what was all the more
shocking, the children of the master, who after all learn by imitation, take the same attitude toward black children, lording it over
them. Thus is perpetuated the depravity of manners and morals
from one generation to the next.[62]

Unlike Rush, Hamilton, and others who judged the black to be
the full intellectual equal of the white, a fact which would be
demonstrated if his environment were changed, Jefferson had a
deep-seated suspicion that the Negro was inferior. Jefferson
thought the Negro was not equal to the white in his ability to
reason and use his imagination, although he judged him to be
equal in the "faculty" of memory.[63] But in an attempt to be fair,
Jefferson pointed out that those interested in natural history had
not studied the matter systematically in the century and a half of
American experience so he could hazard it "as a suspicion only,
that the blacks, whether originally a distinct race, or made distinct by time and circumstances, are inferior to the whites in the
endowments both of body and mind."[64] Since he had lived intimately with them for most of his life, Jefferson's judgment was
bound to be more influential than that of Northerners such as
Rush who, at most, owned a household slave and dealt with
others much less frequently than did a Southern planter. As expressed in his influential *Notes*, Jefferson's thoughts on the matter
were bound to feed the prejudices of those who were less enlightened.

These beliefs, coupled with his conviction that the black was
too scarred by the injustices done him to be able to live as a free
man side by side with the white in American society, led Jefferson to advance the idea of colonization. But it was not only the
attitude of the black that would make such coexistence impossible. He believed that racial prejudice was too deeply imbedded
in the white man to be overcome. So on both scores, he thought
it best to remove the blacks and encourage whites from across the
water to take their place. In his *Notes* he writes of Virginia, but it
is a fair presumption that he saw this as a solution for all of the
slaveholding states.

To prepare the Negro for colonization, he would educate the
children of the present slaves, teaching them crafts and agriculture. When they were of age he would transport them, well-
equipped with tools, domestic animals, and other necessities, to
another place.[65] Where this other place would be he did not say.

It was in the nineteenth century that efforts were made to create a home for colonized blacks in Africa.

Like Jefferson, Madison believed that prejudices were such that peaceful coexistence would be impossible: "The objections to a thorough incorporation of the two people are, with most of the whites, insuperable; and are admitted by all of them to be very powerful."[66] This prejudice could be observed in the condition of the free blacks in American society. They labored under legal and social discrimination in all of the states. Madison believed collision between the two races very possible. To eliminate the danger he supported the idea that the nation take on the financial responsibility of emancipating all blacks,[67] rather than leave the task to private sources. Enormous sums could be gained by selling the extensive vacant lands. In this way, he thought, two laudable objects could be achieved at once: the peopling of the extensive territories with a free people and the freeing of another people to take up residence in Africa.[68]

Through much of the first quarter of the nineteenth century Jefferson lamented the failure of the Revolutionary generation to solve the problems of emancipation. He thought the members of the colonial generation of his youth too used to the degradations of slavery to act. He had had high hopes, however, for the youth who had grown up in the heat of the struggle for American independence. But on his return from Europe to take up a position in the new government in 1789 and for the next twenty-five years, he was not able to ascertain that they had indeed reached the point of sympathizing "with oppression wherever found. . . ." "Yet," he could write in 1814, "the hour of emancipation is advancing, in the march of time."[69] By 1820, however, his hopes and the hopes of the surviving figures of the Enlightenment were all but gone. In the debate leading to the Missouri Compromise of that year, Jefferson believed he saw slavery being used by the North as a political weapon with which to beat the South. There was little or no chance now that the reason of the Enlightenment would solve this final great problem in the way of completing the establishment of the rights of man. ". . . This momentous question, like a fire-bell in the night, awakened and filled me with terror. I considered it at once as the knell of the Union."[70]

CHAPTER 4

The Science of Government

I must study politics and war that my sons may have liberty to study mathematics and philosophy. My sons ought to study mathematics and philosophy, geography, natural history and naval architecture, navigation, commerce, and agriculture, in order to give their children a right to study painting, poetry, music, architecture, statuary, tapestry, and porcelain.

—John Adams[1]

Only slowly did the Americans come to the point where they willingly would throw off the royal rule which they had been reared to respect. With such impositions of the home government as the Stamp Act (1765), the Townshend Acts (1767), and the Coercive Acts (1774), many were driven to the conclusion that the British government was in the hands of men who were intent on depriving them of their rights as Englishmen, rights which they claimed their forebears had brought with them when they had exercised their right of emigration and had moved across the ocean to the American strand.

In the first stage of the argument with the mother country, the Americans disputed the authority of Parliament to tax them, asserting that their own legislatures stood in the same relation to the throne as did Parliament itself. In the second stage, the colonists made their points against the monarch, asserting that he was guilty of tyranny and thereby had forfeited their allegiance. The strain which finally broke the filial ties occurred in 1775 when King George declared his American subjects to be in open rebellion against him.

93

It can be argued that separation would have occurred eventually in any case. The experience of the colonials in their New World environment bred a psychology of independence. Thomas Paine was probably not exaggerating when he said that he had not met anyone who did not think that America sooner or later would become independent. It is possible, of course, that a more understanding and flexible response by the home government to the complaints of the Americans could have avoided a final break, but George III and his ministers in this regard were found wanting. The dominion system which could have saved the colonies for Britain developed after the American Revolution proved successful and was, in effect, in response to it. The crown and Parliament had, too late, learned their lesson.

With the outbreak of the Revolution some Americans, such as David Rittenhouse, would conclude that they had always held republican principles. Rittenhouse said the only person he knew who had agreed with him was his brother-in-law "who had been a republican above twenty years."[2] Dr. Benjamin Rush, who claimed he had thought his way through to republican principles when a medical student in Edinburgh, and never believed he would have the occasion to live under a republican form of government, was "daily nourished" by discussions with Samuel and John Adams—who as fellow members of the Continental Congress made his home in Philadelphia their center—and with Rittenhouse and Owen Biddle, "all of whom appeared to be republicans by choice."[3]

Those Americans who could not bring themselves to accept the idea of rebellion and republicanism chose to leave the land of their birth or adoption and migrate to the colonies in Canada or the West Indies, which remained part of the empire or to return "home" to Britain. No doubt a sizeable number chose to keep their loyalist sentiments to themselves and remain in the United States.

The choice for independence having been made, the colonial leaders set about the heady task of making new constitutional arrangements. It was in this sphere that the men of the American Enlightenment made their most pronounced contribution to thought. More than a generation was consumed by the task, and constitution-writing became a basic ingredient in the American outlook on life. Here, for one of the few times in history, men had the opportunity consciously to weigh alternative approaches and to devise frames of government which would express the emerging ideals of a new nation. "When, before the present epocha," asked John Adams, "had three millions of people full power and a fair opportunity to form and establish the wisest and happiest government that human wisdom can contrive?"[4] Americans had great expectations of these documents. It was as though a utopian society could be reduced to writing and then implemented. John Adams was fond of making a distinction between the war for independence and the Revolution. In this he was joined by his dear friend Benjamin Rush. "There is nothing more common," wrote Rush, "than to confound the terms of American Revolution with those of the late American war." The war was over but not so the Revolution. "It remains yet to establish and perfect our new forms of government, and to prepare the principles, morals, and manners of our citizens for these forms of government after they are established and brought to perfection."[5]

Since the nation had been born in revolution against men who had abused power, it was inevitable that the frames of government devised by the Americans would jealously guard their rights against like abuse. It must be made clear beyond any doubt that power resided in the people and that public office was a trust, violation of which could not be tolerated. One way of establishing this would be to reduce tenure in office to the barest minimum. They were sure that the corruption which led to the undermining of British liberty was due to the practice of infrequent elections. Whereas elections to Parliament had earlier been held triennially, the septennial act of 1716 had altered this. Such long tenure in office allowed bribery and other forms of corruption to control the actions of men who supposedly represented their constituencies. "As standing water soon stinks . . . so a standing house of commons will ever be a standing pool of corruption." The British historian who made that point reminded his audience that their Saxon ancestors had practiced annual elections. The stagnant Parliamentary pool could be purified by an "annual current."[6]

The result was that the earliest American constitutions severely limited tenure in office. It was believed healthy for a public official to have to face the voters so often that he could not get out of touch with the desires of his constituents. Colonel George Mason of Virginia, in a statement before the Independent Company of Militia in 1775 supporting the idea of annual election of officers in the Company, stated the principle in no uncertain terms: "We came equals into this world and equals we shall go out of it. All men are by nature born equally free and independent. To protect the weaker from the injuries and insults of the stronger were societies first formed: when men entered into compacts to give up some of their natural rights that by union and mutual assistance they might secure the rest; but they gave up no more than the nature of the thing required." Government is designed for the "good and safety of the community," and elected officials should exert authority with that end in mind and should hold office only long enough to complete a particular task. ". . . Whenever any power or authority whatever extends further, or is of longer duration than is in its nature necessary for these purposes, it may be called government, but it is in fact oppression." Since "all power was originally lodged in, and consequently is derived from, the people," Mason insisted that public officers had to appeal to the "body of the people . . . for their approbation or dissent" with great frequency.[7]

John Adams stated the same principle when George Wythe, looking forward to the writing of a constitution for Virginia, asked him for advice. Adams suggested an annual election of the governor on the grounds that under these terms he is more likely to have "reverence and affection for the people. . . ." Adams, in fact, recommended annual election for all executive officers and for the representatives of the people as well, "there not being in the whole circle of the sciences a maxim more infallible than this, 'where annual elections end, there slavery begins.' "[8] Adams's advice was put in pamphlet form as *Thoughts on Government* (1776)[9] and had a marked effect on the thinking of constitution writers in several of the states.

That elected officials forget their place was made clear by Jefferson in his *Notes on the State of Virginia* (1785). Jefferson was very indignant at the fact that when Virginia in 1776 (and later in 1781) was in dire wartime circumstances, it was proposed, and came within a few votes of passage in the legislature, that all government power, including the determination of life and death, be placed in the hands of a dictator. Jefferson declared that representatives elected by the people had no right to contemplate such a measure, no matter how dire the seeming necessity. They were elected to perform a representative function and cannot delegate it to someone else. He insisted that, if, from necessity, a government dissolves, the powers devolve back upon the people from whence they came. Jefferson was all the more upset; for, as he pointed out, Massachusetts, Rhode Island, New York, New Jersey, and Pennsylvania, all survived invasions without abandoning republican principles. He insisted that the sentiment in Virginia for dictatorship was "treason against the people. . . ."[10]

It was to insure the liberty of the people against the encroachments of unauthorized power that the men of the American Enlightenment gave much thought to the distribution of authority in government and built into the system checks and balances and a separation of powers. Of all of the thinkers of the day John Adams was the most consistent and persistent in this regard. The power of government must be distributed among different branches because power—as was said in a later century—tends to corrupt: "It is the insatiability of human passions that is the foundation of all government. Men are not only ambitious but their ambition is unbounded; they are not only avaricious but their avarice is insatiable." This being true of common people as well as kings and gentlemen, there is a need to "place checks upon them all."[11]

Adams had several opportunities over the years to express his theories of government in writing and one grand opportunity, in his draft of what became the Massachusetts constitution of 1780, to put them into practice. His most extended commentary on the proper distribution of governmental power was published in response to criticisms by the late French statesman Anne Robert Jacques Turgot and Dr. Richard Price of the constitutions which had been adopted in the various states. In what they believed to be "pale imitation" of the English division of powers among king, lords, and commons, the typical American state constitution featured an executive (governor) and a bicameral legislature. Turgot and Price believed the popular will could best be expressed through a legislature of one house.[12]

Most of the states, indeed, had chosen to adopt bicameral legislatures; the notable exception was Pennsylvania, which was under the influence of Tom Paine and Benjamin Franklin, who believed the most democratic arrangement was to be found in one house where the people's representatives could speak decisively without being checked by an undemocratic, aristocratic, upper house.

John Adams had a low opinion of both Paine and Franklin. Although he conceded that Paine was a keen writer, he believed

him "very ignorant of the Science of Government." As for Franklin, the more Adams saw of him the more he had cause for dis-
like. Their differences on political philosophy were accentuated
by personal antagonism. They knew each other in the early days
of the Continental Congress and were thrown together in intimate circumstances when they served on the commission to
negotiate British-American peace in Paris. Adams, with many of
the Bostonian Puritan qualities Franklin had long since outgrown,
was upset with what he judged laziness and evasiveness, and particularly with the manner in which the old sage allowed his many
female admirers to take liberties with him. Franklin's attitude toward Adams is probably best summarized in his comment that he
"means well for his country, is always an honest man, often a
wise one, but sometimes and in some things absolutely out of his
senses."

The Pennsylvania constitution of 1776 called for a unicameral
legislature, but it did establish a Council of Censors whose job it
was to review the workings of the government periodically to insure that it was not acting in an unconstitutional manner. This
document was argued over for years, with political parties forming to defend it and to denounce it. Many friendships were
strained as a result. David Rittenhouse the astronomer, now active in political matters, supported it. His friend Dr. Benjamin
Rush thought it absurd. [13]

Adams, minister to the Court of St. James at the time, decided
to oppose the democratic centralization advocated by Turgot and
Price and to defend the principle of the separation of powers for
fear their influence might encourage the Americans to go in the
direction of Pennsylvania. Adams's three-volume *Defence of the
Constitutions of Government of the United States of America* was
published in London in 1787 and 1788.

Three-quarters of the work was borrowed—with and without
attribution—from the writings of historians of Europe. [14] Adams
ransacked their works to demonstrate that wherever and
whenever governments were not blessed with the feature of separation of powers and checks and balances, the people were in
turmoil—this from the dawn of civilization to Adams's own day.
The grand exceptions were Britain and, Adams hoped, the new
United States. Yet, Monsieur Turgot was critical of the Americans
because they did not centralize power in one legislature.

Adams, who from time to time expressed a less than optimistic view of human nature, is more sanguine concerning the make-up of man than one might expect. The dour Puritan view of man's ability, a part of his New England heritage, gives way to the more positive view of the Enlightenment. He believed that men could not be entrusted with unlimited power, not because they are wicked but because they are weak. The passions of mankind—the love of gold, of praise, and of ambition—"are all unlimited. . . ." And they grow as they are indulged.[15] Men "were intended by nature to live together in society, and in this way to restrain one another, and in general they are a very good kind of creatures; but they know each other's imbecility so well that they ought never to lead one another into temptation. The passion that is long indulged and continually gratified becomes mad; it is a species of delirium; it should not be called guilt, but insanity." Should a nation trust itself to be governed by a single assembly which has nothing to check its appetite for power? It would be like trusting one's "life, liberty, and property" to an assembly of madmen.[16]

Adams believed that his analysis of the workings of power and authority was not based on personal preference but rather was grounded in the very nature of things. He asserted "that three branches of power have an unalterable foundation in nature; that they exist in every society natural and artificial; and that if all of them are not acknowledged in any constitution of government, it will be found to be imperfect, unstable, and soon enslaved. . . ."[17] As he had done in writing the constitution of Massachusetts, he recommends that the executive function be separated from the legislature and that the latter be divided into two houses, one representing the ordinary citizen, the other the rich and influential in society. This latter feature is crucial to tranquility in the state. If the rich and influential are allowed into the same house with the common people, they will dominate its deliberations. If they do not get their way they will exert force. But if you separate them out and put them in a house of their own, their power can be checked by the lower house and meanwhile their genuine abilities can be utilized for the good of the state.[18]

Essential to the Adamsian system was the veto power. Each of the entities of government should jealously maintain a separate identity and function and must be able to protect its interests from the others. Although this principle was to be generally accepted, Adams's granting of an absolute veto to the executive over the acts of the legislature in his draft of the Massachusetts constitution caused much controversy and was not adopted.[19]

The judiciary was also made independent and thus was designed to ward off encroachments by the other branches. The judges were to hold tenure during good behavior; in other words, for life.[20]

Adams, when he completed the first volume of his *Defence* was happy to send a copy across the English channel to Jefferson, who was in Paris as American minister to the French court. Jefferson, in thanking him for his kindness, took occasion to agree with him that good government must be divided into executive, judicial, and legislative branches—with the latter consisting of two or three houses.[21] As Chinard has pointed out, Jefferson was not the ideologue his enemies represented him to be but a practical politician interested, as he himself once put it, in the "real business of life" and suspicious of untried theories.[22] His praise of Adams's work should be considered in the light of his own criticisms of the constitution adopted in Virginia in 1776. Although in his *Notes on the State of Virginia* Jefferson excused its inadequacies on the basis that it was the first adopted among the new states at a time when his fellow-countrymen "were new and unexperienced in the science of government,"[23] he did not hesitate to include extensive criticisms of its workings. It is possible that some of his complaints influenced the warnings Adams included in his *Defence*.

Jefferson complained that members of the House of Delegates and the Senate in the Virginia General Assembly were chosen from the same level in society and by the same electorate. This system defeated the very purpose of having two houses which are designed to represent in government different interests in society. By the time Jefferson wrote, other states had adopted constitutions (including Adams's in Massachusetts) which had distinguished between membership in two houses on the basis of possession of property. But in Virginia "wealth and wisdom" have a chance for admission to both houses.[24]

Jefferson was further disturbed at the fact that the executive, legislative, and judicial powers were all in the hands of the legislature. The governor, his council, and the judiciary were all chosen by the General Assembly. Jefferson believed that such was the definition of "despotic government." In this arrangement there are no checks or restraints on the power of one branch by another. He added, "It will be no alleviation that these powers will be exercised by a plurality of hands, and not by a single one. One hundred and seventy-three despots would surely be as oppressive as one."[25] Because the present assembly is not disposed to abuse its power should be no comfort, even to its members. They should look forward to the day when corruption will have entered the situation. The same abuse of power by the moneyed interests which has been evidenced in history from the days of Caesar to modern England will seize "the heads of government and be spread by them through the body of the people. . . . The time to guard against corruption and tyranny is before they shall have gotten hold of us. It is better to keep the wolf out of the fold than to trust to drawing his teeth and talons after he shall have entered."[26]

In the suggested draft of a constitution Jefferson sent to Virginia in June of 1776, when he was serving in the Congress in Philadelphia, he had clearly provided for the separation of the legislative, executive, and the judicial elements. The legislature was to be divided into a house of representatives and a senate; the representatives to be chosen annually; the senators, in turn, to be chosen by the representatives to serve for nine years. This method removed from the populace direct influence over the senate. Jefferson believed men of greater wisdom would be chosen, as a result. They would supposedly be in a better position to think and act independently. The executive function was to be carried on by an "administrator" who would be annually appointed by the house of representatives but with the limitation that he could not be reappointed for the succeeding three years. He was to possess "the powers formerly held by the king," but he would not have veto power over legislation. The judicial system provided for trial by jury and a system of county courts.[27]

Membership in the two houses of Jefferson's proposed legislature would depend on the amount of property a person owned. He would have done in Virginia, if he had had his way, what Adams later did in the Massachusetts constitution and which he justified in the *Defence*. He would have set off the representatives of the wealthy in a house of their own in order to keep corruption by money out of the system. As Jefferson warned, "With money we will get men, said Caesar, and with men we will get money."[28] The desideratum in a republican America had to be wealth, since there was no other means to distinguish among men; it was against republican principle to distinguish "quality" among various individuals.[29] But Jefferson would have insured participation in government by all taxpayers by a provision that the franchise be held by all mature males with property of at least fifty acres. Those who fell short of this requirement would have their holdings supplemented by an allotment made by the state,[30] thus assuring they have a "stake in society." Needless to say, this radically democratic proposal was spurned by the conservative elements who dominated Virginia's political life.

As he neared the conclusion of the third volume of his *Defence*, Adams informed his readers that late dispatches from America had brought word that allowed him to conclude his lengthy work with "unexpected dignity."[31] He was referring to those two great accomplishments of the year 1787, the Northwest Ordinance adopted by the Congress in July and the new Constitution proposed by the Convention which had met at Philadelphia all of that summer. Both of these documents contained the features dear to the heart of John Adams: a separation of powers among various branches of government and a resultant series of checks and balances.

During the course of his *Defence*, Adams several times referred to the constitution of the United States then in force. The Articles of Confederation violated most, or all, of the principles he was setting forth. But, he explained that this was perfectly proper, for the United States as then constituted was a confederation of sovereign states, like those ancient and modern, which for convenience had thrown in their lot together. The Congress of this body was not a legislature in the strict sense of the word, as those in the individual states, but rather a diplomatic body which served to harmonize their various interests for the sake of the whole, so it could not be expected to contain separate houses of legislation or a strong executive.[32]

The Articles of Confederation had been developed by the Continental Congress during the course of the Revolution. As Adams indicated, they were designed to hold in unison former colonies which had mostly pursued their own destinies in the past and were uniting for the common end of throwing off the British yoke. The Articles had seen the states through war successfully, but, with the restoration of peace, a dissatisfaction developed over what was considered their weakness. Since each state, large and small, had an equal vote in the confederacy and a three-quarters majority was required for action, it was often slow in coming. At times it was difficult even to achieve a quorum for any action at all. Although the confederation assumed responsibility for issues of war and peace, foreign relations, a common coinage, the operation of a post office, and like matters, it had no control over commerce, and, since it could not tax the people directly, it was dependent on the states for its income—support which was often slow in coming.[33]

There had been a certain amount of discussion during the early days of the Revolution concerning the possible creation of a strong, central government with the states being recognized as subdivisions, but this talk produced no results. With the growth of dissatisfaction, however, some minds inevitably turned in that direction again. The immediate cause for concern was the outbreak of "anarchy" in Massachusetts. Since that commonwealth had experienced much mob action in the years leading up to the Revolution, it should have been no surprise when Dan Shays and disgruntled farmers in western Massachusetts resorted to direct action. Massachusetts, attempting to liquidate its wartime debts, had imposed heavy taxes which were too great a strain on common folk to pay. The result was foreclosures on property by the county courts. Shays and friends forcibly kept the courts from meeting.

Shays's Rebellion as this minor incident was called, became notorious throughout the states and caused many perturbations of heart. Some tried to put the best face possible on this and other troubles of the confederation. As Rush wrote Dr. Price, "The kingdoms of Europe have traveled into their present state of boasted tranquillity through seas of blood. The republics of America are traveling into order and wise government only through a sea of blunders."[34] But the cry for a strengthening of the Articles became insistently louder. Typical of those calling for a stronger government was Robert R. Livingston in an oration before the Society of the Cincinnati on the fourth of July, 1787. He said he was sickened by what he saw when he looked at the federal government: "Nothing presents itself to my view but a nerveless council, united by imaginary ties, brooding over ideal decrees which caprice or fancy is at pleasure to annul or execute! I see trade languish, public credit expire, and that glory which is not less necessary to the prosperity of a nation than reputation to individuals a victim of opprobrium and disgrace."[35]

Whatever the problems of public credit, there were those who thought alarm over Shays's Rebellion much overdone. Jefferson, at a safe distance in Paris, may have been more sanguine than he would have been at home. In letters to Madison he downgraded the disturbance and put it in historical perspective in characteristic Jeffersonian prose. He did not shrink from occasional rebelliousness on the part of the people but thought it healthy: "I hold it that a little rebellion now and then is a good thing and as necessary in the political world as storms in the physical." Rebellion calls attention of the people to public affairs and "prevents degeneracy of government. . . ." Republican governments, therefore, should respond mildly, rather than harshly, to such upsets.[36] "Energetic government," he thinks, tends to be oppressive. Shays's Rebellion has been taken too seriously: "Calculate that one rebellion in 13 states in the course of 11 years is but one for each state in a century and a half. No country should be so long without one." Furthermore, noted Jefferson, oppressive governments, such as those of France and Turkey, have more insurrections, thus demonstrating that oppressiveness does not prevent them.[37]

Those who cried alarm won out, however, and a convention to strengthen the Articles of Confederation was called at the behest of Congress and met at Philadelphia in May of 1787. The convention interpreted its mandate quite liberally, however, and presented at the end of the summer to Congress and to the American people a new frame of government. But it was not entirely new. The experience of the state governments with their constitutions was in the background; and some, like Benjamin Rush, were convinced that the first volume of Adams's *Defence*, which had reached Philadelphia in the spring and which he sponsored in an American edition, played an important part in preparing the minds of the members of the convention for their task.[38]

The resultant document certainly seemed to reflect Adams's views, even though the thinking of the delegates went through various stages and it was a product of several important compromises. Since the delegates were concerned that any word of what was occurring which might leak from the state house would mislead the people in what to expect in the finished document, they adopted a rule of secrecy. Some delegates made notes which have been preserved, and James Madison kept an extensive journal of the debates. Madison, who had prepared for the event by a scholarly review of the history and theory of government, was to emerge as one of the most persuasive debaters at the convention. The whole convention was one of notables. Dr. Rush reported that Franklin told him it was "the most august and respectable assembly he ever was in in his life. . . ."[39] The debates were often heated—no doubt exacerbated by the hot Philadelphia summer—but with George Washington, silent and serious, presiding; with the presence of the venerable Franklin; and, especially, with the presence of many politicians experienced in the art of compromise, the result was a document which had an even chance of acceptance by the states.

The debate went through various crucial stages. The Virginia delegation, having arrived in Philadelphia earlier than others, met in caucus and early in the convention seized the initiative with a plan that would have created a strong national government. When the other delegates recovered from their surprise, the Virginia plan was countered by one from the New Jersey delegation which was closer to the mandate of the convention in that it proposed a strengthening of the Articles of Confederation. At play was the concern of the smaller states that they would be dominated by the larger in a strong, central government. Although the reasonable question was asked as to how anyone could be swallowed up in a government which united small and large into one entity, the answer apparently could not overcome deep-seated suspicion and distrust.

The resulting compromise was designed to protect the interests of both large and small, what Madison described as a government that was "partly federal, partly national." To maintain a balance of power among the states it was stipulated that the legislative branch would represent the interests of both. It would be bicameral with a House of Representatives, places in which would be apportioned among the states according to their population (a concession to the large states), and a Senate which would be made up of two members from each state (a concession to the small states). The House of Representatives would be elected directly by the people, the "popular" branch being responsible for the initiation of money bills and thus insuring that there would be no taxation without representation. The Representatives would

serve for two-year terms, all chosen in the same election. The
Senators were to be chosen by the state legislatures for terms of
six years, the terms to be staggered.

The Convention created an executive officer to be called a
"president," whose responsibilities were not carefully defined, in
part at least because it was assumed among most or all of the
members that Washington would initially fill the post. The term
of office was set at four years but no limit was placed on the
number of terms a person could serve. The election of the president was removed as far as possible from influence by the people
at large. He was to be chosen by electors who were themselves
appointed by the legislatures of the individual states. Each state
was entitled to an electoral college as large as the total of the
number of seats it held in the Senate and the House of Representatives.

Since abuse of power by George III was fresh in the minds of
the members of the Convention, they struggled at length with
the question of how the Union should deal with similar abuse by
its chief executive officer. The solution of impeachment after the
well-established English manner was finally adopted, with George
Mason, well-versed in the laws and practices of the mother country, supplying the formula.[40] The president, as well as the vice
president and other civil officers, was to be removed from office
for "treason, bribery, or other high crimes and misdemeanors,"
with the vote of a majority of the House being necessary for impeachment and two-thirds of the Senate for conviction.

Among the powers of the president specifically prescribed was
control of the military, thus insuring civilian direction, and the
direction of foreign policy, with the Senate giving its advice and
consent in the making of treaties.

A judicial branch with a Supreme Court at the apex of the
pyramid was devised, but details of the size of the Court and
subordinate circuits were left to be worked out in congressional
legislation. Although the president was granted the power of veto
over legislation—a veto which could be overridden by a two-
thirds vote of both houses of the Congress—it was implied, but
not clearly stated, that the Court would have the ultimate power
to rule on the constitutionality of legislation. Since the members
of the Court were to serve for life, or during good behavior, the
ultimate check on possible excesses of democracy was put in the
hands of men who presumably could not be swayed by the "leveling," "democratical" interests feared by so many.

The "genius" of the document, which probably more than any other feature has insured its survival, was the provision for amendment. With the approval of two-thirds of both houses of the Congress, an amendment could be proposed. It would take effect if three-quarters of the state legislatures, or conventions specifically called for the purpose, concurred. It was also provided—in a procedure not yet used—that Congress could call a convention for consideration of amendments if two-thirds of the state legislatures were to petition for such. The amendment feature insured that the Constitution would remain a "living" document, capable of evolution and growth with changing times and circumstances.

The venerable Franklin had his doubts about the wisdom of many provisions in the proposed document but he had lived long enough, and had experienced too many changes, not to doubt the validity of his own doubts. He attempted to put the best face on things, however, and, as members of the Convention were affixing their names to the document, in his inimitable manner commented on the picture of the sun painted on the back of the Convention President's chair. He said, according to Madison's account, that "painters had found it difficult to distinguish in their art a rising from a setting sun. I have . . . often and often in the course of the session, and the vicissitudes of my hopes and fears as to its issue, looked at that behind the President without being able to tell whether it was rising or setting. But now at length I have the happiness to know that it is a rising and not a setting sun."[41]

It has been said that the separation of powers built into this proposed government, and the checks of the various branches of the government over the others, was not a presupposition of the delegates when they gathered but grew out of the discussions. It is difficult to believe, however, that there was not a subliminal, if not conscious, appreciation of the provisions that John Adams had written into the constitution of Massachusetts of 1780, even if the Philadelphia version of volume one of his *Defence* was not bedside reading for all of the delegates to the Convention. And certainly Jefferson's strictures on the inadequacies of the Virginia constitution expressed in his *Notes* would have been known to a number of the participants. Therefore, although Adams and Jefferson were across the sea at the time of the writing, in another sense they were present at the Philadelphia Convention in the summer of 1787.

It goes without saying that Adams was encouraged by the product of the Convention. As he implied in the closing pages of his *Defence*, without bluntly saying it, he saw it as a justification of his own handiwork, the constitution of Massachusetts, and the political theory which he had explicated at such exhaustive length in this work. Jefferson, too, was pleased with certain features of the document. He applauded the separation of the government into legislative, judicial, and executive branches, but he had serious reservations about some other features. He thought it dangerous that a limit was not placed on the number of terms the executive could serve, believing this violated the principle of rotation in office. Under its provisions, he was afraid the president would be elected for life, thus opening the door to a homegrown monarchy after Americans had suffered much to throw off the yoke of the British king.

Jefferson was also quite concerned that the document did not contain a bill of rights, the lack of which was to cause great controversy in many of the states. ". . . A bill of rights," he wrote Madison, "is what the people are entitled to against every government on earth, general or particular, and what no just government should refuse, or rest on inference." He listed the rights that should have been enumerated: "freedom of religion, freedom of the press, protection against standing armies, restriction against monopolies, the eternal and unremitting force of the habeas corpus laws, and trials by jury in all matters of fact triable by the laws of the land and not by the law of nations."[42]

Jefferson by then would have known that that respected proponent of the rights of man, George Mason, had left the Convention without signing the document because he, too, objected to the absence of a bill of rights. Mason had tried to get action by pointing out that "a bill might be prepared in a few hours" if the state declarations of rights were used as a basis. He rejected the excuse that those same state bills gave adequate protection, because the new Constitution was to be the supreme law of the land. Mason received support only from Governor Edmund Randolph of Virginia and Elbridge Gerry of Massachusetts—no state delegation being willing to pursue the matter.[43] This reluctance was probably due, in part, to the fact that states such as Massachusetts, Connecticut, and New Hampshire had every intention of maintaining established churches and the delegates did not want to become enmeshed in the thicket of religious controversy.

(When a bill of rights was added to the Constitution as the first ten amendments it was carefully stated that *Congress* would make no law respecting the establishment of religion, thus leaving the state-supported churches intact. Not until 1833 did Massachusetts pass legislation separating church and state, the last state to do so.)

"Col. Mason left Philada. in an exceeding ill humour indeed," noted James Madison.[44] Mason's ill humor was due to more than the lack of a bill of rights, but this lack became one of the rallying cries of those who opposed the Constitution. There began a long and often acrimonious debate over adoption. Congress in transmitting the work of the Philadelphia Convention to the states recommended that the various legislatures call conventions to consider ratification. This feature met the desires of those who believed such consideration could only be given the document by conventions elected by the people specifically to deal with the matter and not by the legislatures which were elected for a very different function. On the other hand, it also skillfully removed from the legislatures supremacy over the proposed national government. If a legislature could approve a national constitution, it implicitly could also withdraw its approval later. The ratifying conventions went out of existence once their deliberations had ended and could not pose such a threat.

The new Constitution was accepted by the state ratifying conventions, often, however, with embarrassingly small margins. North Carolina did not approve it until the new government was in operation. Rhode Island held out even longer, once more living up to its reputation for contentiousness. But even that little rebel gave in when it appeared that she might be treated by the Union as a foreign power.

It was a hope of many on the formation of the new government that a united front could be maintained, without the factionalism of political parties. This pious, if naive, hope did not last long. Although President Washington deplored the struggles of rival factions in his government and stressed the need for harmony, it was unrealistic to think that a large, diverse country, with many contending interests, could become such a political Eden. Then, as now, the accusation of political partisanship was hurled at persons who happened to hold a view contrary to that of the accuser.

One of the most persuasive arguments used in behalf of the adoption of the Constitution was that a mixed government could balance contending interests in the country. James Madison had written that "It may be a reflection on human nature that such devices should be necessary to controul the abuses of government. But what is government itself but the greatest of all reflections on human nature? If men were angels, no government would be necessary."[45] But men were clearly not angels and were often factious.

The *Federalist*, newspaper essays which Hamilton, Madison, and Jay wrote in the heat of the contest over ratification in New York but which were published throughout the states, rank with Adams's *Defence* as an excellent example of the political theory of the American Enlightenment. The tenth in the series, written by Madison, is the best brief exposition of the theory behind the new Constitution. Madison made it clear that a far-flung country was bound to have diverse and contending factions or parties; this was a fact of life which should be seen as an advantage. It was the very size of the country and its very diversity which would be the salvation of the republic. In this Madison was deliberately contradicting Montesquieu who had insisted that a republic—or at least a democracy—could only survive in a relatively small land mass. So many factions would be present in a large republic, wrote Madison, that a sufficient number of them could not effectively unite to trample the rights of others: "The influence of factious leaders may kindle a flame within their particular states, but will be unable to spread a general conflagration through the other states. A religious sect may degenerate into a political faction in a part of the confederacy, but the variety of sects dispersed over the entire face of it must secure the national councils against any danger from that source. A rage for paper money, for an abolition of debts, for an equal division of property, or for any other improper or wicked project, will be less apt to pervade the whole body of the Union than a particular member of it; in the same proportion as such a malady is more likely to taint a particular county or district than an entire state."[46] The chosen representatives in such an extensive republic would be able to take a broader view of the public welfare in the issues which came before them simply because they themselves would be members of many varied factions.

The writers of the *Federalist* were frank to state that one of the most important reasons for the government proposed was to protect property. They recognized that manufacturing and mercantile concerns were bound to be different from the landed or agrarian interest. No one of these interests is likely to take an impartial view of other contenders. "It is vain to say," wrote Madison, "that enlightened statesmen will be able to adjust these clashing interests and render them all subservient to the public good. Enlightened statesmen will not always be at the helm. . . ."[47]

The argument over ratification did not end the struggle. The new Constitution was a piece of paper, a mere outline for what should be done. Those who were delegated control of the government in the first years would determine the shape of the future. Would the United States become a strongly centralized government with the role of the states made minimal? Or would it remain, as under the Articles, a decentralized government with much of the initiative of the people being expressed in the context of their state and local governments? This was one of the main issues in the debate leading up to ratification and it would remain a live issue for years to come.

In the two administrations of President Washington the issue would be joined in the persons of Jefferson of Virginia as Secretary of State and Hamilton of New York as Secretary of the Treasury. Hamilton, who had left the Constitutional Convention in despair that a sufficiently strong government would be created, eventually returned and was to emerge in the new government as a strong force for centralization. Jefferson, on the other hand, sought to protect the states and the people against an encroachment on their liberties by the central government. He was convinced that a group led by Hamilton was seeking to read into the Constitution features not there, their interpretations leading to a much more powerful central government than the framers had intended. When Washington favored the advice of Hamilton over that of his fellow Virginian, the basis was set for the emergence of the party system. Jefferson withdrew from the government in 1793, claiming like Cincinnatus of old a desire to return to his plow. Some, such as John Adams, serving as Vice President, did not believe him for a moment, thinking that Jefferson was returning to Monticello until the opportune time presented itself for a party move.[48]

Many passages of the *Federalist*, especially essay number ten, were prophetic of what would actually occur during the early years under the new Constitution. The various factions for and against the adoption of the instrument were transmuted into the

Federalist and Republican parties with Hamilton and Jefferson at their respective heads. The broad issue, with many lesser issues subsumed, was the question of who would control the government, the moneyed, influential members of society, or "the people."

Much of the debate inevitably centered on the definition of the role of the president, deliberately left quite vague by the framers. John Adams, on the formation of the new government, considered the United States a "limited monarchy" or a "monarchical republic." Attempting to convert his friend from Continental Congress days, Roger Sherman of Connecticut, to his view, he wrote that the president, although elected for terms of four years, has great power. He correctly predicted that the American people would be jealous of this power; but he himself not only thought it was necessary but was in favor of amending the Constitution to strengthen the president's hand. The alternative, he thought, would be inevitable anarchy. Adams believed that the presidency was too limited in such areas as war making, the making of treaties, and appointments to office. Since they were capable of overriding him, the president was not really equal to the House and Senate. The result would be encroachment on the power of the executive[49] and an unbalancing of the mechanism.

Because of his outspoken position on the question, Adams was accused of being a monarchist. The accusation came not only from his political enemies but from his friends who, he claimed, misconstrued his remarks and should know his true views from his writings. "My friend Dr. Rush will excuse me," he wrote, "if I caution him against a fraudulent use of the words *monarchy* and *republic*. I am a mortal and irreconcilable enemy to monarchy. I am no friend to *hereditary limited* monarchy in America. This I know can never be admitted without an hereditary Senate to control it, and a hereditary nobility or Senate in America I know to be unattainable and impracticable. I should scarcely be for it if it were." But Adams reiterated his belief that the executive power should be strengthened so that the president can maintain a balance between the Senate and the House, "between the aristocratical and democratical interests."[50]

To his skeptical cousin Sam, who was for a freer rein in these matters than John, he wrote that the masses have generally chosen comfort rather than liberty so that a frame of government is vital to preserve liberty.[51] Although he favored education of the people—he after all had written provisions for it into the constitution of Massachusetts—he did not believe it enough to overcome "human appetites, passions, prejudices, and self-love. . . . We must not, then, depend alone upon the love of liberty in the soul of man for its preservation. Some political institutions must be prepared to assist this love against its enemies. Without these, the struggle will ever end only in a change of impostors."[52]

Jefferson had much to say on the subject also. He was sure there was a plot afoot to institute English monarchical forms. In thanking Tom Paine for a copy of the second part of the *Rights of Man*, he wrote, "It is but too true that we have a sect preaching up & pouting after an English constitution of king, lords, & commons, & whose heads are itching for crowns, coronets & mitres. But our people, my good friend, are firm and unanimous in their principles of republicanism & there is no better proof of it than that they love what you write and read it with delight."[53]

If anything, Jefferson's concern over the matter was to grow. One of his recent biographers has written that his concern with what he considered a growing monarchical sentiment was due to the proclivities of New York City, which was serving as the temporary first capital of the new government.[54] Jefferson thought he saw the rise of "an Anglican monarchical aristocratical party" which was working to institute the substance, as it had already introduced the forms, of the British government. But he was sure that the people "remain true to their republican principles. . . ." Those on the land (the "landed interest") and the intellectuals (the "great mass of talents") remain republican. The culprits he identified as the bankers, the speculators, and "all timid men who prefer the calm of despotism to the boisterous sea of liberty . . . ."[55]

Adams and Jefferson had been growing apart philosophically for some years. The thought of John Adams had evolved markedly since the days of 1776 when he had recommended annual rotation in office. His experience in Europe as a diplomat and his extensive reading in history had convinced him—as is clear in his *Defence*—that the class structure of society was inherent in the nature of things and, therefore, must be accepted by all men who had the courage to look reality unblinkingly in the face. He scoffed at the fuzzy-headed democrats who had convinced themselves that any man had the ability to perform any function in government. This was folly and madness and was part and parcel of what he christened "the age of Paine." Given his penchant for blunt speaking, it is not surprising that his critics would class him among the pretended aristocrats and derisively christen him the "Duke of Braintree."

Jefferson, on the other hand, became increasingly "democratical" as he grew older, convinced that "the people" could be trusted to hold the reins of government without the help of what he considered a pseudoaristocratic element. He came to hope that the people would rule every level of government from the most local to the state and the national and that all levels would work together in harmony: "I dare say that in time all these as well as their central government, like the planets revolving round their common sun, acting and acted upon according to their respective weights and distances, will produce that beautiful equilibrium on which our Constitution is founded, and which I believe it will exhibit to the world in a degree of perfection unexampled but in the planetary system itself. The enlightened statesman, therefore, will endeavor to preserve the weight and influence of every part, as too much given to any member of it would destroy the general equilibrium."[56]

These years of party turbulence strained and then broke the ties of friendship. Adams thought that Jefferson had completely given way to factious party politics. With the election of Adams to the presidency in 1796 and the subsequent passage of the Alien and Sedition Acts which were primarily aimed at democratic supporters of Jefferson, Jefferson believed Adams guilty of oppression. From his vantage point in the vice presidency, Jefferson cautioned his supporters to remain calm, believing that the voters would be appalled at these examples of oppression and would register their disgust at the polls. With his own election to the presidency in 1800 and the ascendance of the Republicans over the Federalists, Jefferson was convinced the cause of liberty had been vindicated, that a new revolution had taken place and that the government was now safe—since it was in his hands.

The republic survived. And after years of rupture, the friendship of these two great statesmen of the American Enlightenment was made whole in 1812 through the good offices of Dr. Rush. During the last dozen years of their lives, Adams and Jefferson, both settled again on their farms, refought the old battles, in a much more philosophical manner, in one of the classic correspondences of American history. They at last had the time to explain each to the other.

Jefferson wrote that neither of them at heart had wanted to become heads of parties. Circumstances and their supporters had put them into that unnatural position. ". . . Neither decency nor inclination permitted us to become the advocates of ourselves, or to take part personally in the violent contests which followed. We suffered ourselves, as you so well expressed it, to be passive subjects of public discussion."[57]

CHAPTER 5

The Religion of Humanity

I do not believe in the creed professed by the Jewish Church, by the Roman Church, by the Greek Church, by the Turkish Church, by the Protestant Church, nor by any church that I know of. My own mind is my own church.

—*Thomas Paine*[1]

Among the most prized of the natural rights of man the men of the Enlightenment counted the freedom to accept those religious doctrines which made most sense to one's reason and conscience. Freedom of religious belief was one of the more difficult to achieve, however, since most of the American colonies had a tradition of support of religious establishments. The idea that a society or government could exist without support of a church was one of the more radical positions of the American Enlightenment. Heretofore it was the conventional wisdom that the fate of the state and the church were intimately entwined. Enlightened men not only contravened this proposition but even went so far as to assert that the state should recognize that the individual is free to refuse to profess any religion at all.

Although most of the leaders of enlightened thought were believers in religion, their statement of man's natural right to free belief was strengthened by the abysmal record of church-sponsored persecution of nonconformity. Europe had been racked by "religious" wars in the sixteenth and seventeenth centuries. Persecution had been a strong, sometimes dominant, motivation for the immigration of certain groups to the New World. Although America escaped the excesses of religious warfare, some colonies, such as Puritan Massachusetts, had formal policies of intolerance of diversity in the seventeenth century. The memory of Quakers hanged on Boston Common was a repulsive one.

In all consistency it was impossible for men of the Enlightenment to advocate adventurous thinking and exploration in matters of science and to accept the claims of religious groups to complete certainty of the truth of their doctrines. The spirit of inquiry which was opening new areas of knowledge in the physical world was applied also to the realm of the spirit. The radical transformation in world view which resulted from the rise of modern science inevitably had its effect on men's religious beliefs. Many of them no longer believed the old doctrines of the Christian faith. As phenomena which heretofore had seemed mysterious and threatening were probed and explained in natural terms, it became extremely difficult to maintain the existence of a supernatural world which was beyond man's ken. In a universe operating by natural—mechanical—law, there was no place for the supernatural or the claims of Christians that the deity was free to intervene in the workings of such a machine at will. The God of the Enlightenment was, among many other things, a predictable God who would not allow Himself such an unnatural action.

A concomitant of this world view was the belief that religion, too, was natural. It was not something foreign to man's life, but was, like physics, a part of the natural world in which he lived. It was not something that one accepted from the outside but was something that one possessed as part of his humanity. If man's reason was capable of evaluating the empirical evidence gained in scientific pursuit, it certainly had the ability to evaluate the claims of contending religious groups and weigh them against experience. This reasonable approach to religion led to the rejection of religious claims based on "revelation" and also to rejection of claims based on "authority." The man of the Enlightenment no more accepted the divine right of the priest than he accepted the divine right of kings.

The clergy of the established churches of the American colonies, although they had achieved a fair measure of influence and privilege, did not acquire the deep-seated power base in society which was enjoyed by their European brothers, who had had centuries of opportunity to entrench themselves. Furthermore, the American experience of the frontier presented less of an opportunity for the development of a distinctive clerical order in society. The early Puritan view that a minister was a layman set apart to perform a particular function in the church, after which he returned to the ranks of the laity, although never fully developed in practice, created an attitude toward the ministry which was shared by many of the religious sects. To take one example, the Baptist farmer-preacher who had to labor day to day along with his flock presented much less of a target for anticlerical sentiment than was true of the entrenched priesthood of Europe.

As a result, the anticlerical sentiments which were part of the outlook of the men of the American Enlightenment were much less bitter than those of the European *philosophes*. Nonetheless, the clergy were resented as a party of privilege and were held suspect. As we have seen, Cadwallader Colden, son of a Scottish clergyman who himself had contemplated a career in the ministry, had warned his grandson of the deleterious effect exercised by priestcraft on the minds of men.[2] The belief was firmly rooted that the clergy perpetuated superstition for their own ends: to control the minds of men. The Jeffersonian philosopher John Taylor of Caroline could write, as late as 1814, that "The art of governing the deity is cultivated for the sake of governing men."[3] But Taylor did not limit his attack to the clergy. Religion was often used by others for foul ends: "As a cunning government uses religion to cheat a nation, a cunning man will use it to cheat his neighbour."[4]

The writings of enlightened Americans abound in anticlerical statements. The only safe course for America, if it was to avoid the religious sins of Europe, was to protect the individual against the encroachment of government and of the church on his right to think in religious matters as he himself chose. Religious belief had to be protected as a private matter. As Paine put it: "Religion is a private affair between every man and his Maker, and no tribunal or third party has a right to interfere between them. . . . It is not otherwise an object of just laws than for the purpose of protecting the equal rights of all, however various their belief may be."[5] Jefferson's statement expresses bluntly the more practical aspects of the question: "The legitimate powers of government extend to such acts only as are injurious to others. But it does me no injury for my neighbour to say there are twenty gods, or no god. It neither picks my pocket nor breaks my leg."[6]

From this perspective, religion is not the cement that holds society together. It can safely be left, therefore, to the individual. As these men read history, there was nothing to bolster the idea that religion had served as this unifying element. The history of Christianity was replete with examples of division over doctrine and of brutal suppression of dissent. But, said Jefferson, "we have not advanced one inch towards uniformity." The effect of suppression has been "to make one half the world fools, and the other half hypocrites."[7] But an appeal to history was only half the justification. The experience of Jefferson's own Anglican church in Virginia had been the same. Uniformity had never been achieved. Dissenters, such as the Presbyterians, had constantly clamored for freedom to worship as they pleased. Countless examples could also be drawn from the experience of the other colonies—the majority of them—that had attempted to suppress dissent from their established churches.

The same impulse which had prompted Jefferson to return to Virginia from the Continental Congress in 1776 to work for the overthrow of aristocratic privilege by reform of law in the legislature, led him to the attempt to protect by law the natural religious rights of man. George Mason's Declaration of Rights of that year had asserted the principle of freedom of religion, but the fact of the political situation in Virginia was quite different. The Anglican (Episcopal) establishment was well protected by law and custom. It was one thing to state the general principle of religious freedom but quite another to alter the old practices of privilege. The idea that state support should be withdrawn from the churches and clergy and that they should be left to the fate of voluntary contributions was disturbing both to the majority of the clergy and, one can assume, to the laity as well.

In 1779 Jefferson proposed to the legislature an "Act for Establishing Religious Freedom" which declared that "Almighty God hath created the mind free" and that it was the "impious presumption of legislators and rulers" that they must impose by coercion a particular belief on the people. Since they themselves were "fallible and uninspired men" the result had been the imposition of "false religions over the greatest part of the world . . . through all time. . . ." It is instructive that Jefferson chose to justify this view with an appeal to natural philosophy. ". . . Our civil rights have no dependence on our religious opinions, more than our opinions in physics or geometry. . . ." For the state to support or impose a particular point of view or to support financially the ministry—and burden the citizens with this—tended "to corrupt the principles of that very religion it is meant to encourage. . . ." The only protection for true religion is in the exercise of reason. The state should only step into religious matters if it should become necessary to protect warring groups from each other. The faith of the American Enlightenment was ringingly affirmed in Jefferson's peroration that "truth is great and will prevail if left to herself, that she is the proper and sufficient antagonist to error, and has nothing to fear from the conflict, unless by human interposition disarmed of her natural weapons, free argument and debate, errors ceasing to be dangerous when it is permitted freely to contradict them."[8]

The struggle for the adoption of Jefferson's bill was a long and hard one. He himself was not on the scene when the Virginia legislature finally was persuaded to accept it. While he served as United States minister in Paris, his colleague Madison continued the campaign for adoption. Madison was as intensely interested in the principles involved as was Jefferson. One of the first acts of his career as a legislator had involved the very issue of freedom of religion. In the debates over Mason's Declaration of Rights, Madison moved that toleration of freedom of conscience in Mason's draft be changed to recognize it as a natural and absolute right.[9] Mason had accepted the revision and was to support Madison in his efforts in behalf of Jefferson's Bill for Establishing Religious Freedom.

Madison's campaign was almost lost when Patrick Henry decided to support efforts to preserve certain features of the establishment by spreading benefits among all recognized denominations. A "Bill for Establishing a Provision for Teachers of the Christian Religion" proposed to pay the salaries of the ministers of the various groups. Such a beguiling prospect naturally won over some dissenters who had earlier been clamoring for an overturn of the established church. Madison's response to these efforts was a brilliant contribution to the literature of religious freedom, "A Memorial and Remonstrance on the Religious Rights of Man," addressed to the General Assembly of Virginia and assiduously circulated throughout the state. Madison contended that freedom of religious belief is an "unalienable right" which cannot be abridged by legislative action. The duty which the individual owes to his Creator "can be directed only by reason and conviction, not by force or violence. . . . It is the duty of every man to render the creator such homage, and *such only*, as he believes to be acceptable to him; this duty is precedent, both in order of time and degree of obligation, to the claims of civil society. Before any man can be considered as a member of civil society, he must be considered as a subject of the governor of the universe. . . . We maintain, therefore, that in matters of religion no man's right is abridged by the institution of civil society; and that religion is wholly exempt from its cognizance." Were the legislature to encroach on these prior religious rights of man it would be guilty of tyranny. The Americans had recently concluded a revolution to establish their claims to freedom; they should not now allow the beginnings of infringement of rights so dearly won. If the Virginia Assembly could insist on the support of "Teachers of the Christian Religion," it could just as easily later impose one of the churches on the whole citizenry.

Although Madison pitched his argument on the high plain of rights, he did not hesitate to appeal to Virginia's practical interests. He pointed to the fact that the Quakers and the Mennonites had successfully supported their organizations by voluntary contributions, without the help of the state. Furthermore, there were sufficient examples in history to indicate that "ecclesiastical establishments" had had a deleterious effect on religion, corrupting it by encouraging "pride and indolence in the clergy; ignorance and servility in the laity; in both, superstition, bigotry, and persecution." Another practical effect would be the turning away of immigrants from foreign oppression who would not look to Virginia as a refuge. If the arguments from principle did not take with some, this last would be a serious consideration, given the desire of Americans to multiply their numbers.[10]

Madison thwarted Henry and those who would use tax money for the support of the Christian ministry and then pushed home his advantage by again calling Jefferson's bill to the floor at the right psychological moment. Virginia in 1786—seven years after Jefferson began the campaign—became the first of the states with establishments to separate church and state. The Assembly —consistent with Jefferson's proposition that one generation should not seek to tie the hands of a future one—recognized that it could only speak for the present; but it declared, in Jefferson's words, that "if any act shall be hereafter passed to repeal the present [one] or to narrow its operation, such act will be an infringement of natural right."

Jefferson was delighted with news of Madison's success and

wrote home that the Act was received well in Europe, with am-
bassadors and ministers of various nations at the French court
asking for copies to transmit to their sovereigns. It was published
entire in several books.[11]

Jefferson was also pleased to hear that an attempt to insert the
name Jesus Christ in the bill had been defeated. He saw this as a
great victory: "Where the preamble declares that coercion is a
departure from the plan of the holy author of our religion, an
amendment was proposed by inserting the word 'Jesus Christ,' so
that it should read, 'a departure from the plan of Jesus Christ,
the holy author of our religion;' the insertion was rejected by a
great majority, in proof that they meant to comprehend within
the mantle of its protection the Jew and the Gentile, the Christian and Mahometan, the Hindoo, and Infidel of every
denomination."[12]

Madison continued his concern with the principle of religious
freedom and sought to implement it on every possible occasion.
In the new Congress organized under the Constitution of 1787,
he opposed the proposal to pay chaplains of the House of Representatives out of the public treasury.[13] He lost the argument
but, as he said, "It would have been a much better proof to their
constituents of their pious feeling if the members had contributed
for the purpose a pittance from their own pockets."[14] During his
terms as President of the United States, although he followed the
precedent of his predecessors in issuing proclamations on holi-
days, Madison tried to word them in such a way that they were
"merely recommendatory" and did not imply the sanction of the
government of a particular form of religion. He was bothered by
the vestigial remains of religious observance by government and
was convinced that the separation of church and state could only
be maintained in the new republic if government officials were
scrupulously impartial in matters of religion. "We are teaching
the world the great truth that gov^{ts}. do better without kings &
nobles than with them. The merit will be doubled by the other
lesson that religion flourishes in greater purity without than with
the aid of gov^{t}."[15]

The action of Virginia in disestablishing the church served as
an inspiration for similar moves in other states with establishments. Although Massachusetts and Connecticut held out until
well into the nineteenth century, dissenting religious groups constantly hammered away at the privileges of the establishments

and gained such concessions as the diversion of their own tax money from support of the Congregational establishment to the churches of their own choice and recognition of the validity of marriages performed by their ministers. The legislatures of the Southern states followed the lead of Virginia and rid themselves of official churches. The new state of Vermont, which was admitted to the Union in 1791, proclaimed religious freedom and separation of church and state in its constitution. The opening West, which was luring Easterners across the Appalachian chain, was guaranteed freedom from past mistakes by the enlightened Northwest Ordinance of 1787, which provided that "No person, demeaning himself in a peaceable and orderly manner, shall ever be molested on account of his mode of worship or religious sentiments in the said territory."[16]

Such places as Rhode Island and Pennsylvania, of course, had served as experiments in religious freedom since the days of Roger Williams and William Penn. But in a day of constitution writing it was considered crucial that assurances be put on paper. It comes as no surprise that Franklin was among the supporters of a specific guarantee written into the constitution of Pennsylvania in 1776.[17]

When by conquest New Netherland had become New York in the late seventeenth century, some English sentiment was in favor of an Anglican establishment to replace the Dutch Reformed Church. But, as historian William Smith pointed out in 1757, it was unrealistic to refer to the Dutch Reformed and the Presbyterians as dissenters, since they far outnumbered the Anglicans. He noted that the vast majority of the people wanted toleration of Protestants. They were "utterly averse to any kind of ecclesiastical establishment." Smith was convinced that, although some English governors had exerted pressure in favor of the Anglican church, should a governor actually make an attempt to establish that church, he would do so at the cost of a great upheaval in the colony.[18] The diversity so obvious in New York in religious as well as other matters made it imperative that a religious freedom clause be included in its constitution in 1777.

As has already been noted in our discussion of the federal Constitution of 1787, George Mason and others had attempted to induce their fellow conventioneers to write into the proposed framework of government a guarantee of the liberties of the people. Since their efforts failed, it was left to the individual states to insist as a price for their approval of the new charter that the first Congress tend to that business immediately. Madison, who had won approval for the Constitution over the opposition of Mason in Virginia, stood for election to the new Congress on a platform which included the immediate adoption of a Bill of Rights. Madison was largely responsible for the adoption of that Bill in the first ten amendments to the Constitution which were ratified by the states and took effect in 1791. The first amendment included protection for the right he had fought so hard to achieve in Virginia: "Congress shall make no law respecting an establishment of religion, or prohibiting the free exercise thereof. . . ." This was the culmination of the struggle by the forces of enlightenment for recognition of "the religious rights of man."

Intimately associated with the campaign for freedom of belief and toleration of differences was the religion of enlightenment called Deism, a catenation of beliefs which developed as one result of the radical scientific shift in world view. One of the best outlines of deistic belief was set forth by Benjamin Franklin in a letter to the Reverend President Ezra Stiles of Yale, written a little more than a month before the old sage died in 1790. Because he was ailing and so close to the end and because Yale had been the first institution to recognize his accomplishments with an honorary degree, Franklin was more frank concerning his belief than he likely would have been otherwise. Like other leaders of enlightened thought he believed his religion to be nobody's business but his own; he told Stiles that he never before had been questioned on it and, characteristically, he expressed hope that Stiles would keep the views expressed in this letter to himself. He outlined for Stiles what he called his creed: "I believe in one God, Creator of the universe. That he governs it by his providence. That he ought to be worshipped. That the most acceptable service we render to him is doing good to his other children. That the soul of man is immortal and will be treated with justice in another life respecting its conduct in this."[19] In this summary Franklin reflected the classic five points of Deism, as set forth by the English Lord Herbert of Cherbury, one of the original exponents of the belief. Franklin, as did other Deists, insisted that these were the basic beliefs of all "sound religion. . . ."

Franklin did not skirt the specific issue of the nature of Christ, his view of which Stiles was particularly interested to know. He came down on the side of his old friend, the English Unitarian

Priestley: ". . . I think the system of morals and his religion, as he left them to us, the best the world ever saw or is likely to see; but I apprehend it has received various corrupting changes, and I have, with most of the present Dissenters in England, some doubts as to his divinity. . . ." But with exquisite diplomacy Franklin sweetened the pill for Stiles by adding: ". . . tho' it is a question I do not dogmatize upon, having never studied it, and think it needless to busy myself with it now, when I expect soon an opportunity of knowing the truth with less trouble."[20]

It was typical of the practical Franklin that he did not see any harm in people believing in the divinity of Christ—"if that belief has good consequence. . . ." Nor did he notice that the Creator ever visited "unbelievers in his government of the world with any peculiar marks of His displeasure."[21] Religious belief did not matter to this most utilitarian of sons of the Enlightenment. What did matter was how people behaved. In the age-old argument over which was more important, faith or good works—an argument which had often shaken Christianity to its foundations —Franklin and the Deists came down on the side of works. They found it exceedingly difficult to believe that the God of the magnificent Newtonian universe could become exercised over the paltry doctrinal differences of supposedly religious men. But how men acted was another matter; for the Creator was a believer in order and design, which was apparent from the mechanism which He had devised.

Franklin, at the end of a long life in which he had seen much of the world and had associated with many of its most brilliant men, was probably the most tolerant man of his age. Over the years he had contributed his financial support to the building of various churches in Philadelphia—without making distinctions. But he had not always been so. In his early years he reacted with vigor to the strict doctrines of Calvinism which were still dominant in the Boston of his birth. His father had originally slated him for the ministry; and he had spent much time reading books on "polemic divinity" in his father's library, time he later regretted he had not spent reading more "proper books."[22] Franklin found it hard to swallow the Calvinistic beliefs that pictured God as having slated some persons to salvation and others to damnation, irrespective of merit, before the world began.[23] His rejection of these harsh doctrines led to doubts concerning revelation itself. When reading a defense of Christianity against the attacks of the

Deists, he became convinced that the stronger argument was on the side of the latter.[24] As a young journeyman printer in London he had attacked the Christian religion and taken up the cudgels in behalf of materialism and was generally contentious on the subject. The pamphlet which he published containing his views he later classed as one of the "errata" of his life. He mellowed over the years. Whatever reservations he may have had about the beliefs of his fellows, he chose not to express. Efforts to get him to attend church failed; he used that time for study. He actually did attend the Presbyterian church in Philadelphia for five consecutive Sundays; but when he concluded that the object of the minister was to make good Presbyterians rather than good citizens, he went back to his books.[25]

His tolerance for others' views made him strange bedfellows. It is still a wonder that the rationalist Franklin could have had for a friend the most fervent preacher of the age. But he got on with George Whitefield because he believed that, in his way, he was serving mankind. It would be a mistake, however, to conclude that Franklin was indifferent to religion. He had carefully worked through his own beliefs and kept by him over the years the notebook in which he had jotted down his own articles of belief.

Like Franklin, John Adams had been headed for a career in the ministry, and like him he read widely in the Christian polemics of the day. Adams turned to a career in law instead because he was disturbed by the theological controversy which he thought was carried on "with an uncharitable spirit of intolerance. . . ."[26] It is likely that Adams was siding with the liberals in the Congregational churches and had no stomach for the controversy which might arise over his views were he to be settled as minister of a church.[27] The church in his native Braintree was evolving into what would later be labeled Unitarianism. Similar strains were being experienced by many of the old-line Puritan churches.

Adams was strongly influenced by deistic views; but, with his sense of the importance of tradition, he did not stray as far from the Christian fold as did his Virginia friend Jefferson. As was true of Washington, Mason, and many other prominent figures of the day, Jefferson maintained his nominal connection with the established Anglican church of his native state, but his views from the days of his study at William and Mary were highly unorthodox.

Since he believed strongly that religion was a private concern, he only once expressed himself publicly on the subject in any detail and that was unintentional. Since *The Notes on the State of Virginia* were not originally designed for publication, such statements as to his indifference whether a neighbor believed in twenty gods or in no god may have been stronger than they would have been otherwise. The *Notes* provided his enemies among the clergy, especially the New England Federalist clergy, a mine of material with which to confront him in the presidential election of 1800.

As Jefferson made clear in the *Notes*, he believed that reason and free inquiry are the only bases for the emergence of truth in religion, as in other areas of life.[28] Therefore, he could not honor the claims made by Christians for the Bible. As he advised his nephew, one should read the Bible as one would Livy or Tacitus. Subject it to the powers of reason, for reason is "the only oracle given you by heaven. . . ."[29]

Jefferson was more influenced by the writings of Epicurus and Epictetus than by the Judeo-Christian Scriptures. However, he ranked with the thoughts of the great Epicureans and Stoics those of Socrates and Jesus. Jesus, he thought, had sought to recall the Jews "to the principles of pure deism, . . . to reform their moral doctrines to the standards of reason, justice and philanthropy, and to inculcate a belief in a future state."[30]

Jefferson's attachment to what he considered to be the pure teachings of Jesus grew with the passage of years. He was influenced by the several historical writings of Dr. Priestley which traced the "corruptions of Christianity" over the centuries and thought that an effort should be made to separate the wheat from the chaff in the Gospels. With scissors and paste he made such an attempt. On several evenings in the White House after days spent on Presidential business, he went through the Gospels cutting up the pages, removing the sayings of Jesus from the miraculous, superstitious settings and pasting them in a notebook for his own personal use. "The Life and Morals of Jesus of Nazareth" has become known as the "Jefferson Bible."[31]

Jefferson concluded that, as wise as were Epictetus and Epicurus, Jesus was the superior teacher. The great philosophers had given mankind admirable advice on how the individual should govern himself, but Jesus had taught men how they should behave toward one another. In this insight of Jefferson, we have another instance of the concern of the Enlightenment with men's behavior.[32]

The rejection of the divinity of Christ was widespread among the enlightened. Those with formal church connections sometimes were taken to task as a result. John Bartram was disowned by Quakers of the Darby, Pennsylvania, meeting in 1757 for his failure to accept Jesus as the Son of God. His fellow Friends attempted to "labor" with him but he rejected their efforts to correct his unbelief.[33] He, like others, concentrated his worship on the Creator. For Bartram, the telescope became a substitute for orthodox revelation: "It is through the telescope I see God in his glory."[34] He saw signs of the "Grand Giver and Supporter of universal life" all around him, in animal and mineral; but it was when he gazed at the heavens that he was overwhelmed by a sense of God's presence: "Vast are the bodies which roll in the immense expanse! Orbs beyond orbs, without number, suns beyond suns, systems beyond systems, with their proper inhabitants of the great Jehova's empire. How can we look on these without amazement, most humble adoration. Esteeming ourselves, with all our wisdom, but as one of the smallest atoms of dust praising the living God, the great I AM."[35]

Bartram's was an emotional expression—possibly mystical is a better word—of what other Deists would express in more intellectual terms. They recognized that a great force was at work in the universe, that it was on the side of order and symmetry, and that man through the use of reason was capable of understanding at least in a limited manner how he fit into the scheme of the Great Creator.[36]

Certainly the Deists mentioned so far would have preferred to be left alone in their own belief. However, the last quarter of the eighteenth century and the first of the nineteenth saw the publication of works by several militant Deists who sought to discredit the claims of Christianity and to convince the Americans of the truth of this new religious approach. The proponents did not claim originality for their views. As with reformers of the past, they believed theirs was the true belief which had been corrupted over the centuries by the machinations of priestcraft.

Ethan Allen had migrated from Connecticut up the Connecticut River Valley to what was to become the state of Vermont. He won initial fame as the leader of a guerilla band called the

"Green Mountain Boys," which sought to establish the validity of the land grants made by New Hampshire in this disputed border area with New York. Allen and his boys used terror tactics to rid the area of "Yorkers" and to establish their own claims to the land. He won intercolonial attention when in the early days of the Revolution he took part with Benedict Arnold in a raid on the strategic Fort Ticonderoga, which Allen proclaimed he captured in the name of the "Great Jehovah and the Continental Congress."

Allen, because of his rough life style, vigorous tongue, and rhetoric, was considered by many a profane frontier braggart. Often encouraged by the imbibing of "spirituous liquors," he loudly denounced Christianity and especially the Congregational "priests" of the region. His rough, tough approach to life often won him grudging admiration, however, and not only from the Green Mountaineers. Allen, who was carried off to England after the ill-fated attempt to take Montreal, captured the imagination of many by his *Narrative of Colonel Ethan Allen's Captivity* which recounted his experiences as a prisoner of war.[37] On his exchange by the British, he met General Washington who said, "There is an original something in him that commands admiration; and his long captivity and sufferings have only served to increase, if possible, his enthusiastic zeal."[38] Jeremy Belknap, minister and historian, made a similar evaluation: "I think him an original in his way, but as rough and boisterous as the scenes he has passed through."[39]

When it became known in the early 1780s that Allen was at work on a book on philosophy and religion, the orthodox Christians were understandably concerned. If they thought that Allen would heap torrents of abuse on them and their beliefs, they were correct. But Allen's *Reason the Only Oracle of Man*[40] contained much more. As a young man in Connecticut he had spent much time with the itinerant physician Thomas Young, who introduced him to the writings of the English Deists. It is thought by some scholars that Allen incorporated much of Young's own writing in his book.[41] Certainly the book is checkered in character. It contains both ponderous philosophical propositions and amusing, sometimes hilarious, comments on orthodox Christian belief. The first characteristic may reflect the material inherited from Young, the second Allen's own writing. There is no question, however, that Allen considered himself a philosopher

—referring to himself as such in correspondence—and fully capable of dealing with abstruse subjects. No matter how deficient in education, he had the bumptious, democratic attitude which was characteristic of the American frontier. He believed he had every right to express his ideas in print. If some did not like his views, they could show him where he was wrong.

"Ethan Allen's Bible," as it was called, alternates a vigorous attack on Christian belief with an exposition of natural religion. As is often the case in such works, the irreverent, destructive sections make more interesting reading than the constructive ones. Allen meets his Christian neighbors and does battle with them on their own territory. If they choose to accept the Bible literally, so will he—with devastating results. He, for example, speculates that on Mt. Sinai Moses must have looked on the "Back-parts" of God, since the Old Testament says that no man may look on the face of God and live![42] If the Christians base their belief in original sin on the events in the Garden of Eden, Allen asks why it is such a place has never been found, despite the fact that it was in a heavily populated part of the world? Conclusion: there is no such thing as original sin![43] He scoffed at those who could take seriously the Scripture which he considered a collection of fables.

Allen's more serious passages, however, set forth in detail the belief of the Deists. His attack on Christianity was made in an attempt to free the minds of his readers from the superstition drummed into them since childhood by the "priests." He was convinced that the application of reason would make it clear that the Calvinistic beliefs concerning God and man were erroneous. It is a democratic God who emerges from Allen's pages, One who loves all mankind. The idea that God had predestined a small group of Elect for eternal happiness and the rest of men for eternal perdition, he found repugnant. Reason should reveal that the God of the universe is a universal God, whose object is to "happify" all men.

It is reason which allows man to understand his place in God's scheme of things, declares Allen. The deity created the universe and governs it by natural law. By observation of God's ways reflected in creation, man can tell what is lawful and what is not. This is a process of trial and error; therefore man is bound to sin as he goes through life. Each man is responsible for his own sin, or mistakes, however, and sin cannot be attributed to a mythical "fall" in the Garden of Eden. Sin is due to man's limitations as a finite being. If he were capable of comprehending all, he would be infinite and therefore coequal with God—an obviously fatuous idea. But Allen's God is infinitely understanding of man's short-comings. Because He is an infinitely benevolent being, He will give man another chance to succeed, both in this world and the next.

Allen expressed his greatest moral repugnance over the doctrine of atonement. It was heinous to believe of God that He was so angry with Adam for eating fruit that He condemned all his progeny to everlasting agony and then sent His own Son into the world to die to reclaim some of them. The idea that one man can die for another man's sin went against all reason and justice. The moral Governor of the universe could not be involved in such a transaction.

Having rid theology of the need for atonement, Allen then set about the job of dismantling the trinity, a doctrine intimately associated with it. If God did not need to send to earth His own essence in the form of the Son to perform the soteriological act, was there need to believe the Son (and, for that matter, the Holy Ghost) was coequal with the Creator? Allen sought to destroy the dogma by subjecting it to rational examination. If God were infinite, how could He be three? The idea of a "plurality of infinites" was not logical: "A personal or circumscribed God implies as great and manifest contradiction as the mind of man can conceive of; it is the same as a limited omnipresence, a weak Almighty, or a finite God."[44]

So, one by one, Allen attacked prized Calvinist beliefs and replaced them with what the Deists considered a reasonable approach to religion. Allen's belief was the most democratic of the age. A man who had spent much of his life fighting for the rights of Vermonters was not likely to brook the idea of special privilege in philosophy or religion. All vestiges of a spiritual aristocracy were removed in his religion, just as he believed they would be in everyday American life.

When word of the contents got around, Allen was reviled as a Mohammedan and an infidel. He was attacked in pulpit, newspaper, and pamphlet. Since Allen relished a good argument, he was not cowed. His response was to set to work on a sequel.[45]

Allen's book created a great stir. How many persons actually read it, however, cannot be determined. The first and only edition during his lifetime suffered certain misfortunes which the orthodox considered due to the interposition of the deity. Lightning struck the print shop and consumed many of the copies. To make things more difficult, the printer was converted to Methodism and decided to consign the remaining copies to the fire because of its "atheistical" content. That some escaped these holocausts Allen could well have considered a miracle—but he, of course, did not believe in such things. The copies which survived passed from hand to hand and the book did make an impact on the thinking of many.

By far the most influential of the expositions of Deism came from the pen of the great defender of the rights of man, Thomas Paine. As early as 1776 Paine had told John Adams of his intention someday to publish a work on religion. It seems that he believed it better to wait till his old age, intending it to be his last work.[46] Franklin, who apparently had heard of his intention, cautioned him against any such venture on the ground that it was unwise to disturb the simple people in their beliefs.[47]

When Paine got into trouble with the English authorities because of his publication of *The Rights of Man*, he fled to France where he initially became the darling of the Revolution. As the Revolution deteriorated into the Reign of Terror Paine, because he opposed the execution of Louis XVI, was jailed as a moderate. It was on the eve of his imprisonment that he hurriedly produced *The Age of Reason*. Ironically, it was intended as a conservative work. He was concerned that in abolishing the national priesthood and in sweeping away the vestiges of priestly privilege, the French might go too far. Events, Paine wrote, "rendered a work of this kind exceeding necessary, lest in the general wreck of superstition, of false systems of government and false theology, we lose sight of morality, of humanity and of the theology that is true."[48]

As did Allen before him, Paine attempted to separate the false from the true in religion. With his Quaker heritage he found it easier than some to reject the intricacies of Christian theology. His attack on the superstitions of Christianity was more devastating, not only because his book was not burned in the print shop, but because of Paine's facile style. The pungent, biting prose which had helped to foment and win a political revolution was put to work in behalf of a religious revolution.

Paine, with all of the skill of an old propagandist, chose to recount a collection of silly stories from the Old Testament in an effort to discredit the idea of revelation. There was no reason to accept such trivia as the word of God, certainly not on the word of unreliable witnesses. "When we contemplate the immensity of that Being who directs and governs the incomprehensible Whole, of which the utmost ken of human sight can discover but a part, we ought to feel shame at calling such paltry stories the Word of God."[49] Paine's attack on Christianity was so sharp that many forgot that half of the book was devoted to a moving exposition of what he called the religion of humanity. He even quotes Addison's paraphrase of the nineteenth psalm (which he says is one of the few deistic passages in the Old Testament):

> The spacious firmament on high,
> With all the blue ethereal sky,
> And spangled heavens, a shining frame,
> Their great original proclaim. . . .[50]

Paine's book wreaked havoc with orthodox belief and was a powerful tract for the times. Dr. Rush, who avoided Paine on his return to America because of it, expressed the opinion that the *Age of Reason* "probably perverted more persons from the Christian faith than any book that ever was written for the same purpose. Its extensive mischief was owing to the popular, perspicuous, and witty style in which it was written, and to its constant appeals to the feelings and tempers of his readers."[51] The poet and journalist Philip Freneau claimed that the popularity of Paine's book was due to the Federalist clergy. The *Age of Reason* "would never have been much known in this country if the clergy had suffered it to rest; but they dragged it into publicity. . . ." Furthermore, in written refutations of the book Christianity suffered at the hands of its defenders who, compared to Paine, were shown up to be "weak, yet conceited friends . . ."[52]

As strong advocates of Deism as were Allen and Paine, they made few efforts to go beyond writing on the subject. The attempt to organize it into a denomination in competition with the Christian churches was the work of the Reverend Elihu Palmer. Palmer, who went through Presbyterian and Baptist phases, ended in a rejection of Calvinism entirely. In the 1790s and early 1800s he organized Deist churches in New York and Philadelphia and founded two short-lived newspapers to propagate the belief.

He lost his eyesight, as well as his wife, in an outbreak of yellow fever in Philadelphia in 1793, but these misfortunes did not blunt his enthusiasm.

Palmer's most effective publication appeared in 1802. In the *Principles of Nature*[53] he attempted to place moral principle, or virtue, on a basis independent of any theological system.[54] He inevitably deals with many of the same questions as Allen and Paine, but he diverges from them on some important points. He is convinced that man has greater potential than did his predecessors who were careful to stress the limitations of man's finite mind: "The strength of human understanding is incalculable, its keenness of discernment would ultimately penetrate into every part of nature, were it permitted to operate with uncontrolled and unqualified freedom."[55] Man's mind is thwarted in its operation, however, by false theology. This theology which pictures God as indulging in immoral actions perverts "the finest sensations of the human heart" and renders "savage and ferocious the character of man." God is offered to man as a model for worship and imitation. If that model be defective, it has an inevitable effect on man's character, declares Palmer. "If such a Being commit murder, or at any time gives orders to the human race to perform such cruel act, the order once given is the signal for military assassination, national vengeance, or the exercise of domestic resentment. The world becomes a field of blood, and man is slaughtered in the name of heaven."[56]

If man would be happy and develop a "pure and genuine morality," he must put aside the demeaning views of God and life propagated by the orthodox and, instead, turn to a contemplation of nature, says Palmer. ". . . Admire her splendid beauties, develop truth from the permanence of her laws, cultivate real virtue, improve and exalt thy character, extend the sphere of thy utility. . . ."[57]

Allen and Paine had held a very high opinion of Jesus, whom they considered to be the teacher of a great moral system, although they insisted that he had no intention of establishing a new religion. They, of course, rejected the idea of his resurrection from the dead and the other miraculous elements associated with his life; but, as Paine put it, he was "a virtuous and an amiable man."[58] In this area Palmer departed from his fellow Deists. He pictured Jesus as a fraud and ranked him just a little above Moses and Mohammed—two more names on his list of imposters.

In his *Principles* he includes a Christmas discourse which he had delivered in New York in 1796. On that festive occasion, in discussing Christian claims concerning the virgin birth of Jesus, he revived the assertions made by the Jews in the early days of Christianity that Jesus was the offspring of Mary and a Roman soldier and told his congregation that "The simple truth is that their pretended Saviour is nothing more than an illegitimate Jew, and their hopes of salvation through him rest on no better foundation than that of fornication or adultery."[59]

Although the Christian churches were united in their condemnation of Deism, they were experiencing internal strains brought on both by the changed world view of science to which they were struggling to adapt and by the consequences of the Great Awakening which were felt among the various colonies in the 1730s and 1740s. The Great Awakening brought into American Christianity a public display of emotion which was new to the various churches infected by it. For the Puritans and their descendants, to take but one example, the individual's struggle to achieve a sense of salvation was a process he suffered privately and quietly. It was the grace of God working within to overcome past habits of spiritual deadness, apathy, or inability. According to predestinarian theology this conversion process was started in a person at a time foreordained by the deity. There was nothing that could be done by the clergyman or the individual himself to bring it about. Attendance at church, although required in the Puritan colonies, could inform the mind but, without God's direct intervention, it could not lead to conversion.

The conversion experience was fairly common in the early years of Puritanism. Church membership and participation in civil affairs depended on it, since only the sanctified were deemed worthy by the Puritan fathers to guide the commonwealth. When in the second and third generations, however, the number of conversions fell off, the future of both church and state were in doubt, and new approaches were deemed necessary. The "Halfway Covenant," introduced in the 1660s, allowed those who were living exemplary lives but had not experienced conversion to enjoy some, but not all, of the benefits of church membership. This watering down of strict belief created much controversy and can be interpreted as the first stage in the declension of Puritanism. By the turn of the eighteenth century, the churches were seeking new ways to maintain themselves against the worldliness which was a concomitant of the economic success of the Puritan colonies. The people were relatively at ease in Zion, and this ease brought with it snares and temptations.

The emotional upsurge of the Great Awakening was alien to previous Puritan experience, for it externalized what had been an internal experience. The Puritan of the seventeenth century had wrestled with his soul in the privacy of his closet. Only when the process was complete did he stand before the church and recount the struggle which had gone on within him. The preachers of the Awakening, however, encouraged people to wrestle with their souls in public. In order to spur on the process, they colored their rhetoric with dire descriptions of what was in store at the hands of an angry God for those who remained hardhearted. The condemnation by the Deists of the theology which pictured God as full of vengeance and wrath was not spoken in a vacuum; rather it reflected the popular view which was being preached up by the revivalists.

What distinguished the Great Awakening from previous outbreaks of "the Spirit" was a public display of remorse and anguish which often manifested itself in crying out and violent physical contortions. Leaders and churches of various denominations divided on whether this was the Holy Spirit at work or whether this was an example of "enthusiasm," emotionalism run wild. It was controversy on this point which drove Ebenezer Kinnersley out of the Baptist ministry. Against the advice of his friend Franklin, he published an attack which well represents what the argument was all about: "What spirit such enthusiastick ravings proceed from, I shall not attempt to determine; but this I am sure of, that they proceed not from the spirit of God, for our God is a God of order, and not of such confusion. Such whining, roaring harangues, big with affected nonsense, have no other tendency but to operate upon and foster passions, and work them up to a warm pitch of enthusiasm, which when the preacher has done, he has fully gain'd his end, and goes away rejoicing in his triumphant conquests over weak minds. . . ."[60]

The same type of confrontation was experienced in most of the American religious groups. The family argument among the Congregationalists in New England pitted Charles Chauncy of Boston against Jonathan Edwards of Northampton. Edwards was responsible in large part for the revival in western Massachusetts, and he welcomed George Whitefield when Whitefield toured the colonies promoting the Awakening.

Although Edwards was concerned with the emotionalism of the revival, he tried to distinguish between the true marks of the spirit and sheer physical emotion.[61] Chauncy denied that such a distinction could be made and traveled widely, witnessing many examples of what he considered pure enthusiasm.[62]

The Awakening spurred the development of rationalism in the New England Congregational churches. In rejecting emotional excess as foreign to the Puritan heritage, Chauncy and others stressed the rationalist strain which was a strong element in the tradition. Chauncy was convinced that Jesus and his disciples had appealed to men through reason. In his campaign he was abetted by the young, brilliant Jonathan Mayhew during his short-lived, controversial career in Boston. Chauncy and Mayhew rejected the vision of an angry God and, in a spirit similar to that of the Deists, stressed His benevolent qualities. Since, unlike the Deists, they accepted the Scriptures as revelation, they sought to interpret them with the use of reason. This method led them to reject among other beliefs the trinity, predestination, and original sin. Although Jesus was a divine being, he was not coequal with the Father. His mission had been to bring man to a new understanding of God. Because man was not tainted with original sin, he had the capacity to help himself in the process of salvation, cooperating with the grace held out to him by a loving deity.[63]

Chauncy, Mayhew, and the rest of the emergent liberal party in New England were the forerunners of the Unitarian movement within the Congregational churches. That movement gained momentum at the turn of the nineteenth century with the dispute between liberals and conservatives over who should fill the chair of divinity at Harvard College. By the 1820s the alienation was so advanced that the formation of a new denomination became inevitable.

Although the liberal party was labeled "Unitarian," it was a term not many of them would at first accept, preferring such designations as "liberal Christian" or even "catholic Christian." Their point was well taken, for the dispute over whether the godhead should be interpreted as a unity or a trinity, while important for its theological implications, was subordinate to the difference over the question of the nature of man. In rejecting original sin and predestination, the Unitarians staked their faith in man's ability to strive for moral perfection. Their nineteenth-century formulation of "salvation by character" had its beginnings in the eighteenth-century rejection of the idea of man's innate depravity and the affirmation of his inherent goodness.

Unitarianism was propagated in Philadelphia by English emigrés. When Priestley fled English persecution in the 1790s he was welcomed by fellow believers who hoped that he would accept the ministry of their church. Although Priestley declined the offer, he did travel from his refuge at Northumberland from time to time to deliver series of sermons in the capital. The English variety of Unitarianism was more theologically radical than that of New England. It rejected the doctrine of the divinity of Christ. Priestley also rejected what he labeled Greek philosophical influences on early Christianity. In contrast to a spiritual view, he held to a materialistic one. His materialism, which included belief in a physical resurrection of the body, was no doubt influenced by his scientific experimentation and was, he thought, quite consistent with the Newtonian universe.

One of Priestley's homiletical series was presented in the Philadelphia meetinghouse of the Universalists. Universalists, as did Deists and Unitarians, rejected the Calvinist doctrine of a salvation limited to the Elect, predestined by God to enjoy that prize. They insisted that all men would be saved. The orthodox could condemn Deism as infidelity because it rejected Scriptural revelation and thus dismiss it out of hand. Their difficulty with the radical Universalists was more serious; for they accepted the Scriptures and considered themselves squarely within the Christian tradition, insisting that Jesus had taught the message of a benevolent God who loved and would save all of His children, and that Jesus and the early Christians were Universalists. The Universalists, as is so often true with reformers, saw themselves as removing one of the corruptions of Christianity in rejecting eternal punishment.

Universalist ideas insinuated themselves into several groups before the emergence of an identifiable denomination by that name. Universal salvation played a part in the thinking of Provost William Smith of the College of Philadelphia and other Episcopal clergymen. It was found among a number of the German pietistic groups which migrated to Pennsylvania.[64] After many years of hesitation, Charles Chauncy among the Congregationalists published anonymously two works on the subject in the 1780s. He had worked through the idea with the help of Professor John Winthrop[65] of Harvard, whose interests were by no means limited to natural philosophy. Chauncy's *Mystery Hid from Ages and Generations . . . or the Salvation of All Men*[66] created much controversy within Congregational circles and was very influential beyond.

Universalism was introduced into Philadelphia enlightenment circles by Elhanan Winchester, who broke away from the Baptists and formed a Universal Baptist Society. He helped convert Dr. Benjamin Rush to the new belief, and Rush was enlisted to polish the Articles of Faith adopted by the emerging denomination when it met in Philadelphia in 1790. Rush's influence on the resolutions adopted at the convention is very obvious, for they contained a call for some of his pet social reforms, including the abolition of slavery.[67] Rush believed this liberalizing view of Christianity supplied a powerful motivation for the transformation of society: "A belief in God's universal love to all his creatures, and that he will finally restore all those of them that are miserable to happiness, is a *polar* truth. It leads to truths upon all subjects, more especially upon the subject of government. It establishes the *equality* of mankind—it abolishes the punishment of death for any crime—and converts jails into houses of repentence and reformation."[68]

Rush had a profound respect for Winchester, echoing the view of his former teacher and colleague, Dr. John Redman, that he was a "theological Newton." Winchester, like Chauncy, believed that the benevolent deity had provided for the salvation of all men, even those guilty of gross sin, after a limited period of punishment in the afterlife. When this purgatorial period was over, the soul was ushered into the presence of God, there to enjoy bliss through all eternity. Most orthodox Christians vehemently rejected this view, claiming that it vitiated morality and allowed the sinner to indulge in theft, rapine, and murder with the full assurance of eventual salvation. The Universalist response was that the orthodox view libeled both man and God. They were sure that God had not burdened man with original sin in the Garden of Eden and that He had sent Jesus to earth not to die for man's sins but rather to convince him that a loving deity wished him well and looked forward to his company in eternity. Acceptance of this belief would be a positive force in man's life.

The Universalists believed that orthodoxy attempted to scare man into heaven with threats of everlasting fire instead of luring him there with appeals to his nature, which they believed to be basically good, and by the example of a loving Father and Jesus.

The most effective organizer of the new movement was the English emigré John Murray, who arrived in America in 1770. A former follower of George Whitefield, he came close to, if he did not equal, his oratorical ability. Murray preached Universalism throughout the colonies for two generations, using Gloucester and then Boston as a base. Although couching his message in biblical language, Murray preached a more radical variety of Universalism than Winchester, insisting that no one would suffer purgatorial fire in the afterlife with the possible exception of the fallen angels.

The Universalism of Winchester and Murray preserved many Calvinistic elements. They had democratized Calvinism by reinterpreting the meaning of the Elect and insisting that a benevolent God had elected all men for salvation. But it was through the thought of Hosea Ballou that the full impact of the Enlightenment was felt in the new denomination. Reared in the frontier area of New Hampshire as a Baptist, he was converted to the new belief in young manhood. In the 1790s Ballou came under the influence of Ethan Allen's *Reason the Only Oracle of Man*. Unlike other Christians, he did not reject Allen's ideas out of hand. Instead he adopted Allen's technique of applying reason to the Scriptures and thought through a new, non-Calvinistic basis for Universalism. Ballou's compelling personality and preaching and his skillfully argued *Treatise on Atonement*[69] of 1805 brought most of the denomination to this position.

Winchester and Murray were Trinitarians. Ballou established Universalism on a Unitarian base. He stressed the subordination of the Son to the Father and interpreted atonement as a reconciliation of man to God. Men had been misled by centuries of corrupted theology into believing that God was a stern, wrathful being. But the use of reason would allow men to sweep this away and recognize His true nature, declared Ballou. God loves man and seeks to win him to Himself through the mediation of the loving Jesus. Jesus did not perform a blood atonement but rather exemplified God's great love for man.

Although initially Ballou accepted the idea of a limited punishment in the afterlife, he eventually came to the conclusion that man receives his reward and punishment in this life. At death he is transformed by the overpowering love of the Father and enters a life of eternal happiness in His presence.

It was the acceptance of the radical idea of no future punishment that separated the Universalists from the Unitarians. In most theological points but this last they saw eye-to-eye. These parallel liberal movements were kept apart, however, by socioeconomic factors as well. In New England, the Unitarians were members of the old, well-established Puritan Congregational churches with their Harvard-educated ministry. They were well-off socially, culturally, and economically. The Universalists emerged from various denominations—especially the Baptists —and, on the whole, had meager educations and were lower down on the socioeconomic ladder. The two just did not mix. This situation can be illustrated by the fact that, although their homes and churches in Boston were only a short distance from each other, Ballou and William Ellery Channing, the most prominent of the Unitarian preachers, never met. Channing, from a prominent family, with a thorough Harvard education, was recognized as a mover in literary and cultural circles; Ballou, from the family of a humble Baptist farmer-preacher, with just a few years of formal education at the secondary level, traveled in a very different circle. The writings of Channing are widely read as products of the American Renaissance of the nineteenth century; the writings of Ballou, while useful to the intellectual historian, are almost completely neglected.

Both Unitarianism and Universalism can be interpreted as compromises between traditional Christianity and Deism. While accepting the application of reason to religion, these groups maintained their faith in the Scriptures as a vehicle of revelation, insisting, however, that they could be understood correctly only if reason is applied to them. Like the Deists they rejected Trinitarianism and the idea of a blood atonement, but unlike the Deists they maintained belief in the miraculous element in Christianity. The designation of supernatural rationalists applied to them by some scholars is a fair one.

The same rationalistic spirit which resulted in the emergence of these two liberal denominations had its effects on other American religious groups as well, most notably the Quakers. The disputes between the evangelical faction and that sympathetic to the views of Elias Hicks led to the division of the various American yearly meetings in the Great Separation of 1828. The Hicksite Friends combined rationalism with the basic Quaker belief in the inner light and resisted the efforts of evangelicals to bring into the denomination a biblicism which they considered foreign to their tradition.[70]

The Enlightenment, where it did not lead to outright Deism, had a profound effect on American religious groups.

Although Elihu Palmer made a contribution to American Deist thought, the Deist churches he organized were short-lived. This can probably be explained by the attitudes of the Deists themselves. Since they were so resentful of "priestcraft" and the institution of the church, they had little heart for such organization. In this sense, Deism was a negative force in American life. In another sense it was quite positive. It freed many men's minds of repressive thought. It helped them break out of a Calvinistic mindset and allowed them to relate their religious beliefs to the scientific world view of the age. They did not have to keep their religious beliefs in one mental compartment and their beliefs concerning the nature of the universe in another.

Although there were notable exceptions, such as Rush and Priestley, who remained within a Christian context, many of the men of the Enlightenment held deistic views. A partial catalogue would include George Wythe, Edmund Randolph, John Randolph, George Washington, George Mason, Francis Hopkinson, Gouverneur Morris, and Robert R. Livingston.

However ineffective the forces of organized Deism, the fact is that deistic views permeated the better-educated levels of American society. The religious books mentioned above, along with English and European productions, were the common topic of conversation, but Deism found its way into other forms of literature as well. The poems of Freneau, for example, are steeped in the thought, as is clear from such titles as "On the Uniformity and Perfection of Nature," "On the Universality and other Attributes of the God of Nature," "On the Religion of Nature," "Belief and Unbelief," the last of which he "Humbly recommended to the serious consideration of creed makers."[71]

The colleges were rife with the belief, students adopting nicknames such as "Voltaire," "Rousseau," "Diderot," "D'Alembert" in tribute to thinkers of the French Enlightenment but also, no doubt, as a means of irritating their professors and administrations. Harvard and Yale students were particularly taken with the ideas of Tom Paine. At Yale the heresy was combatted by the homiletical efforts of Timothy Dwight. At Harvard in 1796 the Corporation subjected each student to an intellectual inoculation in the form of Bishop Watson's *Apology for the Bible*, designed as an answer to Tom Paine. Students at William and Mary were engaged in debating such dangerous questions as "Whether there be a God?" or "Whether the Christian religion had been injurious or beneficial to mankind?"[72]

Although a reawakening of interest in Christianity had begun on the western frontier of Kentucky soon after the turn of the nineteenth century, it did not have as great an impact on the more settled East or on the higher orders in the social scale. As late as 1811 when William Meade (later a bishop) was on his way to church in Williamsburg with Bishop Madison for his ordination to the Episcopal priesthood, he met a number of students out with their guns and dogs for the hunt. He also observed a man taking advantage of the sabbath to fill his ice house. The state of the church building, dilapidated with broken windows, told much regarding the status of organized religion in Virginia at the time. His friends and neighbors, hearing that he had chosen ordination to the priesthood, considered him lacking in common sense or a little mad.[74] Meade, "for some years after," expected every young man of education he met to be "a skeptic, if not an avowed unbeliever."[74]

Ultimately Deism was defeated at the popular level because "the majority were drawn off by an emotional substitute for thought. . . ."[75] Revivalism supplied an emotional outlet which was wanting in a religion which insisted on the use of the mind. The reaction against Deism, however, was more than a popular one. The more educated of the population were to reconcile science with religion by drawing parallels between natural and revealed religion.[76] This provided intellectual justification for mainline Christian beliefs, while the elements of Christianity which had received most ridicule from the Deists were swept under the rug.

The experience of Robert R. Livingston of New York is most instructive. As a recent biographer has pointed out, like other men of science, he "had drifted into an easy deism. . . ." He tended "to regard all formal religion with a detached, tolerant, amused curiosity." We have the testimony of Livingston's sister—which may be tainted by the fact that she was married to

the Methodist minister Freeborn Garretson—that he went
through a change on his deathbed, where he discoursed on Christianity "in such a strain of heavenly eloquence."[77] If this story is
true, it is but one example of an experience which Christians of
the day were convinced was widespread. No man, they believed,
could face his Maker with equanimity if he clung to "infidelity."
When he came to the edge of the great beyond, he would reach
out and cling to the robes of the Son of God, his Savior.

CHAPTER 6

The Diffusion of Knowledge

EUROPE in its present state of political torpor affords no scope for the activity of a benevolent mind. Here [in America] everything is in a plastic state. Here the benefactor of mankind may realize all his schemes for promoting human happiness. Human nature here (unsubdued by the tyranny of European habits and customs) yields to reason, justice, and common sense.

—*Benjamin Rush*[1]

It goes without saying that the men of the Enlightenment in America believed in education. Their hopes for the present and the future of mankind were based on the conviction that the ignorance and superstition which pervaded so much of the world could be eradicated by subjecting it to the penetrating light of reason. Much of their energy, therefore, went into the communication of modern thinking. Knowledge was not to be the exclusive property of an elite group but was to be diffused among all levels in society.

With the achievement of national independence, the establishment of universal education became, in their eyes, a matter of life and death. They were sure a republic could not survive with an uneducated population. Jefferson would go so far as to say that education was necessary to prepare the people to defeat their own government if it got out of their control and hatched wicked designs. So we observe the paradoxical situation of Jefferson proposing a state system of education to prepare the people to resist the state. He saw no inconsistency in this, however; for it was his firm conviction that the government belonged to the people and leaders who betrayed their trust should be deposed.

145

As we observed in chapter 2 above, those interested in the development of science maintained a constant correspondence. This communication was aided by the fact that Franklin as deputy postmaster under the royal government had free access to the mails. He then was called upon to supervise the establishment of a postal service in the early days of the American confederation.

The lack of an organization such as the Royal Society to promote the exchange of ideas was early felt and constantly lamented by the natural philosophers. The establishment of such an organization was proposed from time to time. Cadwallader Colden had suggested to William Douglass in 1728 that Boston would be a logical location for a society which would act as a clearinghouse and publish scientific papers for the consumption of members throughout the colonies. The suggestion, however, was not acted on. The initiative to establish such a group was finally taken in Philadelphia. Although the idea may have been John Bartram's,[2] it was Franklin, with customary vigor, who carried it through. Franklin thought that the colonies were at the stage in their development where they could go beyond concern for the mere necessities of life. There were now many men who were able to devote time to the cultivation of "the finer Arts, and [the improvement of] the common stock of knowledge."[3] Franklin also observed that, because the country was so large, communication among scientists was not likely. He feared that knowledge of important discoveries was often lost with the death of the discoverers.[4] So he proposed the establishment of an organization to be known as the American Philosophical Society to promote communication among "virtuosi" of the several colonies.

When the Society came into being in 1743, it was short-lived. The time needed to promote such an organization and the energy needed to keep it going were apparently lacking among the virtuosi. When the society was revived some years later, it was confronted with a competing group. The competition was caused not so much by the scientific diversity of the various members as by political tensions among Philadelphians. The superior claims of science finally led to peace and harmony and merger of the two organizations in 1768.

The earliest *Transactions* of the two societies were published in 1769, and the following sampling gives a fair idea of the potpourri of interests—most quite utilitarian—of the members: Henry Hollingsworth set forth a prescription for getting rid of "the wild garlic with which the country is in many places infected and which is very pernicious to the grain." Moses Bartram contributed "Observations on the native silk worms of North America." Dr. John Morgan, F.R.S., professor of medicine in the College of Philadelphia, submitted an account of the recent irruption of Vesuvius supplied him by an English friend who observed it. Included also was an extract of a letter from Peter Miller of Ephrata "on the time of sowing pease so as to preserve the crop from being worm-eaten." Dr. Lionel Chalmers of Charles Town, South Carolina, a corresponding member of the Society, contributed an "Essay on the Dry Belly Ach or Nervous Colick."[5]

It is clear from this sample list that the Society, even if strongly oriented toward the solution of American problems, maintained some interest in developments overseas. During the Revolution when the temptation was strong to look inward and to allow patriotism to overwhelm the broader interests of philosophy, the Society eschewed that approach. It declared that, no matter what issues may divide the United States from the mother country, the interests of mankind transcended them. As Jefferson expressed the sentiment, societies of scientists "are always at peace, however their nations may be at war . . . they form a great fraternity spreading over the whole earth."[6]

The internationality of science was justly symbolized on 10 March 1797, when Jefferson, who had come to Philadelphia to be inaugurated Vice President of the United States, assumed the presidency of the American Philosophical Society, to which he had been elected on the death of David Rittenhouse. He was flanked on the platform that evening by the renowned English scientist, Joseph Priestley, a recent refugee from British intolerance, and Le Comte de Volney, the famed French rationalist. The occasion was not purely ceremonial, for Jefferson presented a paper entitled "Memoir on the Discovery of Certain Bones of a Quadruped of the Clawed Kind in the Western Parts of Virginia."[7] His election to the presidency of the Society was no doubt in recognition of his various interests in science, among them his work *Notes on the State of Virginia*, and his improvement of "the most useful of the instruments known to man," the plow. The Jeffersonian moldboard plow, the principles of whose contours Jefferson had figured mathematically, cut furrows deeper and with more ease than older models and won him recognition on two continents. He, incidentally, refused to patent his invention—as had Franklin earlier with his stove—on the grounds that one should not monopolize an idea useful to mankind.[8]

Almost from the beginning, the American Philosophical Society in Philadelphia was envied in other places. John Page, an old and dear friend of Jefferson's from their days at William and Mary, led in the establishment of the Virginia Society for Promoting Useful Knowledge in 1772. John Adams, writing to his wife, Abigail, from Philadelphia in 1776, expressed the hope that one day Boston might enjoy a similar group. The Society, he said, "excites a scientific emulation and propagates their fame."[9] His hope was fulfilled with the establishment of the American Academy of Arts and Sciences in Boston in 1780. Elected first president of the group was James Bowdoin, capitalist, politician, and promoter of scientific endeavors. Although the country was still in the midst of war, Bowdoin outlined an ambitious program for the Academy in his inaugural address. It was to take as its province American antiquities and natural history, mathematics, medical and scientific experimentation, astronomical, meteorological, and geographical observation. It was to seek to improve agriculture, the arts, manufactures, commerce, and to develop natural resources. In the words of the act of the legislature incorporating the Academy, it was "to cultivate every art and science which may tend to advance the interest, honour, dignity and happiness of a free, independent, and virtuous people."[10]

Such scientific societies, of course, stimulated research and discussion among learned men. But the task of propagating interest in science at more popular levels was not neglected. Many men took to the lecture platform, spreading knowledge of scientific discoveries. Benjamin Franklin took credit for starting on his way one of the first and most successful of American scientific popularizers. Ebenezer Kinnersley was born in England and brought to this country by his parents when he was three years old. He intended to establish himself as a Baptist minister, but he became involved in various controversies with leading brethren in the movement. He was ordained in 1743 but was never settled over a parish because he held rationalistic ideas which made it impossible for him to coexist with the more pious of his coreligionists. He took a strong stand against the excesses of the Great Awakening in 1740 and was one of the persons who fell victim to the divisiveness of that emotional outburst. Aside from what is known of his religious ideas, the fact that he became a close friend of Franklin is indication enough that Kinnersley was unorthodox. Although Franklin had taught himself to tolerate all types, it is difficult to believe that he would have had such an intimate relationship with Kinnersley had they not seen eye to eye on very basic matters.

Kinnersley was later to become Professor of English and Oratory in the College of Philadelphia, but he was one of the circle of Franklinian natural philosophers who spent much time carrying on experiments in electricity with the apparatus which Franklin had acquired. Since a preaching career appeared closed to him, Franklin encouraged him to go among the populace lecturing on the wonders of electricity. Initially Franklin put together a couple of lecture-demonstrations for him and set him on the course of his new career. Kinnersley apparently tried his hand at this first in Annapolis in 1749 and then two years later in Philadelphia. In succeeding years, he spent months on the road, giving series of lectures and demonstrations in such places as Boston, Newport, New York, and as far away as the West Indies.[11]

Although his "Course of Experiments on the newly-discovered Electrical Fire" was well received and very entertaining, Kinnersley was not a mere reporter of what was going on; he made definite contributions of his own to the expanding knowledge of electricity. He has been overshadowed by his greater contemporary, but Priestley, for one, rated his work quite positively. In the *History and Present State of Electricity* (London, 1767), he wrote that "if he continue his electrical inquiries, his name, after that of his friend [Franklin], will be second to few in the history of electricity."[12] It could be that Kinnersley did not live up to this promise because of the demands of his lecture schedules and his teaching of nonscientific matters, but he made a significant contribution to the education of the people.

Because he understood the pious mind, Kinnersley was careful to point out the positive religious implications of science. His published lecture prospectus made the point: "As the knowledge of nature tends to enlarge the human mind and give us more noble, more grand and exalted ideas of the Author of Nature, it is presumed that this course of experiments will meet with encouragement as a rational and commendable entertainment. 'The works of the Lord are great and sought out of all them that have pleasure therein.' Psalm CX 1, 2."[13]

Having made his genuflection to piety, in his prospectus, Kinnersley promised not only instruction but a lively show, as is clear from this sampling of topics included in his presentations:

"An experiment showing how houses, ships, &c. may be secured from being damaged by lightning."

"An animal killed by it instantaneously."

"Eight musical bells rung by an electrified phial of water."

"A battery of eleven guns discharged by fire issuing out of a person's finger."

"A battery of eleven guns discharged by lightning after it has darted through ten feet of water."[14]

Such entertaining approaches to science had their constructive uses. Not only were people who were unlikely to understand from the printed page shown the workings of the "fire," but it is a fair conclusion that the study of science was promoted thereby. Franklin, after all, had been inspired to dabble in it by the presentation of an itinerant lecturer. He may have had this influence in mind when he urged Kinnersley to take to the lecture platform.

It appears that electricity had its political uses also. It is known that George III threw his royal weight on the side of blunt-ended lightning rods because that American rebel, Franklin, promoted the use of pointed rods as more attractive to lightning. But electricity had political implications on the other side of the Atlantic as well. When news arrived that Franklin had been abused by Alexander Wedderburn before the Privy Council, Kinnersley made a popular demonstration of the power of electricity by using it to burn the effigies of not only that imperious interrogator but also that cordially hated royal Governor of Massachusetts, Thomas Hutchinson, before a tumultuous crowd in Philadelphia.[15]

Franklin was an old hand at educating the people. One of his most successful educational ventures, one that also turned a pretty penny for him, was his publication of *Poor Richard's Almanac*. The almanac was a well-established genre when Franklin began. Almanacs were published throughout the colonies and were found in most American homes, often taking their place next to the Bible in more modest family libraries. The astronomical tables, weather predictions, articles, and poetry which filled their pages provided many hours of entertainment and instruction in an age when books and newspapers were not easily come by. Nathaniel Ames and his family in New England produced a series of almanacs which continued over a period of fifty years.

In the name of Richard Saunders, an impoverished "philiomath," whose wife was insisting that he make some money, Franklin began the venture in 1732, selling about 10,000 copies a year for twenty-five years.[16]

Each issue featured an inimitable preface by "Poor Richard," except for the year when his wife, disturbed by his statement in a previous edition that his profit on the almanac had gone to buying her a new corset and petticoats, substituted a complaining preface of her own. She assured the reader she had not altered her husband's production beyond the preface, except to change some weather predictions, since the ladies were entitled to more drying days.[17] In the almanac, Franklin allowed his imagination full rein. The sayings of Poor Richard have been among those things which account for his abiding fame. Some were original; many were not. But those he adapted from elsewhere, he sharpened so that they had a real edge.

"Love your enemies, for they tell you your faults."

" 'Tis easier to prevent bad habits than to break them."

"Saying and doing have quarrel'd and parted."[18]

One of Franklin's more imaginative ventures was to gather into the preface of the 1758 edition many of the sayings from over the years and put them into a connected discourse uttered by "Father Abraham" at an auction.[19] This discourse was reprinted many times in many languages: French, German, Italian, Spanish, Swedish, Welsh, Gaelic, Polish, Danish, Russian, Bohemian, Dutch, Chinese, Greek and others;[20] its dissemination goes far toward explaining Franklin's reception in Europe.

Aside from the sayings, the *Almanac* contained the usual tables and pieces on various subjects. Professor Raymond Stearns did a "liberal sampling" of almanacs published between 1740 and 1770 and found that "they continued to perform a role in the popularization of science similar to that earlier in the century. . . ."[21] Although he published fewer strictly scientific articles than some of his competitors, Franklin's *Almanac* reflected his scientific interests and had an effect by "its gentle, though devastating, ridicule of superstition from the pen of the pretended astrologer, Richard Saunders. . . ."[22] In addition, he had great influence on his readers on a whole gamut of subjects. A reading of his newspaper, the *Pennsylvania Gazette*, reveals the extent to which he filled its columns with his own liberal, rationalistic views. His fertile imagination did not hesitate even at using hoaxes to undercut narrow or superstitious attitudes in order to promote the interests of enlightenment.

Formal education became one of the central concerns of the leaders of the American Enlightenment and they made various efforts to promote it. Franklin was among the first with a proposal for the establishment of an academy to educate the youth of Philadelphia. As usual, he promoted the venture from behind the scenes. He published, anonymously, a pamphlet stressing the many advantages to be gained by the boys who attended such a school and those which would accrue to the community itself.[23] The plan of education he suggested stressed the utilitarian subjects which would help young men get on in the world. It is obvious, as one reads his proposal, that he was reflecting on his own experience as he set forth the ideal curriculum for such an institution. As it turned out, Franklin proposed, but others disposed. The academy, when underway in 1751, included much more of the classical in its curriculum than he desired.

When Franklin was surveying possible locations for the school, in the 1740s, he asked his friend Cadwallader Colden in New York for advice. Colden, who had escaped the hurly-burly of Manhattan for the measured calm of his country estate up the Hudson, at the foot of the Catskills, favored a location in the country. He was probably influenced, also, by his concern for the teaching of agriculture, which he, like other men of the Enlightenment, hoped to facilitate as a scientific venture.[24] But he recognized the difficulties he had had raising his own children so far away from the cultural advantages of the city. Still, he believed with effort these disadvantages could be overcome. He told Franklin, "The chief objection to the college's being in the country, I think, is that the schollars cannot acquire that advantage of behavior and address which they would acquire by a more general conversation with gentlemen. But this, I think, may be remedied by obliging them to use the same good manners towards one another, with a proper regard to their several ranks, as is used among well bred gentlemen, by having them taught dancing and other exercises usually taught gentlemen."[25]

As it turned out, Franklin's projected Academy was established in the heart of Philadelphia. Some houses were utilized and the trustees were contemplating the erection of a main building when it became plain that a deal could be worked out for the use of the tabernacle originally built by a nonsectarian group so that the controversial preacher, George Whitefield, could be heard in Philadelphia. This meetinghouse was available, under the terms of its erection, to any preacher who came to town and asked for its use. As the Great Awakening receded, it was no longer in much demand. It happened that Benjamin Franklin was a trustee of the meetinghouse, as he was of the newly established Academy. So he managed, in his cunning way, to bring the two groups together in an arrangement mutually beneficial. The tabernacle became the core building of the Academy in 1751.[26]

The Academy and the College which grew out of it was intended as a nonsectarian venture. Despite Franklin's efforts to keep it so, Provost William Smith, an Anglican clergyman, made every effort to insinuate his sectarian views into its operation. That stormy petrel became one of Franklin's most bitter enemies. Franklin in 1763 explained Smith's animosity in a most interesting manner: "I made that man my enemy by doing him too much kindness. 'Tis the honestest way of acquiring an enemy. And since 'tis convenient to have at least one enemy, who by his readiness to revile one on all occasions may make one careful of one's conduct, I shall keep him an enemy for that purpose. . . ."[27]

Jefferson looked with envy at the public school system of New England. The reforming influence of Horace Mann was more than fifty years in the future; but, with all its inadequacies, the school system which stemmed from the seventeenth-century Puritan desire that all men be taught to read and write so they would understand the Word of God was a vehicle for creating an informed electorate in the new republic. Such a system Virginia lacked. The interests of those who had settled the Old Dominion were very different from those of the Puritan fathers of Massachusetts Bay. In most instances, they made no effort to settle in towns where the Word of God could easily be heard in the meetinghouses. The geography and soil of Virginia dictated a different mode of life. Plantations with extensive landholdings were established along the many navigable rivers. Such a mode of settlement did not lend itself to a system of schools. The formal education which was carried on was by tutors or in plantation schools for the sake of the children of the planters. Education of the great mass of children was not a concern of the leading citizens.

This was the problem Jefferson confronted when he looked to the future of the new republic. As part of the reform of law and custom of Virginia, he proposed the establishment of an extensive school system. He entered into the legislature in 1779 "A Bill for the More General Diffusion of Knowledge Among the People." When he later traveled to Paris to become the American minister plenipotentiary, he became more than ever convinced of the importance of his plan of education. He wrote his collaborator George Wythe that that bill was the most important in the Virginia law code. Wythe would have to see to believe the ignorance of the common people of Europe. They were one thousand years behind Americans, who, fortunately, were cut off from the Old World. Hoping Wythe would continue to exert influence on behalf of the bill, Jefferson stressed that education of the people was vital: "No other sure foundation can be devised for the preservation of freedom and happiness. If any body thinks that kings, nobles, or priests are good conservators of the public happiness, send them here. It is the best school in the universe to cure them of that folly. . . . Let our countrymen know that the people alone can protect us against these evils, and that the tax which will be paid for this purpose is not more than the thousandth part of what will be paid to kings, priests and nobles who will rise up among us if we leave the people in ignorance."[28]

Jefferson's plan called for an educational system that would take care of all levels of Virginia society, rich and poor. To overcome geographical difficulties of such a far-flung commonwealth, he proposed to divide the counties of the state into wards or "hundreds," with population sufficient in each to provide enough pupils for an elementary school. These wards ideally would be about six miles square, inspired by the geographical convenience of the New England town. The school would be placed in a central location. Each ward was to be controlled by three elected aldermen. Overseers or superintendents would be chosen to look after groups of about ten schools in a county.[29]

Jefferson opined that children in the elementary schools were too young to study the Bible; but he did think they were old enough to be exposed to Greek, Roman, European, and American history and to learn the first elements of morality. Of course, the basic job of these schools would be to teach reading, writing, and arithmetic.

For the second level of education, ages eight through fifteen or sixteen, Jefferson would have divided Virginia into twenty districts, in each of which would be located a grammar school. Parents who were financially able would pay for their children's attendance. But Jefferson would have the state support the most talented boys of poor families. Each September the most promising poor boy from each ward would be chosen to attend grammar school for one or two years, depending on his ability. The curriculum of these schools would be one "for the common purposes of life" and would include the classics, grammar, geography, higher mathematics, and languages, both ancient and modern.

Jefferson thought the study of languages ideal for children of this age. They often seem more mature than they really are and should not be exposed as yet to some subjects. But since language study is a matter of memorization, these years are best spent in such an endeavor, declared Jefferson. "If this period be suffered to pass in idleness, the mind becomes lethargic and impotent, as would the body it inhabits if unexercised during the same time." Language study was important for another reason, however; it was a vital tool for later scientific study.

At the end of the second year in grammar school one poor boy would be chosen from each of the twenty districts and supported with public funds for four more years. "By this means," wrote Jefferson, "twenty of the best geniuses will be raked from the rubbish annually." Then, in alternate years, half of the districts would choose their best scholars (one each) for three years at the College of William and Mary. The others would be prepared to serve as grammar school masters.[30]

The study of science was to be the capstone of the Jeffersonian structure. To accomplish this, he hoped to transform his alma mater into a state university. But the Anglican roots of William and Mary ran too deep. Dissenting religious groups, therefore, opposed this part of his plan and the legislation was never acted upon.

Indeed his whole proposal ran into the rock of Virginia conservatism. The plan for the establishment of elementary schools never went into effect because it was amended in the legislature to allow each county court to decide when it would become effective within its jurisdiction. As Jefferson explained it, since the schools were to be supported by county taxes, the more wealthy citizens, who dominated the county courts, blocked implementation lest their taxes be used for the education of the poor.[31] So the good people of Virginia, in checkmating their most enlightened son, took their chances with the future of the republic.

Jefferson's attempts were to be emulated elsewhere. When part of the western territories of Virginia became the state of Kentucky in 1792, forward-looking residents began promoting the idea of an educational system. The state of learning in the opening West can be gauged by the example of a teacher from an "old field" or "hedgerow" school in Kentucky who testified in court that a certain transaction had been accomplished on the thirty-ninth day of the month. Under questioning, the teacher admitted he did not know how many months there were in the year. It was this kind of deficiency which led the legislature in 1821 to appoint a commission to devise a plan for a system of common schools for Kentucky.[32]

The same resistance to the support of public education by the financially well-off residents was registered in Kentucky as in Virginia. They saw no reason why the state should provide education; each should provide for his own children. In answering a questionnaire sent by the commission, James Madison commented that both rich and poor should have an interest in educational institutions at all levels, since the vicissitudes of life often see them exchange places in society. An American rich man today may very well be penurious tomorrow and there were enough examples of people who had had the opposite experience to make Madison's a telling point.[33] Public education, however, was practically nonexistent in Kentucky and much of the West until after the Civil War. Those who received any formal education at all did so at private schools.[34]

Benjamin Rush justified the expenditure of tax money for the development of a system of educational institutions in Pennsylvania on very practical grounds. His expectations of the benefits to be derived have probably never been exceeded, even in a nation which has come to look on education as a panacea. According to Rush, all would benefit, even bachelors and parents without children. The money spent in taxes would more than be compensated by the improvement in all aspects of society: better government, improved manufactures, and more efficient and productive agriculture. In the long run, the tax burden would even be lessened by the gains made in these fields. And the tone of society would be immeasurably improved: ". . . I will go further and add [that] it will be true economy in individuals to support public schools. The bachelor will in time save his tax for this purpose by being able to sleep with fewer bolts and locks to his doors, the estates of orphans will in time be benefited by being protected from the ravages of unprincipled and idle boys, and the children of wealthy parents will be less tempted by bad company to extravagance. Fewer pillories and whipping posts and smaller jails, with their usual expenses and taxes, will be necessary when our youth are properly educated than at present. I believe it could be proved that the expenses of confining, trying and executing criminals amount every year, in most of the counties, to more money than would be sufficient to maintain all the schools that would be necessary in each county. The confessions of these criminals generally show us that their vices and punishments are the fatal consequences of the want of a proper education in early life."[35]

Having failed to transform the College of William and Mary into a state institution at the pinnacle of his complete system of education for Virginia in 1779, Jefferson made a new effort for education in his native state after his retirement as President of the United States. His new university was chartered in 1819 and opened its doors in 1825, just a year before his death. As Rector of the institution he planned and guided the building of the home for the university, planned its curriculum, and supervised the hiring of its faculty. He rated this accomplishment as one of the three most important of his life, the other two being his authorship of the Declaration of Independence and the Statute of Virginia for Religious Freedom.

Jefferson saw to it that the ugly specter of sectarian division was kept outside the walls of his university. His was to be a secular institution, for he was as convinced as ever that organized religion and priestcraft had for centuries exercised tyranny over the mind of man. No sectarian theology would be included in the curriculum of the university. Natural theology and related subjects would be within the province of the professor of ethics. But Jefferson came to the rectorship of the university from a political career and knew that accommodations must sometimes be made. To ease the minds of the less enlightened, he did agree that the various sects could establish their own schools of theology at the perimeter of the institution. This would allow them access to the educational and cultural riches of the university but would not allow them a voice in its management.

Such an accommodation proved acceptable in principle, although no group ever took advantage of it. Jefferson did, how-

ever, still suffer a setback at the hands of the sectarians. He had
attracted to the university what he considered the most able
mind in America: "[Dr. Thomas] Cooper is acknowledged by
every enlightened man who knows him to be the greatest man in
America in the powers of mind and in acquired information and
that without a single exception." John Adams's evaluation of
Cooper was substantially the same but contained a reservation
which may explain to some extent Cooper's controversial career.
He called him "a learned, ingenious, scientific and talented
mad-cap."[36]

Cooper had migrated from England where he had been associated with the same political, scientific, and religious circle as
Joseph Priestley. He had spent some time in France in the midst
of the early revolutionary events. In the United States he soon
became a partisan of the Jeffersonian Republican Party. Cooper,
who was both a physician and a lawyer, lived with Priestley for
an extended period of time at Northumberland, Pennsylvania.
Unlike the latter, however, he became a naturalized American
citizen. This fact saved him from deportation in 1799 under the
Alien Law (which was a threat to Priestley), but he was jailed for
six months and fined four hundred dollars under the Sedition
Law in April of 1800, as punishment for editorial attacks on President John Adams in his *Northumberland Gazette*.[37]

The emotional state of the Federalist administration is well
gauged from a letter written by Secretary of State Timothy Pickering to an influential attorney on the scene: "As to Dr. Priestley,
his conduct in this affair is wholly unpardonable. I once thought
him a *persecuted Christian*, but I am now satisfied that *ambition*
influences him, like the mass of seditious, turbulent democrats;
and that no government which human wisdom could devise
would ever make them contented, unless they were placed at its
head. I am sorry that Cooper, like Priestley, has not remained an
alien. The *indecency* in these *strangers* thus meddling with our
government merits a severe animadversion. . . ."[38]

It was in 1800, the year of the jailing of Cooper, that Thomas
Jefferson was elected third President of the United States and the
Alien and Sedition Laws went to their infamous rest. Cooper was
rewarded by the Republicans of Pennsylvania with a district
judgeship. But even here he was not secure. He was attacked
—irony of ironies—for introducing the formalities of the English
judicial system into the much more informal court system of

Pennsylvania and was removed from the bench by legislative action.[39]

Cooper then entered the final phase of his career, that as a college professor. But the groves of academe were not to be quiet. Despite the fact that he established a first-rate curriculum in science at Dickinson College, to which he brought much of the excellent apparatus of the late Priestley, his appointment was made without the approval of the conservative Presbyterian supporters of the college, who objected to Cooper's Unitarianism and his materialist philosophy. They considered Cooper an infidel who would threaten the Christianity and morals of his students.[40]

Cooper taught at Dickinson from 1811 to 1815 and then briefly at the University of Pennsylvania, where he was also active in the affairs of the American Philosophical Society. He moved to Columbia College (later the University of South Carolina) while waiting for Jefferson's university to be born. While Jefferson strove mightily to arrange his move to Charlottesville, it was not to be. The *odium theologicum* which had pursued Cooper most of his life dogged him still. The Presbyterians, who were a power in the state, threatened to withdraw their support for the university in the state legislature if Cooper were actually hired. Jefferson was bitter over their opposition, describing them as "the most intolerant of all sects, the most tyrannical, and ambitious; ready . . . to put the torch to the pile and to rekindle . . . the flames in which their oracle Calvin consumed the poor Servetus."[41] With anguish Jefferson had to give way. Cooper was to have been the first of a distinguished group of faculty members who would make the University of Virginia second to none in the world. Jefferson was forced to settle for less.

Jefferson suffered no illusion that his persistent badgering of the legislature for money and other favors for his university was greatly appreciated. As he wrote one of his collaborators in the noble effort, "I have been long sensible that while I was endeavoring to render our country the greatest of all services, that of regenerating the public education, and placing our rising generation on the level of our sister states (which they, have proudly held heretofore), I was discharging the odious function of a physician pouring medicine down the throat of a patient insensible of needing it." But in the long run the effort would prove worthwhile, no matter what the temporary discomfort and loss of popularity. "I am so sure of the future approbation of posterity, and of

the inestimable effect we shall have produced in the elevation of
our country by what we have done, as that I cannot repent of the
part I have borne in cooperation with my colleagues."[42]

The standard of quality Jefferson hoped to maintain for the
University of Virginia to a great extent depended on the quality
of the schools which prepared students for entrance. He was
quite conscious that his institution would be a university in name
only unless the state was willing to adopt the other features of his
comprehensive plan which would insure adequate preparation.
He and Cooper compared notes on how rigorous entrance re-
quirements might be. Cooper believed—and Jefferson agreed
—that no one should be allowed in unless he could "read with
facility Vergil, Horace, Xenophon, and Homer; unless he is able
to convert a page of English at sight into Latin; unless he can
demonstrate any proposition at sight in the first six books of Eu-
clid and show an acquaintance with cubic and quadratic equa-
tions." Any standard lower than this would make of the university
"a mere grammar school."[43]

Jefferson had aspired to the establishment of a university which
would be a center of enlightenment to which the whole nation
would look. It would be a national university, attracting students
from all of the states. But as the national trauma of the Missouri
Compromise of 1820 accentuated regional feelings, the University
of Virginia became in his thinking more and more a state, or at
most regional, institution.[44]

What Jefferson sought to accomplish in Virginia, Benjamin
Rush worked for in Pennsylvania. Systematic education was
among the reforms the energetic Doctor advocated in the late
1780s. His plan was as comprehensive as that proposed by
Jefferson.[45] He called for a system of public schools which would
provide a basic education in reading, writing, and arithmetic.
These schools would be conducted in German in those areas of
the state where that language predominated. Beyond the elementary level, Rush advocated the establishment of academies in each
county. These would have the task of teaching the boys "learned
languages" in preparation for college.

Rush called for the establishment of four liberal arts colleges in
the state: in Philadelphia; in Carlisle (Dickinson College, of which
Rush was a founder, was already in operation there); in Manheim
for the German-speaking population; and eventually in the frontier area at Pittsburgh. He believed that four was an ideal

number, for he wanted to restrict them to a manageable size, such as the ones he knew in his own experience in Scotland. He claimed that because Oxford and Cambridge were overcrowded they were "seats of dissipation. . . ."[46] At the pinnacle of his educational pyramid would be the university in Philadelphia, which he would have concentrate on advanced, professional subjects, such as law, medicine, divinity, economics, and "the law of nature and of nations. . . ."[47]

These various attempts to improve education were made with the male population in mind. There was still little thought that institutions should be organized to provide an equal education for women. Franklin, in his *Autobiography*, disapproved of the mindless subjects that were taught women to make them acceptable companions of men. His observation was based on a personal experience. Instead of music and dancing, he thought females should be taught accounting. In this way they could avoid being taken in by crafty, unscrupulous businessmen and could tend their own affairs on the decease of their husbands. He illustrated his point with the story of the wife of a journeyman printer he had staked to a printing shop in South Carolina in 1733. The agreement was that Franklin would get one-third of the yearly profits of the business. The printer, however, never rendered an account. After his death his wife carried on the business quite successfully. She had been educated in Holland, where she was taught what she needed to know to get on in the world of business. She eventually bought out Franklin's share in the shop and set her son up in the business.[48]

Organized efforts to provide females with equal education, however, had to wait until the nineteenth century.

Both Jefferson and Rush provided for public libraries in connection with their school systems. Rush would encourage "Farmers and tradesmen" in proximity to the colleges, academies, and elementary schools to utilize these collections "upon paying a moderate sum yearly. . . ."[49] The idea for subscription libraries had stemmed from the Library Company which had originated in Franklin's Junto. Members of that mutual improvement group had at one point agreed to place their personal libraries together in a collection from which they all could draw. Inevitably, however, some complained that their books were being mistreated. The arrangement, therefore, lasted for just about a year. But the germ was there for something greater. Franklin conceived the idea of the formation of a library which would be supported by subscription. Fifty individuals banded together, paying forty shillings as an initiation fee and then dues of ten shillings a year, the commitment to run fifty years. The number of subscribers was then increased to one hundred and a charter obtained.[50]

By the 1740s the Library Company included "the finest collection of scientific books in the country."[51] This report should not come as a surprise when it is considered that Franklin and a number of his associates were actively interested in investigations of natural philosophy.

The example of the Library Company was followed throughout the colonies. Franklin credited to these subscription libraries important alterations in the outlook and attitudes of the colonists. The libraries "have improved the general conversation of the Americans, made the common tradesmen and farmers as intelligent as most gentlemen from other countries, and perhaps have contributed in some degree to the stand so generally made throughout the colonies in defense of their privileges."[52]

We cannot overestimate the importance men of the American Enlightenment attached to education. John Adams was so convinced of its efficacy that he wrote into his draft of the constitution of Massachusetts (1780) that the legislature of the commonwealth would have as one of its responsibilities the fostering of educational institutions for the people. Adams was worried that this passage would be scoffed at and stricken,[53] but he underestimated his fellow countrymen. Like himself, they had strongly engrained in them the Puritan sense of the need for a literate citizenry. The concern of President John Quincy Adams that the United States government promote the advancement of education, uttered in his first annual message in 1825, was but another expression of the continuing interest of the Adams family.

As we have had occasion to observe several times in this study, the classics were an abiding element in the educational theory of the period. Although they continued to hold an affection in the hearts of the educated well into the nineteenth century, as the Americans faced the prospect of building and maintaining their new republic, their concern for the utilitarian aspects of education became ever stronger. Even men whose thinking and expression constantly conjured up references to the experience and literature of antiquity stressed the desirability of relegating the classics to a subordinate place. Noah Webster, the most influential pedagogue of the early national period, thought the teaching of the classics to certain levels of society literally a waste of time. It took years for a person to learn them well. Anything short of this was superficial and of questionable value. Life was too short to be spent in this manner. Classical learning was of value in the professions, such as law, medicine, and divinity; but the common man needed to be taught how to earn a living. Such subjects as bookkeeping would be much more serviceable to the person who was not slated for a life of scholarship.[54]

Although increasingly critical of the emphasis placed on the classics in education, Benjamin Rush saw the study of the "learned or dead languages" as useful in helping young men develop a sound knowledge of English. He thought such facility important not only for those who were to pursue the professions but for those who were to become merchants. Eloquence in the language could not be valued too highly: ". . . We attribute as much to the power of eloquence as to the sword in bringing about the American Revolution."[55]

Another curricular question which led to sharp disagreement in the early days of the republic concerned the place of religion in education. Since Jefferson, as we have said, did not believe that young children were capable of dealing with the Bible, he would eliminate it in the elementary schools. He would have included, however, basic questions of morality. At the university level, he specifically banned sectarian theology; but presumably the professor of ethics, in dealing with natural theology, would be allowed to make reference to the Scriptures. The students emerging from Jefferson's secularized university would be superior, he thought, to the "pious young monks of Harvard and Yale."[56]

Jefferson's attitude was similar to that of Franklin, who many years earlier had been taken to task by the revivalist George Whitefield for not putting strong accent on the place of the Christian religion in his *Proposals* calling for the establishment of an academy. Whitefield told him he mentioned it too late in the pamphlet and passed over it lightly.[57] Whitefield probably suspected, and rightly, that Franklin was merely paying lip service to the place of Christianity in education. Franklin's deistic attitudes emerge clearly in his statement that "to have in view the glory and service of God, as some express themselves, is only the same thing in other words. For doing good to men is the only service of God in our power; and to imitate His beneficence is to glorify Him."[58]

On this subject, Rush, as usual, parted company from his friends. He insisted that religion was the only proper foundation for education in a republic. He went so far as to say that he would rather see children taught the opinions of Confucius or Mohammed than none at all.[59] Although he did not take a sectarian view, he made it clear that he identified Christianity and republicanism: "A Christian cannot fail of being a republican." He believed that the "humility, self-denial, and brotherly kindness" taught by the Gospels were "directly opposed to the pride of monarchy and the pageantry of a court."[60]

Rush took direct issue with those who advocated leaving the question of religion to be decided by the young person himself when he reached the age of discretion. The child's mind could not be maintained "a perfect blank" on the subject in the meantime; therefore, it was better to teach him the principles of Christianity as he was taught the arts and sciences. He adroitly asked, "Do we leave our youth to acquire systems of geography, philosophy, or politics till they have arrived at an age in which they are capable of judging for themselves?"[61] He disagreed with "those modern writers" who spoke against using the Bible in the public school. Within its pages the pupil would gain more knowledge of the motives and actions of individuals and governments than in any other book of comparable size. He correctly forecast that "if the Bible is made to give way [to other books] . . . it will be read in a short time only in churches and in a few years will probably be found only in the offices of magistrates and in courts of justice."[62]

There was no dispute, however, on the part the study of history should play in education. Although Poor Richard had quipped that "Historians relate not so much what is done as what they would have believed,"[63] Franklin made provision for its study in his plan for an academy. The study of history, which had always loomed large in the minds of the men of the Enlightenment, became crucial with the winning of independence. "Above all," wrote Rush, "let our youth be instructed in the history of the ancient republics and the progress of liberty and tyranny in the different states of Europe." Then they should be instructed in

American history, especially the history of the Revolutionary period.[64]

Noah Webster took the same position. It was obvious to him that the common people were intent on participating in their government. Since they lacked the knowledge to do so well, however, their desire should be accommodated by the public schools.[65] He wrote that the principal textbook should be one that included American geography, a history of the Revolution and its heroes, and the political principles of the federal and state governments. He would create a patriotic American out of every child: "As soon as he opens his lips, he should rehearse the history of his own country; he should lisp the praise of liberty and of those illustrious heroes and statesmen who have wrought a revolution in her favor."[66]

In Jefferson's mind, the study of history was the best insurance the people had against the reinstitution of tyranny. By studying other times and places they would be able to judge "the actions and designs of men; it will enable them to know ambition under every disguise it may assume; and knowing it, to defeat its views." Since every government had in it the seed of corruption, a seed which would develop if the people left control of affairs to their leaders, the people must be prepared by the study of history to be the "guardians of their own liberty."[67]

As they entered old age and a new century, men such as Jefferson, Adams, and Rush thought that the successful American struggle for liberty had taken its place as one of the great events of history. As they had studied the past in order to understand their own situation in the critical days leading up to the great conflict, so Adams in 1818 advocated a study of the Revolution as a means of achieving an understanding of the struggles occurring in South America.

Adams and Rush insisted that a distinction had to be made between the war and the Revolution itself. Adams believed that the Revolution had been accomplished in the "minds and hearts of the people" before the war began. It was effected when the people became convinced that England was not a "kind and tender parent" but rather a "cruel beldam, willing like Lady Macbeth to 'dash their brains out.' . . ." This discovery had alienated the affections of the people, and, though they shared little in common because of thirteen diverse heritages, they united to throw off the yoke of tyranny: "This radical change in the principles, opinions, sentiments, and affections of the people was the real American Revolution. . . . Thirteen clocks were made to strike together—a perfection of mechanism which no artist had ever before effected."

Adams hoped that young scholars would undertake the laborious, but enjoyable, task of collecting "all of the records, pamphlets, newspapers, and even handbills, which in any way contributed to change the temper and views of the people and compose them into an independent nation." It was an important task which would be useful not only to the Americans but to all men, for the Revolution was a leaven still at work. The results of the research of these historians into the American experience, he hoped, would teach men elsewhere a great lesson: "They may teach mankind that revolutions are no trifles; that they ought never to be undertaken rashly; nor without deliberate consideration and sober reflection; nor without a solid, immutable, eternal foundation of justice and humanity; nor without a people possessed of intelligence, fortitude, and integrity sufficient to carry them with steadiness, patience, and perseverance, through all the vicissitudes of fortune, the fiery trials and melancholy disasters they may have to encounter."[68]

From the perspective of old age Adams was but summarizing the list of public virtues which the Revolutionary generation had considered crucial to the success of the republican experiment. The Revolution had been a great transforming event which was thought to have released new moral energy among the people. As the Deist minister, Elihu Palmer, observed, "The moral condition of man will be as essentially renovated by the American Revolution as his civil condition. . . ."[69]

Public virtue, however, could not be left to chance. Men as diverse in their views as Palmer, Rush, and Webster could agree on that much. Just as it was necessary "to establish and perfect" the new governments, thought Rush, it was necessary also "to prepare the principles, morals, and manners of our citizens for these forms of government after they are established and brought to perfection."[70] Webster made the same point. Since the American governments were new and "not yet firmly established" and since "our national character is not yet formed," the establishment of a sound educational system which will mold young Americans into lovers and preservers of virtue and liberty is an undertaking of "vast magnitude. . . ."[71] But, thought Rush, the time was short: "The minds of our people have not as yet lost the yielding texture they acquired by the heat of the late Revolution."[72] With the passage of not many years, he was afraid, the attitudes of Americans might begin to change. Aristocracy, or, for that matter, a "democratic junto," might find the perpetuation of ignorance and vice useful to their own devious purposes.[73] Thus it was crucial that a system of education which would instill in the young the principles of republicanism be established immediately.

In the final analysis, survival of both liberty and the republic depended on the state of readiness of the people. In the early days of the Revolution, Thomas Paine had told the Americans that they had the opportunity to begin the world over again. They must seize that opportunity or it might forever be lost.

Conclusion

THE spirit of improvement is abroad upon the earth. It stimulates the hearts and sharpens the faculties not of our fellow-citizens alone, but of the nations of Europe and of their rulers. While dwelling with pleasing satisfaction upon the superior excellence of our political institutions, let us not be unmindful that liberty is power; that the nation blessed with the largest portion of liberty must in proportion to its numbers be the most powerful nation upon earth, and that the tenure of power by man is, in the moral purposes of his Creator, upon condition that it shall be exercised to ends of beneficence, to improve the condition of himself and his fellow-men.

—*John Quincy Adams*[1]

During much of the eighteenth century, enlightened Americans held to a cyclical view of history. A society was believed to be similar to an organism which was born, went through various stages of growth and development, and then entered old age, declined, and died. As they surveyed the history books, they culled plenty of examples which seemed to substantiate their point of view. In addition, they seemed to have at hand in the various Indian tribes living examples of a people in an early stage of development.

This view of history is clearly evident in Cadwallader Colden's *History of the Five Indian Nations* (1727). The book was conceived because Colden believed it important that the English colonists learn the ways of the Mohawks, Onondagas, Senecas, Oneidas, and Cayugas; for if they treated them well, the Indians could act as a convenient buffer between them and the French in Canada. Franklin evaluated Colden's effort as "a well wrote, entertaining & instructive piece [which] must be exceedingly usefull to all those colonies who have anything to do with Indian affairs."[2] Entertaining and instructive it was, reading like an adventure story, since Colden gave in to the temptation to include many stories of Indian bravery and treachery.

Of significance at this point, however, is what the book reveals

169

of the cyclical view of history. Colden himself believes his study of value, not only for the purposes of state policy but because of what it demonstrates concerning a people at a particular stage of development. In their barbarism, the Indians represent an early stage, much like that the Romans had gone through on their way to civilization. Colden represents the Indians as possessing many virtues, among them courage, resolution, and persistence. But they also have serious flaws of character, the greatest of which is a passion for revenge. They will go to any length to get even with their enemies. His history is replete with fascinating examples of the stamina and cunning of braves carrying out missions of revenge.

Central to the survival of a society, according to the cyclical view, is morality. A nation grows in strength and flourishes as her people are virtuous. Inevitably, Colden seeks an explanation of the downfall and destruction of the Adirondacks, once counted one of six nations, and finds it in their moral failure: "Immorality has ever ruin'd the nations where it abounded, whether they were civilized or barbarians, as justice and strict discipline has made others flourish and grow powerful."[3]

The example of Rome was ever present in the minds of enlightened thinkers, since they had such an intense interest in classical antiquity. In their survey of history they pondered the reasons for the rise, decline, and fall of the republic. It was a common assumption among them that as long as the Romans lived in a virtuous way, the republic had survived. When virtue gave way to corruption, the long decline began.

The same formula seemed to fit innumerable other nations. But how explain the decline of virtue in these cases? Paradoxically, the people had been corrupted by their very success. Industriousness, or hard work, which were cornerstones of success, became their undoing as increasing wealth, in turn, produced luxury, the result of which was, as John Adams put it, "effeminacy, intoxication, extravagance, vice and folly."[4] The distinguished Boston physician John Warren invited to deliver a commemorative address on the fourth of July, 1783, devoted much of his oration to a catalogue of nations and the vices which had led to their downfall: "That virtue is the true principle of republican governments has been sufficiently proved by the ablest writers on the subject, and, that whereas other forms of government may be supported without her, yet that in this she is absolutely necessary to their existence."[5] Warren set forth examples of noble and pat-riotic service, from the time of Sparta to his own day. But, sooner or later, each nation met ruin "in a forgetfulness of those *fundamental principles* on which her happiness depended."[6] The moral was clear. It was the "fatal operation of luxury" which had led to their downfall.[7]

His was not an unrelieved picture of gloom, however. He could hold up to his audience a few, very few, exceptions; states which had preserved their integrity and, thus, their lives. The cantons of Switzerland were a notable example, and the descrip-tion of their virtues is instructive of what Warren hoped for America: "simplicity, honesty, frugality, and modesty." In words borrowed from Voltaire, he pointed out, "They have no corrupt or corrupting court, no blood sucking placemen, no standing army, the ready instruments of tyranny, no ambition for con-quest, no luxury, no citadels against invasion, and against liberty, their mountains are their fortifications, and every householder is a soldier ready to fight for his country."[8]

Considering that the cyclical view of history was prevalent among the enlightened, the anxiety of men like Jefferson and Rush that educational systems be set up to prepare citizens for self-government is better understood. Warren noted this growing concern for education in the new American states and expressed confidence that a well-informed people would be prepared to take the measures necessary to protect their freedoms.[9] But some men had grave doubts that America could defy the forces of history. At this point their nation was in a youthful stage of development, not yet at maturity. But as America grew wealthy and indulged in luxury, it would go the way of the nations before it. "Yet," wrote John Adams to Jefferson, "I believe no effort in favor of virtue is lost, and all good men ought to struggle, both by their counsel and example."[10]

The growing success of America, however, instead of leading to its downfall, led to a discarding of the cyclical view. It began to give way to the growing conviction among Americans that theirs was a unique situation, never before experienced in history. Franklin, in the 1780s, illustrated the point, pointing to the in-vention of printing and the consequent accumulation and diffu-sion of knowledge and the consequent fostering of the spirit of liberty.[11] This new approach becomes more prominent in enlight-ened thought at the turn of the century. Jefferson branded as "cowardly" the idea that the human mind had developed as far as it could and that men should look to former ages for knowledge: "I am among those who think well of the human character generally. . . . I believe also, with Condorcet . . . that his mind is perfectible to a degree of which we cannot as yet form any conception."[12] As long as the mind was free to explore, "the condition of man will proceed in improvement."[13]

In the two decades or so between these expressions of confidence and the formulation of a plan of education for the University of Virginia, Jefferson's optimism grew. He and his fellow commissioners, a group which included Madison, charged with suggesting a site and curriculum for the new institution, condemned the tendency to look backward as a product of the combination of church and state. Men should look to the future. ". . . Each generation succeeding to the knowledge acquired by all those who preceded it, adding to it their own acquisitions and discoveries, and handing the mass down for successive and constant accumulation, must advance the knowledge and well-being of mankind, not *infinitely*, as some have said, but *indefinitely*, and to a term which no one can fix and foresee."[14] The commissioners justified their optimism on the ground that science and technology in the last half-century had brought about a marked amelioration in the conditions of man's life.

As in no previous age in history, men were able to measure within the span of a single lifetime a distinct change in the quality of living. Americans seemed to have everything going for them. Under the circumstances, it is not difficult to understand that optimism became an integral part of their outlook. If the idea of progress could develop in Europe amid wars and turmoil, it was certain to take strong hold in the United States where opportunity for change and improvement seemed. limitless. It was a fitting culmination of the Enlightenment in America, before it was absorbed into the spirit of a new age.

Notes and References

Introduction

1. John Adams to Thomas Jefferson, Quincy, 13 November 1815. *The Works of John Adams*, ed. Charles Francis Adams, 10 vols. (Boston, 1851), X, 174.
2. John Locke, *An Essay on Human Understanding* (1690).
3. Joseph Priestley, *Memoirs*, ed. John T. Boyer (1806; Washington, D. C., 1964), p. 153.
4. J. Hector St. John de Crèvecoeur, *Letters from an American Farmer and Sketches of Eighteenth-Century America* (1782; New York, 1963), p. 64.

Chapter One

1. Thomas Jefferson to James Madison, 20 February 1784. *Papers of Thomas Jefferson*, ed. Julian P. Boyd, 17 vols. to date (Princeton, 1950 –), VI, 550.
2. Frederick Tolles, *James Logan and the Culture of Provincial America* (Boston, 1957), p. 211.
3. A copy of the volume may be seen in the Franklin Collection, American Philosophical Society, Philadelphia.
4. Thomas Jefferson, Autobiography, *The Writings of Thomas Jefferson*, ed. Andrew A. Lipscomb, 20 vols. (Washington, D. C., 1903–05), I, 3.
5. Merrill D. Peterson, *Thomas Jefferson and the New Nation* (New York, 1970), p. 12; Priestley, *Memoirs*, p. 82.
6. Gilbert Chinard, ed., *The Literary Bible of Thomas Jefferson: His Commonplace Book of Philosophers and Poets* (Baltimore, 1928), p. 34.
7. Editor's Introduction. Jefferson, *Papers*, ed. Boyd, I, viii.
8. For instance, Reverend Samuel Seabury, *Letters of a Westchester Farmer* (1774–75) and Richard Henry Lee, *Letters from the Federal Farmer* (1787–88).
9. *The Farmer's Letters to the Inhabitants of the British Colonies*, in *The Political Writings of John Dickinson*, 2 vols. (Wilmington, Del., 1801), I, 144.
10. Cadwallader Colden to William Douglass, 1728 (?). *Letters and*

Papers of Cadwallader Colden [1711-1775], 9 vols. (*New-York Historical Society Collections*, 50–56, 67–68, 1917–23, 1934–35; reprinted., New York 1968), I, 272.

11. Cadwallader Colden, Introduction to the Study of Physics or Natural Philosophy for the Use of Peter De Lancey the Younger [1760?]. Colden MSS, New-York Historical Society, p. 20.

12. Thomas Jefferson, *Notes on the State of Virginia*, ed. William Peden (1954; reprint ed., New York, 1972), pp. 159–60.

13. Colden, Study of Natural Philosophy. Colden MSS, N.-Y. H. S., p. 2.

14. *Ibid.*, pp. 3–4.

15. *Ibid.*

16. Thomas Jefferson to Benjamin Rush, Monticello, 23 September 1800. *Writings*, ed. Lipscomb, X, 175.

17. James Logan to Cadwallader Colden, Philadelphia, 17 March 1719 or 1720 (?). Colden, *Papers*, I, 130.

18. Benjamin Franklin, *Autobiography*, ed. Gordon S. Haight (Roslyn, New York, 1941), p. 53.

19. Quoted by Crane Brinton, "Enlightenment," *The Encyclopedia of Philosophy*, ed. Paul Edwards, 8 vols. (New York, 1967), II, 520.

20. Cotton Mather, *Bonifacius: An Essay upon the Good*, ed. David Levin (Cambridge, Mass., 1966).

21. Franklin, *Autobiography*, pp. 192–95.

22. *Ibid.*, pp. 142–43.

23. For a contemporary account of Franklin's modest demeanor in London, see William B. Reed, *The Life of Esther De Berdt, afterwards Esther Reed, of Pennsylvania* (1853; reprint ed., New York, 1971).

24. Page Smith, *John Adams*, 2 vols. (New York, 1962), I, 330.

25. *Ibid.*, p. 417.

26. Thomas Jefferson to Robert Skipwith, Monticello, 3 August 1771. Jefferson, *Papers*, ed. Boyd, I, 76–81.

27. Richard M. Gummere, *The American Colonial Mind and the Classical Tradition: Essays in Comparative Culture* (Cambridge, Mass., 1963), p. 195.

28. Thomas Jefferson, Syllabus of an Estimate of the Merit of the Doctrines of Jesus, compared with Those of Others. Sent to Benjamin Rush, 21 April 1803. *Writings*, ed. Lipscomb, X, 383.

29. Gilbert Chinard, ed., *The Commonplace Book of Thomas Jefferson: A Repertory of His Ideas on Government* (Baltimore, 1926), p. 48.
"As far as the evidence at hand permits us to draw a conclusion, it may be said that the most famous writer of the eighteenth century had little influence upon Jefferson." *Ibid.*, p. 49.

30. Thomas Jefferson to Peter Carr, Paris, 19 August 1785. *Papers*, ed. Boyd, VIII, 405–08.

31. Jefferson obviously is referring to Spanish possessions in the Americas.

32. Gummere, *American Colonial Mind*, p. 193.

33. *Ibid.*

34. Richard M. Gummere, *Seven Wise Men of Colonial America* (Cambridge, Mass., 1967), p. 72.

35. Gummere, *American Colonial Mind*, p. 193.

36. Number 10. *The Spectator*, ed. Gregory Smith, 4 vols., rev. ed. (1945; reprint ed., New York, 1963–64), I, 31.

37. Bonamy Dobrée, *English Literature in the Early Eighteenth Century, 1700-1740*, vol. VII of *The Oxford History of English Literature*, ed. B. Dobré, *et al.* 12 vols. (New York, 1959), p. 110.

38. James Madison, Autobiography, ed. Douglass Adair, *William and Mary Quarterly*, 3d ser., 2 (April, 1945), 197.

39. Quoted by Ralph Ketcham, *James Madison: A Biography* (New York, 1971), p. 41.

40. The influence of the *Spectator* on Franklin can be seen by a comparison of *Spectator*, no. 1, with the first of the Silence Dogood papers in *The Papers of Benjamin Franklin*, ed. Leonard W. Labaree, 17 vols. to date (New Haven, 1959–), I, 8–11.

41. *Idea of the English School, Sketch'd out for the Consideration of the Trustees of the Philadelphia Academy* (1751) in *ibid.*, IV, 103, 107.

42. Francis Hopkinson, *The Miscellaneous Essays and Occasional Writings*, 3 vols. (Philadelphia, 1792).

43. Plan of Conduct. Franklin, *Papers*, ed. Labaree, I, 99–100.

44. Franklin, *Autobiography*, p. 102.

45. Plan of Conduct. Franklin, *Papers*, ed. Labaree, I, 100.

46. *Ibid.*

47. Franklin, *Autobiography*, pp. 130–31.

48. Smith, *Adams*, I, 548.

49. Thomas Jefferson to Martha Jefferson, Aix en Provence, 28 March 1787. Jefferson, *Papers*, ed. Boyd, XI, 251.

50. Thomas Jefferson to Thomas Jefferson Randolph, Washington, 24 November 1808. *Writings*, ed. Lipscomb, XII, 196–202.

51. *Ibid.*, p. 197.

52. Dumas Malone, *Thomas Jefferson and the Rights of Man*, vol. II of *Jefferson and His Time*, 5 vols. to date (Boston, 1948–74), pp. 369–70.

53. Thomas Jefferson to Peter Carr, Paris, 19 August 1785. *Papers*, ed. Boyd, VIII, 406.

54. Thomas Jefferson to Peter Carr, Paris, 10 April 1787. *ibid.*, XII, 14.

55. Thomas Jefferson to Thomas Law, Esq., Poplar Forest, 13 June 1814. *Writings*, ed. Lipscomb, XIV, 142.

56. Benjamin Franklin to Joseph Priestley, London, 19 September

1772. *The Writings of Benjamin Franklin*, ed. Albert Henry Smyth, 10 vols. (New York, 1905–07), V, 438.

Chapter Two

1. Owen Biddle, *An Oration delivered the Second of March, 1781, at the Request of the American Philosophical Society for Promoting Useful Knowledg᷈ before the said Society and a large and respectable Assembly of Citizens and Foreigners* (Philadelphia, 1781), p. 30.

2. I. Bernard Cohen, *Franklin and Newton: an Inquiry into Speculative Newtonian Experimental Science and Franklin's Work in Electricity as an Example Thereof* (Philadelphia, 1956), p. 9.

3. *Ibid*.

4. Quoted from Benjamin Franklin, *Opinions and Conjectures, concerning the Properties and Effects of the Electrical Matter, arising from Experiments and Observations Made at Philadelphia* (Philadelphia, 1749) by Carl C. Van Doren, *Benjamin Franklin* (New York, 1938), pp. 160–61.

5. See Adolph B. Benson, ed., *The America of 1750: Peter Kalm's Travels in North America*. 2 vols. (New York, 1937).

6. William Douglass to Cadwallader Colden, Boston, 20 February 1720 or 1721 (?). "Letters from Dr. William Douglass to Cadwallader Colden of New York," *Collections of the Massachusetts Historical Society*. 4th ser., 2 (1854), 165–66.

7. Franklin, *Papers*, ed. Labaree, I, 8.

8. Tolles, *Logan*, p. 198.

9. Crèvecoeur, *Letters from an American Farmer*, p. 188.

Ernest Earnest indicates that Crèvecoeur's account has been disputed but he believes it consistent with other stories of Bartram's early interest in plants as medicinals. *John and William Bartram: Botanists and Explorers* (Philadelphia, 1940), p. 15.

10. *Ibid*., pp. 22–23.

11. The full title is *Observations on the Inhabitants, Climate, Soil, Rivers, Productions, Animals, and other Matters worthy of Note, made by Mr. John Bartram in His Travels from Pensilvania to Onandaga, Oswego and Lake Ontario in Canada* (London, 1751).

12. Raymond P. Stearns, *Science in the British Colonies of America* (Urbana, Ill., 1970), p. 585.

13. *Travels through North & South Carolina, Georgia, East & West Florida, the Cherokee Country of the Chactaws; containing an Account of the Soil and Natural Productions of those Regions, together with Observations on the Manners of the Indians*.

14. Earnest, pp. 132 ff.; Thomas H. Johnson, ed., *The Oxford Companion to American History* (New York, 1966), p. 67.

15. Bartram quoted by Earnest, p. 47.

16. Stearns, p. 565; Alice M. Keys, *Cadwallader Colden: a Representative Eighteenth Century Official* (New York, 1906), p. 19.

17. Edmund and Dorothy Smith Berkeley, *Dr. Alexander Garden of Charles Town* (Chapel Hill, N. C., 1969), p. 28.

18. *Ibid.*, p. 40.

19. *Ibid.*, p. 43.

20. Cadwallader Colden to Johann Friedrich Gronovius, New York, 1 October 1755. *Papers*, V, 30.

21. Brooke Hindle, "A Colonial Governor's Family: the Coldens of Coldengham," *New-York Historical Society Quarterly* 45 (1961), 249.

22. Colden, *Papers*, V, 29–30.

23. Hindle, "Colonial Governor's Family," *N.-Y. H. S. Qty* 45 (1961), 249.

24. Berkeley, pp. 47–48.

25. *Ibid.*, p. 161.

26. Stearns, pp. 614–15.

27. Thomas Jefferson, *Notes on Virginia* is available in an excellent version edited by William Peden (1954; reprint ed., New York, 1972).

28. The "Orrery," or mechanical planetarium, takes its name from Charles Boyle, the 4th Earl of Orrery (1676–1731).

29. One face of Rittenhouse's original Orrery is in the possession of Princeton University. His second, or duplicate, missing one of three faces, is on exhibition at the Library of the University of Pennsylvania. An excellent example of an Orrery on a horizontal plane, constructed by the Boston clock-maker, Joseph Pope (1787), can be seen at the Houghton Library, Harvard University.

30.' Minutes of the American Philosophical Society, State House, Philadelphia, 19 April 1768. *Transactions of the American Philosophical Society*, pp. 10–12; appended to *The American Magazine*, Jan.–Sept., 1769.

31. Clifford K. Shipton, *Sibley's Harvard Graduates* (Boston, 1956), IX, 242.

32. *Ibid.*, pp. 250–51.

33. Appendix. John Winthrop, *Relation of a Voyage from Boston to Newfoundland, for the Observation of the Transit of Venus, June 6, 1761* (Boston, 1761), p. 23. See also Winthrop, *Two Lectures on the Parallax and Distance of the Sun, as deducible from the Transit of Venus. Read in the Holden-Chapel at Harvard-College in Cambridge, New-England, in March 1769* (Boston, 1769).

34. Jared Eliot to Ezra Stiles, 24 March 1756, quoted by Brooke Hindle, *The Pursuit of Science in Revolutionary America, 1735–1789* (Chapel Hill, N. C., 1956), p. 95.

35. John Winthrop, *Lecture on Earthquakes. Read in the Chapel of Harvard-College in Cambridge, N. E. November 26th 1755. On Occasion of the great Earthquake which shook New-England the Week before* (Bos-

ton, 1755), Appendix, p. 32.

36. John Winthrop, *A Letter to the Publishers of the* Boston Gazette, *&c. Containing an Answer to the Rev. Mr. Prince's Letter, inserted in said* Gazette, *on the 26th of* January *1756* (Boston, 1756), p. 2.

37. John Winthrop, *Two Lectures on Comets,* cited in Lawrence C. Wroth, *An American Bookshelf, 1755* (Philadelphia, 1934).

38. Stearns, pp. 639–42.

39. *Ibid.,* p. 639.

40. Franklin, *Autobiography,* p. 203.

41. Benjamin Franklin, *An Account of the New Invented Pennsylvanian Fire-Places* (Philadelphia, 1744) in *Papers,* ed. Labare, II, 419–46.

42. Franklin, *Autobiography,* p. 184.

43. Benjamin Franklin to Cadwallader Colden, Philadelphia, 10 July 1746. *Papers,* ed. Labaree, III, 80–81.

44. Benjamin Franklin to Cadwallader Colden, Philadelphia, 16 October 1746. *Ibid.,* III, 91.

45. Stearns, p. 572.

Chapter Three

1. Thomas Jefferson to Roger C. Weightman, Monticello, 24 June 1826. *Writings,* ed. Lipscomb, XVI, 182.

2. See *The Second Treatise on Civil Government* (1690) in John Locke, *On Politics and Education* (Roslyn, N. Y., 1947).

3. Carl L. Becker, *The Heavenly City of the Eighteenth-Century Philosophers* (1932; reprint ed., New Haven, 1960), p. 57.

4. John Dickinson, *A Speech delivered . . . 1764,* quoted by Bernard Bailyn, *Ideological Origins of the American Revolution* (Cambridge, Mass., 1967), p. 187.

5. Otis is here probably quoting directly from *Oceana,* since he praises Harrington in glowing terms in the passages immediately preceding this. James Otis, *The Rights of the British Colonies Asserted and Proved* (Boston, 1764) in Samuel Eliot Morison, *Sources and Documents illustrating the American Revolution, 1764–1788, and the Formation of the Federal Constitution,* 2d ed. (1929; New York, 1967), p. 5.

6. *Ibid.*

7. Thomas Jefferson, *A Summary View of the Rights of British America* in *Writings,* ed. Lipscomb, I, 209.

8. *Ibid.,* p. 186.

9. *Ibid.,* pp. 186–87.

10. *Ibid.,* p. 209.

11. John Adams, *Novanglus,* in *Works,* ed. Adams, IV, 99–121.

12. On this point, see Bailyn, *Ideological Origins,* especially pp. 144–59.

13. George Washington to Joseph Reed, Cambridge, 31 January 1776,

quoted by Samuel Eliot Morison, *Oxford History of the American People* (New York, 1965), p. 220.

14. Benjamin Rush, *Autobiography: His "Travels through Life," together with his Commonplace Book for 1789–1813*, ed. George W. Corner (Princeton, 1948), p. 114.

15. Benjamin Rush, quoted in Alfred Owen Aldridge, *Man of Reason: The Life of Thomas Paine* (London, 1960), p. 35.

16. Thomas Paine, *Common Sense*, in *The Life and Works of Thomas Paine*, ed. William M. Van der Wyde, 10 vols. (New Rochelle, N. Y., 1925), II, 148, 150.

17. *Ibid.*, p. 117.

18. *Ibid.*, p. 150.

19. *Ibid.*, p. 179.

20. *Ibid.*, p. 167.

21. The Virginia Declaration of Rights may be conveniently consulted in Robert A. Rutland, *George Mason: Reluctant Statesman* (N. Y., 1961), pp. 111–14. For various drafts of the document, see *The Papers of George Mason, 1725–92*, ed. Robert A. Rutland. 3 vols. (Chapel Hill, N.C., 1970), I, 274–91. On Mason's possible influence on the French drafters of the Declaration of the Rights of Man, see R. R. Palmer, *The Age of the Democratic Revolution: the Challenge: A Political History of Europe and America, 1760–1800* (Princeton, 1959), pp. 486–88, 518–21.

22. A detailed comparison of the efforts of Mason and Jefferson is found in David Hawke, *A Transaction of Free Men: The Birth and Course of the Declaration of Independence* (New York, 1964), pp. 145 ff.

23. Cf. 2d Paper, 13 January 1777. Paine, *Works*, ed. Van der Weyde, II, 306, 318–19.

24. Thomas Paine, *The Rights of Man* in *Works*, ed. Van der Weyde, VI, 66–67.

25. *Ibid.*, pp. 239–40.

26. *Ibid.*, p. 241.

27. *Ibid.*, p. 243.

28. *Ibid.*, pp. 69–72.

29. *Ibid.*, pp. 172, 20.

30. *Ibid.*, p. 235.

31. Franklin's story, as Jefferson remembered it, is found in Jefferson, *Writings*, ed. Lipscomb, XVIII, 169–70.

32. Thomas Jefferson, Autobiography, *ibid.*, I, 53.

33. *Ibid.*, p. 64.

34. *Ibid.*, p. 60.

35. *Ibid.*, p. 54.

36. For a thorough discussion of the debates on equality in the various states, see Gordon Wood, *The Creation of the American Republic, 1776–1787* (Chapel Hill, N. C., 1969), pp. 70 ff.

37. John Adams, *A Defence of the Constitutions of Government of the*

United States, in *Works*, ed. Adams, IV, 391 ff.

38. Thomas Jefferson to John Adams, Monticello, 28 October 1813. *Writings*, ed. Lipscomb, XIII, 396.

39. John Adams to Thomas Jefferson, 15 November 1813. Paul Wilstach, ed., *Correspondence of John Adams and Thomas Jefferson, 1812–26* (1925; reprint ed., 1966), pp. 98–99.

40. John Adams to John Taylor, 1814. *Works*, ed. Adams, VI, 453–54.

41. Thomas Paine, *The Rights of Man*, in *Works*, ed. Van der Weyde, VI, 92, 94.

42. Quoted in Van Doren, *Franklin*, p. 31.

43. Thomas Jefferson, Anas, *Writings*, ed. Lipscomb, I, 267–68.

44. Thomas Jefferson to George Washington, Paris, 14 November 1786. *Papers*, ed. Boyd, X, 532–33.

45. See Jefferson's expressions of his fear of secret military organizations in *Writings*, ed. Lipscomb, IV, 217–19; XVII, 84–85, 89–90.

46. Benjamin Franklin to Sarah Bache, Passy, France, 26 January 1784. *Writings*, ed. Smyth, IX, 161–68.

47. For his account of the debate on titles, see *The Journal of William Maclay: United States Senator from Pennsylvania, 1789–91* (New York, 1927), *passim*.

48. David Hawke, *Benjamin Rush, Revolutionary Gadfly* (Indianapolis, 1971), p. 104.

49. *The Selected Writings of Benjamin Rush*, ed. Dagobert Runes (New York, 1947), p. 4.

50. *Ibid.*, pp. 13–14.

51. Jefferson, *Writings*, ed. Lipscomb, I, 201.

52. Jefferson, Autobiography, *ibid.*, I, 34–35.

53. *Ibid.*, pp. 72–73.

54. Alexander Hamilton to John Jay, Middlebrook, N. J., 14 March 1779. *The Papers of Alexander Hamilton*, ed. H. C. Syrett, 19 vols. to date (New York, 1961–), II, 18.

55. Helen Hill, *George Mason: Constitutionalist* (1938; reprint ed., Gloucester, Mass., 1966), pp. 202–03.

56. Rutland, *Mason*, p. 86.

57. The Northwest Ordinance, in Morison, *Sources and Documents*, pp. 226–33.

58. Van Doren, *Franklin*, p. 774.

59. *Ibid.*, pp. 774–75.

60. *Ibid.*, p. 775.

61. *Ibid.*

62. Jefferson, *Notes on Virginia*, p. 162.

63. *Ibid.*, p. 139.

64. *Ibid.*, p. 143.

65. *Ibid.*, pp. 137–38. In his Autobiography Jefferson made it clear again that he did not believe whites and blacks could live together under

the same government. "Nature, habit, opinion have drawn indelible lines of distinction between them." *Writings*, ed. Lipscomb, I, 73.

66. James Madison to Robert J. Evans, Montpellier, 15 June 1819. *The Writings of James Madison*, ed. Gaillard Hunt, 9 vols. (New York, 1900–10), VIII, 440.

67. *Ibid.*, p. 441.

68. *Ibid.*, pp. 442–43.

69. Thomas Jefferson to Edward Coles, Monticello, 25 August 1814. *The Writings of Thomas Jefferson*, ed. Paul L. Ford, 10 vols. (New York, 1892–99), IX, 478.

70. Thomas Jefferson to John Holmes, Monticello, 22 April 1820. *Writings*, ed. Lipscomb, XV, 249.

Chapter Four

1. John Adams to Abigail Adams, Paris, 1780. *Familiar Letters of John Adams and His Wife Abigail Adams during the Revolution*, ed. Charles Francis Adams (Boston, 1875), p. 381.

2. As told to Benjamin Rush. *Autobiography*, p. 115.

3. *Ibid.*

4. John Adams, *Thoughts on Government*, in *Works*, ed. Adams, IV, 200.

5. Benjamin Rush, *Defects of Education* in Good, *Benjamin Rush and American Education*, p. 198; quoted in Hawke, *Rush*, p. 341. Another version of this thought is found in Rush to Richard Price, 25 May 1786. *The Letters of Benjamin Rush*, ed. Lyman H. Butterfield, 2 vols. (Princeton, 1951), II, 388–89.

6. Obadiah Hulme, *An Historical Essay on the English Constitution* (London, 1771), pp. 149–50; quoted in H. Trevor Colbourn, *The Lamp of Experience: Whig History and the Intellectual Origins of the American Revolution* (Chapel Hill, N. C., 1965), p. 52.

7. Hill, pp. 118–19.

8. *Works*, ed. Adams, IV, 197.

9. *Ibid.*, pp. 193–200.

10. Jefferson, *Notes on Virginia*, pp. 126–28.

11. John Adams to Thomas Brand-Hollis, Fountain Inn, Portsmouth, England, 5 April 1788, quoted in John Disney, *Memoirs of Thomas Brand-Hollis* (London, 1808), pp. 32–33.

12. Turgot's thoughts, expressed in a letter, were included in Richard Price, *Observations on the Importance of the American Revolution, and the Means of Making It a Benefit to the World* (Boston, 1784). Frederick Rudolph, ed., *Essays on Education in the Early Republic* (Cambridge, Mass., 1965), p. 375, n 6. See, also, Joyce Appleby, "The New Republican Synthesis and the Changing Political Ideas of John Adams," *American Quarterly* 25 (December, 1973), 578–95.

13. For Rittenhouse's support of the constitution, see Brooke Hindle, *David Rittenhouse* (Princeton, 1964), pp. 152 ff. For Rush's opposition, see his *Letters*, I, 114–15, 137, 148.

14. Zoltan Haraszti, *John Adams and the Prophets of Progress* (Cambridge, 1952), pp. 155 ff.

15. Adams, *Defence of the Constitutions*, in *Works*, ed. Adams, IV, 406.

16. *Ibid.*, p. 407.

17. *Ibid.*, p. 579.

18. *Ibid.*, pp. 444–45.

19. Smith, *Adams*, I, 442.

20. *Ibid.*, p. 443.

21. Thomas Jefferson to John Adams, Paris, 28 September 1787. *Papers*, ed. Boyd, XII, 189.

22. Chinard, Introduction, *Commonplace Book of Jefferson*, pp. 25–26.

23. *Notes on Virginia*, p. 118.

24. *Ibid.*, pp. 119–20.

25. *Ibid.*, p. 120.

26. *Ibid.*, p. 121.

27. Jefferson, *Papers*, ed. Boyd, I, 356–64.

28. *Notes on Virginia*, p. 121.

29. On this point, see Wood, *Creation of American Republic*, pp. 206 ff.

30. Jefferson, *Papers*, ed. Boyd, I, 362.

31. Adams, *Works*, ed. Adams, VI, 219.

32. *Ibid.*, pp. 219–20.

33. For the positive accomplishments of the United States government under the Articles, see the works of Merrill Jensen: *The Articles of Confederation: An Interpretation of the Social-Constitutional History of the American Revolution, 1774–81* (Madison, Wisconsin, 1948) and *The New Nation: A History of the United States during the Confederation, 1781–89* (New York, 1950).

34. Benjamin Rush to Richard Price, 27 October 1786. *Letters*, I, 409.

35. Robert R. Livingston, *An Oration delivered before the Society of the Cincinnati of the State of New York; in Commemoration of the Fourth of July* (New York, 1787), p. 12.

36. Thomas Jefferson to James Madison, Paris, 30 January 1787. *Papers*, ed. Boyd, XI, 93.

37. Thomas Jefferson to James Madison, Paris, 20 December 1787. *ibid.*, XII, 442.

38. Benjamin Rush to Richard Price, Philadelphia, 2 June 1787. Max Farrand, ed., *The Records of the Federal Convention of 1787*, 3 vols. (New Haven, 1911), III, 33.

39. *Ibid.*

40. *Ibid.*, pp. 550 ff.

41. James Madison, *Notes on Debates in the Federal Convention of 1787* (Athens, Ohio, 1966), p. 659.

42. Thomas Jefferson to James Madison, Paris, 20 December 1787. *Papers*, ed. Boyd, XII, 440.

43. Rutland, *Mason*, p. 89.

44. *Ibid.*, p. 90.

45. Federalist Paper, no. 51. Alexander Hamilton, James Madison, and John Jay, *The Federalist*, ed. Jacob E. Cooke (Middletown, Conn., 1961), p. 349. Cooke's reasons for attributing no. 51 to Madison are found in his Introduction, pp. xxvii ff.

46. *Ibid.*, pp. 64–65.

47. No. 10, *ibid.*, p. 60.

48. For Adam's attitude on Jefferson's retirement from office, see Smith, *Adams*, II, 845 ff.

49. John Adams to Roger Sherman, Richmond Hill, N. Y., 18 July 1789. *Works*, ed. Adams, VI, 429–31.

50. John Adams to Benjamin Rush, New York, 18 April 1790. *Ibid.*, IX, 566.

51. John Adams to Samuel Adams, New York, 18 October 1790. *Ibid.*, VI, 418.

52. *Ibid.*, pp. 414–18.

53. Thomas Jefferson to Thomas Paine, Philadelphia, 19 June 1792. *The Works of Thomas Jefferson*, ed. Paul L. Ford, "The Federal Edition;" 12 vols. (New York, 1904–05), VII, 121.

54. Peterson, pp. 405 ff.

55. Thomas Jefferson to Philip Mazzei, Monticello, 24 April 1796. *Writings*, ed. Lipscomb, IX, 335–36.

56. Thomas Jefferson to Peregrine Fitzhugh, 23 February 1798. Quoted in Herbert W. Schneider, *A History of American Philosophy* (New York, 1946), pp. 46–47.

57. Thomas Jefferson to John Adams, Monticello, 27 June 1813. *Writings*, ed. Lipscomb, XIII, 281.

Chapter Five

1. Thomas Paine, *The Age of Reason*, in *Works*, ed. Van der Weyde, VIII, 4–5.

2. See chapter 1 above.

3. John Taylor, *An Inquiry into the Principles and Policy of the Government of the United States* (1814), p. 455; quoted by Eugene T. Mudge, *The Social Philosophy of John Taylor of Caroline: A Study in Jeffersonian Democracy* (New York, 1939), p. 200.

4. *Inquiry*, p. 461; quoted in *ibid*.

5. Thomas Paine, *A Letter to Thomas Erskine*, in *Works*, VIII, 342.

6. Jefferson, *Notes on Virginia*, p. 159.

7. *Ibid.*, p. 160.

8. Thomas Jefferson, An Act for Establishing Religious Freedom, in Joseph L. Blau, ed., *Cornerstones of Religious Freedom in America* (Boston, 1950), pp. 74–75.

9. Ketcham, *Madison*, pp. 72–73.

10. James Madison, *A Memorial and Remonstrance on the Religious Rights of Man*, in Blau, pp. 81 ff.

11. Thomas Jefferson to George Wythe, Paris, 13 August 1786. *Papers*, ed. Boyd, X, 244.

12. Jefferson, Autobiography, *Writings*, ed. Lipscomb, I, 67.

13. James Madison, *Autobiography*, ed. Douglass Adair, in *William and Mary Quarterly*, 3d ser., no. 2 (April, 1945), 204.

14. James Madison to Edward Livingston, Montpellier, 10 July 1822. *Writings*, ed. Hunt, IX, 100.

15. *Ibid.*, pp. 102–3.

16. Morison, *Sources and Documents*, p. 230.

17. Woodbridge Riley, *American Thought: From Puritanism to Pragmatism and Beyond* (1915; reprint ed., Gloucester, Mass., 1959), p. 87.

18. William Smith, *The History of the Province of New-York from the First Discovery to the Year 1732* (London, 1757), p. 218.

19. Benjamin Franklin to Ezra Stiles, Philadelphia, 9 March 1790. *Writings*, ed. Smyth, X, 84.

20. *Ibid.*

21. *Ibid.*

22. Franklin, *Autobiography*, p. 18.

23. *Ibid.*, p. 126.

24. *Ibid.*, pp. 87–88.

25. *Ibid.*, p. 127.

26. John Adams to Skelton Jones, Quincy, 11 March 1809. *Works*, ed. Adams, IX, 611.

27. 22 August 1756. *Diary and Autobiography of John Adams*, ed. Lyman H. Butterfield, 4 vols. (Cambridge, Mass., 1961), I, 43.

28. Jefferson, *Notes on Virginia*, pp. 159–60.

29. Thomas Jefferson to Peter Carr, Paris, 10 August 1787. *Papers*, ed. Boyd, XII, 15, 17.

30. Thomas Jefferson to Joseph Priestley, 9 April 1803. *Writings*, ed. Ford, VIII, 224 n.

31. For a discussion of the "Jefferson Bible" and his view of Jesus, see Peterson, pp. 955–61.

32. Thomas Jefferson to Benjamin Rush, Washington, 21 April 1803. *Writings*, ed. Lipscomb, X, 381–85.

33. Earnest, p. 66.

34. *Ibid.*, p. 64.

35. *Ibid.*, pp. 65–66.

36. For examples of how some of the natural philosophers reckoned

with this force, see Cadwallader Colden to Alexander Garden, 1757. *Papers*, V, 153–54. The views of David Rittenhouse are summarized in Hindle, *Rittenhouse*, pp. 117 ff.

37. *A Narrative of Colonel Ethan Allen's Captivity* (1779; New York, 1961).

38. Quoted by John Pell, *Ethan Allen* (Boston, 1929), p. 133.

39. *Ibid.*, pp. 169–70.

40. Ethan Allen, *Reason the Only Oracle of Man, or a Compenduous* [sic] *System of Natural Religion. Alternately Adorned with Confutations of a Variety of Doctrines incompatible to It; deduced from the most exalted Ideas which We are able to form of the Divine and Human Characters, and from the Universe in General* (1784; facsimile reprint, New York, 1940).

41. For a discussion of the authorship of the book, see George Pomeroy Anderson, "Who Wrote 'Ethan Allen's Bible'?" *New England Quarterly* 10 (December, 1937), 685–96. The problem is put in a lively perspective by Dana Doten, "Ethan Allen's 'Original Something,' " *ibid.*, 11 (June, 1938), 361–66.

42. For an analysis of the book, see Ernest Cassara, "Ethan Allen as Philosopher," *Vermont History* 35 (Autumn, 1967), 208–21.

43. Allen, p. 363.

44. *Ibid.*, pp. 345–46.

45. Allen's sequel was entitled "An Essay on the Universal Plenitude of Being and on the Nature and Immortality of the Human Soul and its Agency." It was not published until 1873, when it appeared in the *Historical Magazine*. It is included in the 1940 facsimile edition of *Reason the Only Oracle of Man.*

46. John Adams to Benjamin Rush, Quincy, 12 April 1809. *Works*, ed. Adams, IX, 617. See also Thomas Paine, Introduction to Part 2 of the *Age of Reason. Works*, ed. Van der Weyde, VIII, 103.

47. Benjamin Franklin to Thomas Paine [date uncertain]. *The Works of Benjamin Franklin*, ed. Jared Sparks, 10 vols. (Boston, 1840), X, 281–82. Also *Writings*, ed. Smyth, IX, 521–22. Herbert Morais dates Franklin's letter in 1786. *Deism in Eighteenth Century America* (1934; reprint ed., New York, 1960), p. 20 n.

48. Thomas Paine, *The Age of Reason*, in *Works*, ed. Van der Weyde, VIII, 4.

49. *Ibid.*, p. 23.

50. *Ibid.*, p. 46.

51. Entry on death of Thomas Paine, 8 June 1809, Commonplace Book. *Autobiography*, p. 323.

52. Philip Freneau, *Letters on Various Interesting and Important Subjects* [originally published in the *Aurora*], pp. 37-38; quoted in Nelson F. Adkins, *Philip Freneau and the Cosmic Enigma* (New York, 1949), p. 48. See also Morais, p. 153.

53. Elihu Palmer, *Principles of Nature; or a Development of the Moral Causes of Happiness and Misery among the Human Species* (1802; reprint ed., London, 1819).

54. Preface. *Ibid.*, iv.

55. *Ibid.*, pp. 5, 200.

56. *Ibid.*, p. 12.

57. *Ibid.*, p. 50.

58. Paine, *Works*, ed. Van der Weyde, VIII, 11.

59. Palmer, *Principles of Nature*, p. 25.

60. Quoted from Kinnersley's sermon in the Philadelphia Baptist Church, included in "A Letter from Ebenezer Kinnersley to His Friend in the Country," postscript to the *Pennsylvania Gazette*, 15 July 1740. It was negative reaction to this inflamed piece which led Franklin to write his defense of a free press, "Statement of Editorial Policy." *Papers*, ed. Labaree, II, 259–61.

61. Jonathan Edwards, *The Distinguishing Marks of a Work of the Spirit of God, Applied to that uncommon Operation that has lately appeared on the Minds of many of the People in New-England: With a Particular Consideration of the extra-ordinary Circumstances with which this Work is attended* (Boston, 1741).

62. Charles Chauncy, *Seasonable Thoughts on the State of Religion in New England, A Treatise in five Parts* (Boston, 1743).

63. This position was labeled "Arminianism" after the Dutch theologian Jacobus Arminius (1560–1609), who rejected the Calvinist doctrine of predestination and insisted men, cooperating with divine grace, could achieve salvation.

A good example of Mayhew's outspoken departure from orthodox interpretation is to be seen in his *Two Sermons on the Nature, Extent, and Perfection of the Divine Goodness* (Boston, 1763). Charles W. Akers, *Called Unto Liberty: A Life of Jonathan Mayhew, 1720–1766* (Cambridge, Mass., 1964) presents Mayhew's career in the context of religious and political developments of his day.

64. Richard Eddy, *Universalism in America: A History*, 2 vols. (Boston, 1884–86), I, 4 ff.

65. Shipton, IX, 251.

66. Charles Chauncy, *The Mystery Hid from Ages and Generations, Made Manifest by the Gospel-Revelation: or, the Salvation of All Men the Grand Thing Aimed at in the Scheme of God, as Opened in the New-Testament Writings, and Entrusted with Jesus Christ to Bring into Effect* (London, 1784).

67. Eddy, I, 301.

68. Rush, *Letters*, I, 583–84.

69. For a summary of Ballou's thought, see Ernest Cassara, *Hosea Ballou: The Challenge to Orthodoxy* (Boston, 1961).

70. For an account of the various divisions among the Friends, and for

an account of the evolution of Hicks's thought, see Bliss Forbush, *Elias Hicks: Quaker Liberal* (N. Y., 1956).

71. Philip Freneau, *A Collection of Poems*, 2 vols. (New York, 1815).

72. William Meade, *Old Churches, Ministers, and Families of Virginia* (1872; Philadelphia, 1906), p. 29.

73. *Ibid.*, pp. 30–31.

74. *Ibid.*, p. 29.

75. Riley, p. 94.

76. *Ibid.*

77. George Dangerfield, *Chancellor Robert R. Livingston of New York, 1746–1813* (New York, 1960), p. 438.

Chapter Six

1. Benjamin Rush to Charles Nisbet, 1783. Quoted by Lyman H. Butterfield, Introduction, *Plan of Education, 1785, as Drafted by Benjamin Rush for the Trustees of Dickinson College* (Carlisle, Pa., 1973), p. 7.

2. Franklin, *Papers*, ed. Labaree, II, 378 n.

3. *Ibid.*, p. 380.

4. *Ibid.*, p. 381.

5. *Transactions of the American Philosophical Society* (January-September, 1769), pp. 29, 1, 22 ff., 44, 95.

6. Quoted in Peterson, p. 590.

7. *Ibid.*, pp. 576–77.

8. *Ibid.*, pp. 589–90.

9. John Adams to Abigail Adams, 4 August 1776. *Familiar Letters*, p. 207.

10. James Bowdoin, *A Philosophical Discourse addressed to the American Academy of Arts and Sciences* (Boston, 1780), p. 8.

11. Franklin, *Papers*, ed. Labaree, IV, 192 n.

12. *Ibid.*

13. Ebenezer Kinnersley, *A Course of Experiments in that Curious and Entertaining Branch of Natural Philosophy, called Electricity; accompanied with explanatory Lectures: in which Electricity and Lightning, will be proved to be the same Thing* (Philadelphia, 1769), p. 2.

14. *Ibid.*, pp. 5–8.

15. Joseph A. Leo Lemay, *Ebenezer Kinnersley, Franklin's Friend* (Philadelphia, 1964), p. 86.

16. Franklin, *Autobiography*, p. 148.

17. Preface, *Poor Richard's Almanac*, 1738. Franklin, *Papers*, ed. Labaree, II, 190–91.

18. Thomas H. Russell, ed., *The Sayings of Poor Richard: Wit, Wisdom, and Humor of Benjamin Franklin in the Proverbs and Maxims of Poor Richard's Almanacks for 1733 to 1758* (n. p., 1926), pp. 20, 30, 31.

19. *Ibid.*, pp. 34–39.

20. Introduction. *Ibid.*, p. 2.

21. Stearns, p. 506.

22. *Ibid.*

23. Franklin, *Autobiography*, p. 155. See, also, his *Proposals for the Education of Youth in Pennsylvania* (1749; Ann Arbor, Michigan, 1927).

24. Louis L. Gitin "Cadwallader Colden, as Scientist and Philosopher," *New-York History* 16 (1935), 177.

25. Cadwallader Colden to Benjamin Franklin, November, 1749, in Franklin, *Papers*, ed. Labaree, III, 431.

26. Franklin, *Autobiography*, pp. 185 ff.

27. Thomas Fleming, ed., *Benjamin Franklin: A Biography in His Own Words* (New York, 1972), p. 123.

28. Thomas Jefferson to George Wythe, Paris, 13 August 1786. *Papers*, ed. Boyd, X, 244–45.

29. A Bill for the More General Diffusion of Knowledge, in Appendix, Roy John Honeywell, *The Educational Work of Thomas Jefferson* (1931; reprint ed., New York, 1964), p. 200.

30. *Ibid.*, p. 11.

31. Jefferson's plan for education is outlined both in his *Notes on Virginia*, pp. 146–49, and in his Autobiography, *Writings*, ed. Lipscomb, I, 70–72.

32. Thomas D. Clark, *A History of Kentucky* (New York, 1937), pp. 312–13.

33. James Madison to William T. Barry, 4 August 1822. *Writings*, ed. Hunt, IX, 108.

34. F. Garvin Davenport, *Ante-Bellum Kentucky: A Social History, 1800–1860* (Oxford, Miss., 1943), p. 60.

35. Benjamin Rush, *A Plan for the Establishment of Public Schools and the Diffusion of Knowledge in Pennsylvania, to which are added, Thoughts upon the Mode of Education Proper in a Republic. Addressed to the Legislature and Citizens of the State* (Philadelphia, 1786), in Rudolph, pp. 6–7.

36. Charles F. Himes, *Life and Times of Judge Thomas Cooper, Jurist, Scientist, Educator, Author, Publicist* (Carlisle, Pa., 1918), pp. 1, 3.

37. *Ibid., passim.*

38. Timothy Pickering to Charles Hall, Esq., Philadelphia, 1 August 1799. Priestley MSS Collection, Dickinson College.

39. Himes, pp. 25–28.

40. *Ibid.*, p. 36.

41. Quoted in Dumas Malone, *The Public Life of Thomas Cooper, 1783–1839* (1926; reprint ed. Columbia, S.C., 1961), p. 243.

42. Thomas Jefferson to Joseph C. Cabell, Monticello, 7 February 1826. Nathaniel Francis Cabell, *The Early History of the University of Virginia as contained in Letters of Thomas Jefferson and Joseph C.*

Cabell (Richmond, 1856), p. 366. See, also, Jefferson to Cabell, Monticello, 11 January 1825. *Ibid.*, p. 332.

43. Gummere, *American Colonial Mind*, p. 57.

44. Peterson, p. 981.

45. Rush, *Public Schools*, in Rudolph.

46. *Ibid.*, p. 4.

47. *Ibid.*

48. Franklin, *Autobiography*, pp. 152–53.

49. Rush, *Public Schools*, in Rudolph, p. 8.

50. Franklin, *Autobiography*, pp. 106–07.

51. Hindle, *Pursuit of Science*, p. 65.

52. Franklin, *Autobiography*, p. 107.

53. Smith, *Adams*, I, 443–44.

54. Noah Webster, *On Education of Youth in America* (Boston, 1790), in Rudolph.

55. Rush, *Public Schools*, in Rudolph, p. 19.

56. Riley, p. 85.

57. George Whitefield to Benjamin Franklin, Plymouth, 26 February 1750. Franklin, *Papers*, ed. Labaree, III, 467.

58. Franklin, *Proposals for Education of Youth*, p. 33 n.

59. Rush, *Public Schools*, in Rudolph, p. 10.

60. *Ibid.*, p. 11.

61. *Ibid.*

62. *Ibid.*, p. 13.

63. Quoted in Cohen, p. 27.

64. Michael Kraus, *The Writing of American History* (Norman, Oklahoma, 1953), p. 59.

65. Webster, *Education of Youth*, in Rudolph, pp. 66–67.

66. *Ibid.*, p. 65.

67. Jefferson, *Notes on Virginia*, pp. 148–49.

68. John Adams to Hezekiah Niles, Quincy, 13 February 1818. *Works*, ed. Adams, X, 282–84.

69. Elihu Palmer, *Inquiry relative to the Moral and Political Improvement of the Human Species* (New York, 1797), quoted in Schneider, *History of American Philosophy*, p. 69.

70. Rush, *Defects of Education*, in Hawke, *Rush*, p. 341.

71. Webster, *Education of Youth*, in Rudolph, p. 45.

72. Rush, *Public Schools*, in *ibid.*, p. 22.

73. *Ibid.*

Conclusion

1. John Quincy Adams, First Annual Message, in James D. Richardson, ed., *A Compilation of the Messages and Papers of the Presidents, 1789–1897*, 10 vols. (Washington, D. C., 1896–99), II, 316.

2. Colden, *Papers*, IV, 6.

3. Cadwallader Colden, *The History of the Five Indian Nations depending on the Province of New-York in America* (New York, 1727), p. 19.

4. John Adams to Thomas Jefferson, 18 December 1819, in Wilstach, p. 170.

5. John Warren, *An Oration, Delivered July 4th, 1783 . . . in Celebration of the Anniversary of American Independence* (Boston, 1783), reprinted in Gordon S. Wood, ed., *The Rising Glory of America, 1760–1820* (New York, 1971), p. 56.

6. *Ibid.*, p. 58.

7. *Ibid.*, p. 59.

8. *Ibid.*, p. 61 n 2.

9. *Ibid.*, p. 61 n 1.

10. John Adams to Thomas Jefferson, 18 December 1819. Wilstach, p. 170.

11. Stow Persons, "The Cyclical Theory of History," in Cushing Strout, ed., *Intellectual History in America: Contemporary Essays on Puritanism, the Enlightenment, and Romanticism*, 2 vols. (New York, 1968), pp. 61–62.

12. Thomas Jefferson to William Green Mumford, Monticello, 18 June 1799. Adrienne Koch, ed., *The American Enlightenment: The Shaping of the American Experiment and a Free Society* (New York, 1965), p. 340.

13. *Ibid.*, p. 341.

14. Report of the Commissioners appointed to Fix the Site of the University of Virginia, &c., in Cabell, p. 436.

Selected Bibliography

The Notes and References reflect the specific sources used in this study. The following list is merely suggestive of the wide variety of materials available to those who desire to study the American Enlightenment in greater detail.

PRIMARY SOURCES

A study of the collected papers of the persons who figure most prominently in these pages is the most fruitful approach to an understanding of the *Weltanschauung* of the Enlightenment in America.

Several projects are presently underway which, when finished years hence, will provide complete editions of the writings of the leaders of the movement. The Jefferson papers, for example, will run to sixty volumes.

Adams Family Correspondence. Edited by Lyman H. Butterfield. 4 vols. to date. Cambridge, Mass., 1963–.
The Diary and Autobiography of John Adams. Edited by Lyman H. Butterfield. 4 vols. Cambridge, Mass., 1961.
The first fruits of the mammoth edition of the Adams Family Papers, these two sets, along with the legal papers cited below, provide an excellent insight into the development of the mind and personality of John Adams.

The Earliest Diary of John Adams. Edited by Lyman H. Butterfield. Cambridge, Mass., 1966.
Discovered after the diary above had been put in press.

The Adams-Jefferson Letters. Edited by Lester J. Cappon. 2 vols. Chapel Hill, N. C., 1959.
Includes the famous exchange of the last fourteen years of their lives, as well as earlier correspondence, including letters exchanged by Thomas Jefferson and Abigail Adams.

Correspondence of John Adams and Thomas Jefferson, 1812–26. Edited by Paul Wilstach. 1925. Reprint. New York, 1966.

191

Excerpts from their letters with commentary by the editor.

Legal Papers of John Adams. Edited by L. K. Wroth and H. B. Zobel. 3 vols. Cambridge, Mass., 1965.
John Adams's legal battles, with vignettes of James Otis and other leading figures of the Revolutionary period.

The Works of John Adams. Edited by Charles Francis Adams. 10 vols. Boston, 1851.
The standard edition of John Adams's writings which will remain useful until the new Adams papers are complete.

Colden Letter Books. Vols. 9 & 10, *New-York Historical Society Collections*, 1876–77.
Letters and Papers of Cadwallader Colden. Vols. 50–56, 67–68. *New-York Historical Society Collections*, 1917–23, 1934–35. Reprint (9 vols. in 4). New York, 1968.
These two collections are rich in material concerning colonial America from 1711 to 1775. Colden's varied interests as politician and scientist are expressed in an extensive correspondence with many of the leading figures of the day.

"Letters from Dr. William Douglass to Cadwallader Colden of New York," *Collections* of the Massachusetts Historical Society, 4th ser., 2 (1854), 164–89.

Douglass, William. *A Summary, Historical and Political, of the First Planting, Progressive Improvements, and Present State of the British Settlements in North-America.* 2 vols. Boston, 1749–51.
Although rare, well worth searching out. Douglass, fellow Scot emigré of Colden, gives his prescription for the future government of America, which, he believes, is fast coming of age. The only history published before the Revolution to look at America as a whole.

The Autobiography of Benjamin Franklin. Edited by Gordon S. Haight. Roslyn, N. Y., 1941.
One of innumerable editions of this classic expression of the American Enlightenment.

Benjamin Franklin: A Biography in His Own Words. Edited by Thomas Fleming. New York, 1972.
The autobiography supplemented by extracts from his correspondence and other writings. Richly illustrated.

The Papers of Benjamin Franklin. Edited by Leonard W. Labaree. 17

vols. to date. New Haven, 1959–.
A new, exhaustive edition, excellently presented. Until it is completed, the following two editions will remain useful.

The Works of Benjamin Franklin. Edited by Jared Sparks. 10 vols. Boston, 1840.

The Writings of Benjamin Franklin. Edited by Albert Henry Smyth. 10 vols. New York, 1905–07.

The Papers of Alexander Hamilton. Edited by H. C. Syrett. 19 vols. to date. New York, 1961–.

The Works of Alexander Hamilton. Edited by Henry Cabot Lodge. 12 vols. New York, 1904.

Jefferson, Thomas. *Notes on the State of Virginia*. Edited by William Peden. 1954. Reprint. New York, 1972.
A classic of the American Enlightenment.

Papers of Thomas Jefferson. Edited by Julian P. Boyd. 18 vols. to date. Princeton, 1950–.
A definitive edition, projected at sixty volumes. Until it is completed, the following editions will remain vital in any study of the period.

The Writings of Thomas Jefferson. Edited by Andrew A. Lipscomb. 20 vols. Washington, D. C., 1903–05.
This so-called Memorial Edition is more inclusive and carefully edited than the following.

The Writings of Thomas Jefferson. Edited by Paul L. Ford. 10 vols. New York, 1892–99.

The Works of Thomas Jefferson. Edited by Paul L. Ford. 12 vols. New York, 1904–05 [The so-called Federal Edition].

The Papers of James Madison. Edited by William T. Hutchinson, *et al*. 8 vols. to date. Chicago, 1962–.

The Writings of James Madison. Edited by Gaillard Hunt. 9 vols. New York, 1900–10.

The Papers of George Mason, 1725–92. Edited by Robert A. Rutland. 3 vols. Chapel Hill, N. C., 1970.
The only edition of the papers of a central figure in the struggle for

the Rights of Man. Well annotated.

The Complete Writings of Thomas Paine. Edited by William M. Van der
  Weyde. 10 vols. New Rochelle, N. Y., 1925.

Rush, Benjamin. *Autobiography: His "Travels through Life" together
  with his Commonplace Book for 1789–1813*. Edited by George W.
  Corner. Princeton, 1948.
Rush casts light on his own development and characterizes many of
the leading figures of the age.

Letters of Benjamin Rush. Edited by Lyman H. Butterfield. 2 vols.
  Princeton, 1951.
A prolific letter writer who reflected the idealism of the Enlight-
enment in a Christian context.

The Selected Writings of Benjamin Rush. Edited by Dagobert Runes.
  New York, 1947.
A collection of his tracts and articles in periodicals: A more definitive
edition needed, but meanwhile a useful volume.

SECONDARY SOURCES

Since the men of the Enlightenment had a wide variety of interests,
there is no neat way in which biographies can be distributed among the
chapters below. I have tended to list them under the headings of the
chapters in which the individuals play a substantial part.

Chapter One

For general background on America in the eighteenth century, consult
the following:
KRAUS, MICHAEL. *Intercolonial Aspects of American Culture on the Eve
  of the Revolution with Special Reference to the Northern Towns*.
  New York, 1928.
SAVELLE, MAX. *Seeds of Liberty: The Genesis of the American Mind*.
  New York, 1948.

The cultural life of the colonial towns and cities is given detailed
  treatment in the following:
BRIDENBAUGH, CARL. *Cities in Revolt: Urban Life in America,
  1743–1776*. 1955. Reprint. New York, 1964.
BRIDENBAUGH, CARL and JESSICA. *Rebels and Gentlemen: Philadelphia
  in the Age of Franklin*. 1942. Reprint. New York, 1965.

The place of classical history and literature in the thinking of eighteenth-century Americans is set forth by an expert classicist:

GUMMERE, RICHARD M. *The American Colonial Mind and the Classical Tradition: Essays in Comparative Culture.* Cambridge, Mass., 1963.

——. *Seven Wise Men of Colonial America.* Cambridge, Mass., 1967.

A discussion of the American literature being read by the colonists at midcentury is found in

WROTH, LAWRENCE C. *An American Bookshelf, 1755.* Philadelphia, 1934.

The following is a list of helpful biographies of leading figures dealt with in this chapter:

CLARKIN, WILLIAM. *Serene Patriot: A Life of George Wythe.* Albany, 1970.

MALONE, DUMAS. *Jefferson and His Time.* 5 vols. to date. Boston, 1948–.

PETERSON, MERRILL D. *Thomas Jefferson and the New Nation: A Biography.* New York, 1970.

SMITH, PAGE. *John Adams.* 2 vols. New York, 1962.

TOLLES, FREDERICK B. *James Logan and the Culture of Provincial America.* Boston, 1957.

VAN DOREN, CARL C. *Benjamin Franklin.* New York, 1938.

Chapter Two

HINDLE, BROOKE. *The Pursuit of Science in Revolutionary America, 1735–1789.* Chapel Hill, N. C., 1956.
Developments in the American colonies in the period of rapid growth of interest in science is set forth with skill.

STEARNS, RAYMOND PHINEAS. *Science in the British Colonies of America.* Urbana, Ill., 1970.
Setting forth developments in a much broader time frame, Stearns depends heavily on Hindle where their works overlap. A work of depth and great interest.

BOORSTIN, DANIEL J. *The Lost World of Thomas Jefferson.* 1948. Reprint. Boston, 1960.
Traces the development of a "Jeffersonian circle" of scientists and the influence each had on the others.

COHEN, I. BERNARD. *Franklin and Newton: An Inquiry into Speculative*

Newtonian Experimental Science and Franklin's Work in Electricity as an Example Thereof. Philadelphia, 1956.

Biographies:

BERKELEY, EDMUND, and DOROTHY SMITH BERKELEY. *Dr. Alexander Garden of Charles Town.* Chapel Hill, N. C., 1969.

EARNEST, ERNEST. *John and William Bartram: Botanists and Explorers.* Philadelphia, 1940.

HERBST, JOSEPHINE. *New Green World.* New York, 1954.
  A biography of John Bartram.

HINDLE, BROOKE. *David Rittenhouse.* Princeton, 1964.

KEYS, ALICE M. *Cadwallader Colden: A Representative Eighteenth Century Official.* New York, 1906.

Chapters Three and Four

Since the questions dealt with in these two chapters are so closely related, books for suggested reading are treated together here.

BAILYN, BERNARD. *Ideological Origins of the American Revolution.* Cambridge, Mass., 1967.

A work that grew out of his editing of the pamphlet volume listed below. Bailyn has isolated the main threads of the argument between the colonies and the mother country as they appeared in the tracts of the pre-Revolutionary period.

COLBOURN, H. TREVOR. *The Lamp of Experience: Whig History and the Intellectual Origins of the American Revolution.* Chapel Hill, N. C., 1965.

A study of the history books read by the American colonists and how they constructed their case against Britain with the help of Whig historiography. Includes lists of historical works in libraries of colleges, towns, etc.

POLE, J. R. *Political Representation in England and the Origins of the American Republic.* New York, 1966.

A comparative study which traces the development of the ideology of representative government and how it was implemented both in England and in the American states.

ROSSITER, CLINTON. *Seedtime of the Republic: The Origin of the American Tradition of Political Liberty.* New York, 1953.

A rambling but stimulating discussion of the issues leading to the Revolution, with chapters devoted to a selection of important, representative, thinkers.

WOOD, GORDON. *The Creation of the American Republic, 1776–1787.* Chapel Hill, N. C., 1969.

An exhaustive consideration of the ideology of American republicanism. Excellently conceived and executed.

The following works deal specifically with the Declaration:

BECKER, CARL L. *The Declaration of Independence: A Study in the History of Political Ideas.* 1922. Reprint. New York, 1942.

HAWKE, DAVID. *A Transaction of Free Men: The Birth and Course of the Declaration of Independence.* New York, 1964.

Becker deals primarily with the text and the ideas which were incorporated therein. Hawke approaches his study through the developing careers of Adams and Jefferson and their convergence in Philadelphia.

The following series of primary works, not listed above, is central to any consideration of the American Revolution and the formation of the Constitution of 1787:

BAILYN, BERNARD, ed. *Pamphlets of the American Revolution, 1750–1776.* [The first volume of a projected series.] Cambridge, Mass., 1965–.

FARRAND, MAX, ed. *The Records of the Federal Convention of 1787.* 3 vols. New Haven, 1911.

MADISON, JAMES. *Notes of Debates in the Federal Convention of 1787.* Athens, Ohio, 1966.

Madison's version of what happened. "The Father of the Constitution" kept the most extensive journal of the debates. His notes and those of other participants are included in Farrand above, along with correspondence, etc.

HAMILTON, ALEXANDER-MADISON, JAMES-JAY, JOHN. The *Federalist.* Edited by Jacob E. Cooke. Middletown, Conn., 1961.

The classic apologia for the Constitution. The editor assigns the disputed papers among the three and gives reasons for doing so.

There are many useful studies of the convention which drafted the Constitution. Three of the best are the following:

FARRAND, MAX. *The Framing of the Constitution of the United States.* 1913; Reprint. New Haven, 1967.

ROSSITER, CLINTON. *1787: The Grand Convention.* New York, 1966.

VAN DOREN, CARL. *The Great Rehearsal: The Study of the Making and Ratifying of the Constitution of the United States.* New York, 1948.

Biographies:

ALDRIDGE, ALFRED OWEN. *Man of Reason: The Life of Thomas Paine.* London, 1960.

BRANT, IRVING. *The Fourth President: A Life of James Madison.* In-
dianapolis, 1970.
   A condensation of his six-volume biography.
HAWKE, DAVID. *Benjamin Rush, Revolutionary Gadfly.* Indianapolis,
1971.
HILL, HELEN. *George Mason: Constitutionalist.* 1938. Reprint. Glouces-
ter, Mass., 1966.
KETCHAM, RALPH. *James Madison: A Biography.* New York, 1971.
KOCH, ADRIENNE. *Jefferson and Madison: The Great Collaboration.*
1950; Reprint. New York, 1964.

Chapter Five

Two well-established works tracing the rise and influence of Deism in
American life are:
KOCH. G ADOLF. *Republican Religion: The American Revolution and the
Cult of Reason.* 1933. Reprint. Gloucester, Mass., 1964.
MORAIS, HERBERT. *Deism in Eighteenth Century America.* 1934. Re-
print. New York, 1960.

Still the best treatment of the life of that frontier hero and disturber of
the peace is
PELL, JOHN. *Ethan Allen.* Boston, 1929.

A discussion of the development of Jefferson's religious views is in-
cluded in
KOCH, ADRIENNE. *The Philosophy of Thomas Jefferson.* 1943. Reprint.
Chicago, 1964.

The orthodox Christian viewpoint is developed at length in
HEIMERT, ALAN. *Religion and the American Mind: From the Great
Awakening to the Revolution.* Cambridge, Mass., 1966.

For the development of the liberal movements within Christianity, see
the following:
AKERS, CHARLES W. *Called Unto Liberty: A Life of Jonathan Mayhew,
1720–1766.* Cambridge, Mass., 1964.
CASSARA, ERNEST. *Hosea Ballou: The Challenge to Orthodoxy.* Boston,
1961.
WRIGHT, CONRAD. *The Beginnings of Unitarianism in America.* Boston,
1955.

Chapter Six

CABELL, NATHANIEL FRANCIS. *The Early History of the University of Virginia as contained in the Letters of Thomas Jefferson and Joseph C. Cabell*. Richmond, 1856.
A valuable exchange of letters between Jefferson and his cohort in the legislature. Appendix includes the Report of the Commissioners appointed to Fix the Site of the University of Virginia which sets forth in detail Jefferson's thinking on the ideal university curriculum.

HONEYWELL, ROY JOHN. *The Educational Work of Thomas Jefferson*. 1931. Reprint. New York, 1964.
An able explanation of Jefferson's comprehensive ideas on education. Appendix includes A Bill for the More General Diffusion of Knowledge, etc.

RUDOLPH, FREDERICK, ed. *Essays on Education in the Early Republic*. Cambridge, Mass., 1965.
A valuable collection of tracts by Rush, Webster, and others.

Biographies:
LEMAY, JOSEPH A. LEO. *Ebenezer Kinnersley, Franklin's Friend*. Philadelphia, 1964.
A slim volume but one which covers adquately Kinnersley's career as a popularizer of the new views of electricity.
MALONE, DUMAS. *The Public Life of Thomas Cooper, 1783–1839*. 1926. Reprint. Columbia, S. C., 1961.

The career of the stormy petrel from his early years of radicalism in England and France to his late years as a proponent of states' rights.

Index

Adams, John, 24, 29-30, 82, 94; believes American Revolution accomplished before the war, 165-166; on class structure, 113-14; influence of classics on, 42; on constitutions of the new states, 95; on Thomas Cooper, 158; includes support of education in Massachusetts Constitution, 162; on the eighteenth century, 15; on annual elections, 96; on equality, 83-84; on Franklin, 98; Franklin's opinion of, 98; on human nature, 99; corresponds with Jefferson, 23, 114-15; political disagreements with Jefferson, 114; on Jefferson's resignation as Secretary of State, 111; on establishment of learned society in Boston, 148; on dangers of luxury to a republic, 170; labeled monarchist, 112; on Paine, 97-98; challenges Parliament's authority over colonies, 72; on need for strong political institutions, 112-13; on his study of politics and war, 93; elected president, 114; on presidency as "limited monarchy," 112; on terms of respect for president, 86; and Joseph Priestley, 19; religious beliefs of, 126; self-doubts of, 34; on separation of powers, 97-100; on virtue, 171; *Defence of the Constitutions of Government of the United States, A*, 37, 83, 98-100, 102, 104, 108; *Novanglus*, 72; *Thoughts on Government*, 96

Adams, John Quincy, 37, 83; on government support of education, 162; on improvement of mankind, 169

Adams, Samuel, 94, 112

Addison, Joseph: *Guardian, The*, 42; *Spectator, The*, 42-44; *Tatler, The*, 42

Alien and Sedition Acts, 114, 158

Allen, Ethan: Jeremy Belknap on, 129; on Jesus, 134; military career, 128-29; Washington on, 129; *Narrative of Colonel Ethan Allen's Captivity, A*, 129; *Reason the Only Oracle of Man*, 129-32, 140

American Academy of Arts and Sciences: established, 148

American Philosophical Society, 66; established, 146; declares science transcends national differences, 147; *Transactions*, 146-47

American Revolution, 21; in education, 165-67; justification of, 17-18

Ames, Nathaniel, 150

Anglican Church: in New York, 123; in Virginia, 119

Articles of Confederation, 89; provisions of, 102-103

Atonement: doctrine of, 16-17; Ethan Allen on, 131

Ballou, Hosea: on Universalism, 140-41; *Treatise on Atonement, A*, 140

Baptists, 118

Bartram, John, 20-21, 26, 50, 65, 146; on first interest in botany, 53, 176n9; botanical explorations in New York, 53; establishes botanical garden, 53-54; appointed Royal Botanist, 54; publishes catalogue of work, 57; on Colden, 54; Linnaeus on, 54; on his religious beliefs, 128; *Observations on Travels from Penn-*

silvania to Onandaga, Oswego and Lake Ontario, 53
Bartram, John (son), 54
Bartram, Moses, 147
Bartram, William, 21; influences poetry of Coleridge and Wordsworth, 54; *Travels through North & South Carolina, Georgia, East & West Florida,* 54
Benezet, Anthony, 87
Bernard, Francis, 60
Biddle, Owen, 94; on advancement of science, 49; in observation of Transit of Venus, 59
Bill of Rights, 22; advocated by Jefferson and Mason, 108; prohibits establishment of religion, 22, 109, 124; influenced by Virginia Declaration of Rights, 76. *See also* Constitution of the United States *and* Constitutional Convention
Bowdoin, James, 60, 62; on role of American Academy of Arts and Sciences, 148
Buffon, Count George Louis Leclerc de: on animal life in America, 56; *Natural History,* 56
Burke, Edmund: prevents publication of Paine's *Rights of Man,* Part 2, 80; *Reflections on the Revolution in France,* 77, 78, 79, 80

Chalmers, Lionel, 147
Channing, William Ellery, 141
Chauncy, Charles, 60; opposes Great Awakening, 136-37; theology of, 137; on Universalism, 138-39; *Salvation of All Men, The,* 139
Christianity: theology of, 15, 16-17
Church of England, *See* Anglican Church
Cincinnati, Society of the, 85-86
Cincinnatus: American view of, 30
Classics: in America, 41-42, 162-63. *See also* Education *and* Literature
Colden, Cadwallader, 18, 20, 62; publishes catalogue of work, 57; builds "Coldengham," 29; corresponds with Douglass, 51-52; advises

Franklin on site of college, 152; corresponds with Franklin, 52; on intellectual cultivation, 31; proposes learned society, 146; work recognized by Linnaeus, 54; corresponds with Logan, 52; a Loyalist, 66, 67; on the free mind, 31-32, 118; on pleasures of nature, 29; on scientific pursuits, 29; on women in botany, 55; *Explication of the First Causes of Action in Matter, An,* 65-66; *History of the Five Indian Nations, The,* 169-70
Colden, Jane: botanical studies of, 55
Collinson, Peter, 26, 62; publishes Franklin's papers on electricity, 62; influences science in America, 51
Congregational churches, 122-23, 137
Connecticut: established church of, 122-23
Constitution of the United States, 22; *The Federalist* on, 110-11; provisions of, 104-107; ratification of, 109; separation of powers in, 102, 107; prohibits importation of slaves, 89. *See also* Bill of Rights *and* Constitutional Convention
Constitutional Convention: proceedings of, 104-107, 108; on slavery, 88-89, 90. *See also* Bill of Rights *and* Constitution of the United States
Cooper, Thomas: John Adams on, 158; at Columbia College (S.C.), 159; at Dickinson College, 159; on educational standards, 160; removed from Pennsylvania judiciary, 158-59; at University of Pennsylvania, 159; jailed under Sedition Law, 158; prevented from joining University of Virginia, 159
Copernicus, Nicolaus, 32; cosmology of, 15-16
Crèvecoeur, J. Hector St. John de, 21; on Bartram's discovery of botany, 53; *Letters from an American Farmer,* 21, 53

Declaration of the Rights of Man: influence of the Virginia Declaration of Rights on, 75, 179n21

Deism, 22, 34, 124-35, 141, 142-43

Dickinson, John: on natural rights, 69; *Framer's Letters to the Inhabitants of the British Colonies, The,* 28-29

Dickinson College, 159, 160

Douglass, William, 20, 29, 146; corresponds with Colden, 51-52; corresponds with Franklin, 52, contributes to James Franklin's *New England Courant,* 52; sceintific investigations of, 52

Dutch Reformed Church: in New York, 123

Education, 152-67; classics in, 41-42; in Enlightenment, 37-38, 145; history in, 164-67; religion in, 163-64; and public virtue, 166

Edwards, Jonathan: and the Great Awakening, 136-37

Elections: frequency of, 95-97

Empiricism: in Enlightenment, 16, 49, 52

Episcopal Church. *See* Anglican Church

Equality: in Declaration of Independence, 17; John Adams and Jefferson on, 83-84; Mason on, 96

Euler, Leonhard, 66

Evans, Lewis, 53, 65

Fauquier, Francis, 28

Franklin, Benjamin, 29, 31, 59; proposes Philadelphia academy, 152-53; on John Adams, 98; John Adams's opinion of, 98; proposes American Philosophical Society, 146; invents bifocals, 64; ridicules Society of the Cincinnati, 86; corresponds with Colden, 52; on Colden's *First Causes of Action in Matter,* 65; on Colden's *History of the Five Indian Nations,* 169; "plan of conduct" of, 44-47; at Constitutional Convention, 105, 107; corresponds with Douglass, 52; education of, 34; experiments in electricity, 61-63; es-

teemed in Europe, 67; frugality of, 44-45; on study of history, 164; on human felicity, 63-64; criticized for publication of Hutchinson letters, 36; advises Jefferson on drafting papers for public bodies, 80-81; forms Junto, 27; encourages Kinnersley to lecture on electricity, 148-49; on Latin and modern languages, 42; forms subscription library, 161-62; invents lightning rod, 63; Logan on, 26; manipulation of public by, 35-36; on "moral algebra," 48; influenced by Cotton Mather, 27-34; on natural law, 50; encourages Paine to emigrate to America, 19; moves to Philadelphia, 26; on progress, 171; on limits of reason, 33; on religion in proposed academy, 163-64; supports clause on freedom of religion in Pennsylvania Constitution, 123; religious beliefs of, 34-35, 124-26; against slavery, 89-90; on Smith as enemy, 153; has illegitimate son, 47; influenced by *Spectator,* 43-44; invents new type stove, 64-65; improves street lights, 64; on titles, 85; Turgot on, 67; vegetarian, 33; virtue in life of, 44-47; on education of women, 161; *Account of the New Invented Pennsylvania Fire-Places, An,* 64-65; *Autobiography,* 34, 35, 44-45, 161; *Experiments and Observations on Electricity,* 62; *On the Slave Trade,* 90; *Pennsylvania Gazette,* 151-52; *Poor Richard's Almanac,* 44, 150-51; *Proposals for the Education of Youth in Pennsylvania,* 152, 163-64; "Silence Dogood Papers," 43

Franklin, William: a Loyalist, 67

Freneau, Philip: Deism in poetry of, 142; on popularity of Paine's *Age of Reason,* 133

Friends, Society of: antislavery in, 87; Hicksite, 141-42

Galilei, Galileo, 15, 31, 32

Garden, Alexander, 20; on meeting
Bartram, 54-55; biological investigations of, 52; Linnaeus names "Gardenia" for, 55; a Loyalist, 67;
zoological explorations of, 55-56

George III, King, 94; appoints Bartram
Royal Botanist, 54; opposes
Franklin's pointed lightning rods,
150; declares American subjects in
rebellion, 93

Gerry, Elbridge, 108

God: benevolence of, 16-17; natural
rights from, 17; nature as handiwork of, 16; man's reason from, 16;
in universe, 15

Godfrey, Thomas: invents seaman's
quadrant, 26

Great Awakening, 135-38

Great Britain: policy toward colonies,
18

Hamilton, Alexander: on blacks, 91; for
centralized government, 111; on
slaves in Revolutionary army, 88;
Federalist Papers, The, 22, 110-11

Harvard College: influence of Deism
on, 142-43

Henry, Patrick: proposes tax support of
clergy in Virginia, 120

Hicks, Elias, 141-42

History: cyclical view of, 169-71; in
education, 164-66; Jefferson recommends books on, 39, 40; progress in, 171-72

Hollingsworth, Henry, 146-47

Hopkinson, Francis, 31, 142; emulates
Spectator, 44; writings of, 44; "Over
the hills far away," 44

Hutchinson, Thomas, 36, 150

Jay, John: *Federalist Papers, The*, 22,
110-11

Jefferson, Thomas, 29-30; corresponds
with John Adams, 23, 114-15; political disagreements with John
Adams, 114; on Alien and Sedition
Acts, 114; president of American
Philosophical Society, 147; on "aristocracy of virtue and talent," 82-84;
on abilities of blacks, 91; on colonization of blacks, 91-92; refutes Buffon on animal life in America, 56;
on separation of church and state in
Virginia, 119-20; on Society of the
Cincinnati, 85; influence of classics
on, 42; cirticizes draft of U.S. Constitution, 108; drafts constitution for
Virginia, 101-102; on the Virginia
Constitution, 100-101; On Thomas
Cooper, 158; drafts Declaration of
Independence, 75-76, 87-88; democratic tendencies of, 114; on proposed dictatorship in Virginia, 96-97;
education of, 27-28; on Bible in
education, 163; on history in education, 165; advises nephew on education, 40-41; on need of education in
republic, 145; plans universal education in Virginia, 153-55; on
Europe, 21, 30-31; on ignorance of
common people in Europe, 154; on
exercise, 41; on fiction, 38-39; opposes centralized government, 111;
on study of history as antidote to
tyranny, 165; on honesty, 47-48; on
Lord Kames, 40; on languages, 40;
on ideal library, 38-41; proposes
public libraries, 161; on free mind,
31, 32; on perfectibility of human
mind, 171-172; on Missouri Compromise, 92; on monarchical tendencies, 113; on education for morality, 48; love of music, 28; on
natural rights, 71-72; on Plato, 39,
40; invents moldboard plow, 147-
48; on Presbyterian intolerance,
159; elected president, 114; and
Preistley, 19, 30; opposes primogeniture and entail, 81-82; on re-
bellions, 104; on freedom of religion, 118, 119; religious beliefs of,
126-28; proposes Act for Establishing Religious Freedom, 119-120;
121-122; on Paine's *Rights of Man*,
113; on rights of man, 68, 71-72;
resigns as Secretary of State, 111;
on American self-sufficiency, 47;
opposes slavery, 87-88, 90-91, 92,

180n65; on William Small, 27; on rational society, 25; on the *Spectator*, 43; on Stoics, 39, 40; versatility of, 28; recodifies Virginia law, 81; founds University of Virginia, 157-60; on legislature's support of University of Virginia, 159-60; not influenced by Voltaire, 40; "Life and Morals of Jesus of Nazareth, The" ("The Jefferson Bible"), 127; *Notes on the State of Virginia,* 20, 56-57, 90-91, 96-97, 100, 127, 147; *Summary View of the Rights of British America, A,* 71-72, 87

Kalm, Peter: tours American colonies, 51

Kentucky, 143; education in, 156

Kinnersley, Ebenezer: lectures on electricity, 149-50; opposes Great Awakening, 136, 148-49; Priestley on, 149

Library Company, 161-62

Linnaeus, Carolus, 20-21, 57; corresponds with American scientists, 51; on Bartram, 54; names genus for Colden, 54; names "Gardenia" for Garden, 55; believes swallows hibernate under water, 49

Literature: in Enlightenment, 38-44; Jefferson on, 38-42. *See also* Classics

Livingston, Robert R.: on Articles of Confederation, 103-104; religious views of, 142, 143-44

Locke, John: influences American political thought, 68-69, 76; psychology of, 16; on social contract, 68; *Essay on Human Understanding, An,* 16; *Second Treatise on Civil Government,* 76

Logan, James: aids Bartram, 52, 53; translates Cicero, 26; corresponds with Colden, 52; on Franklin, 26; on limits of reason, 32-33; encourages scientific investigations, 26; scientific studies of, 52

Maclay, William: opposes John Adams on terms of respect for president, 86

Madison, James, 30; works for Bill of Rights, 124; on colonization of blacks, 92; opposes public support of chaplains in House of Representatives, 122; campaigns for separation of church and state in Virginia, 120-22; on Constitution, 105; prepares for Constitutional Convention, 37; on importance of education, 156; on political factions, 109-11; opposes religious observance by government, 122; influenced by *Spectator,* 43; a commissioner of University of Virginia, 172; *Federalist Papers, The,* 22, 110-11; *Memorial and Remonstrance on the Religious Rights of Man, A,* 120-21

Mason, George, 81, 126, 142; opposes aristocracy in Virginia, 82; proposes Bill of Rights at Constitutional Convention, 108-109; influences Declaration of Independence, 75-76; drafts Virginia Declaration of Rights, 75, 76, 179n21; on annual elections, 95-96; opposes slavery at Constitutional Convention, 88-89, 90

Massachusetts: established church of, 122-23; constitution of, 99-100

Mather, Cotton: influences Franklin, 27, 34; *Bonifacius: An Essay upon the Good,* 34

Mayhew, Jonathan, 60; theology of, 137

Meade, William: on state of religion in Virginia, 143

Morgan, John, 147

Murray, John: Universalist views of, 140

Natural law: Franklin on, 50; established by God, 50; and natural rights, 69-70; in universe, 69, 117

Natural rights: and American Revolution, 21, 70-72; in Declaration of Independence and Virginia Declaration of Rights, 76; Dickinson on, 69;

Jefferson on, 71-72; and natural law, 69-70; Otis on, 70-71; in Paine's *Rights of Man*, 77-80. *See also* Rights of man

Nature, 16, 29

New York: in eighteenth century, 25; freedom of religion in, 123

Northwest Ordinance of 1787; freedom of religion in, 123; provides for separation of powers, 102; prohibits slavery, 89

Optimism: in eighteenth century, 17; in Jefferson's thought, 172

Original sin, 16; Allen on, 130. *See also* Christianity

Orrery, 58

Otis, James: on natural rights, 70-71; 178n5; *Rights of the British Colonies Asserted and Proved, The*, 70, 178n5

Page, John, 148

Paine, Thomas, 20, 113; emigrates to America, 19; refutes Edmund Burke on French Revolution, 77; on classical education, 41; and French Revolution, 19; influences Harvard and Yale students, 142-43; on Jesus, 134; on freedom of religion, 116, 118; charged with sedition in England, 80; on titles, 84-85; *Age of Reason, The*, 19, 132-33; *Common Sense*, 19, 73-75, 77, 80; *Crisis Papers, The*, 19, 77; *Rights of Man, The*, 77-80

Palmer, Elihu: on American Revolution and man's moral condition, 166; propagates Deism, 133-34, 142; on Jesus, 134-35; *Principles of Nature*, 134-135

Pendleton, Edmund, 81; desires to maintain primogeniture, 82

Pennsylvania: Constitution of 1776, 97, 98; freedom of religion in, 123

Philadelphia: in eighteenth century, 25

Pickering, Timothy: on Priestley and Cooper, 158

Presbyterians: in New York, 123; in Virginia, 119

Presidency of the United States, 106; John Adams on, 112; debate over terms of respect for, 86

Price, Richard, 79; on American state constitutions, 97; defends French Revolution, 78

Priestley, Joseph, 48, 80, 124-25, 127, 147, 158; warned by John Adams, 19; emigrates to Pennsylvania, 19, 30; supports Jeffersonian Republicans, 19; theology of, 138, 142; *History and Present State of Electricity, The*, 149

Prince, Thomas: *Earthquakes the Works of God and Tokens of His Just Displeasure*, 60-61

Progress: idea of, 17, 171-72

Ptolemaeus, Claudius: cosmology of, 15

Puritanism, 118, 135-36

Quakers. *See* Freinds, Society of

Randolph, Edmund, 108, 142

Reason: in Enlightenment, 33; limits of, 32-33; in man's life, 16; and progress, 17; in religion, 22

Revolution, 17-18. *See also* American Revolution

Rhode Island: freedom of religion in, 123

Rights of man, 17, 77. *See also* Natural rights

Rittenhouse, David, 31, 98, 147; ignorant of classics, 41; makes clocks and instruments, 57-58; education of, 57; builds Orrery, 58, 177n29; on his republicanism, 94; observes Transit of Venus, 58-59

Royal Society of London: American members of, 51; chartered, 50-51; *Philosophical Transactions*, 51, 62

Rush, Benjamin, 98; reunites John Adams and Jefferson, 114; on influence of John Adams's *Defence of the Constitutions*, 104; on plasticity of America, 145; believes American Revolution ongoing, 165; on blacks, 91; on classics in education, 41,

163; on problems of the Confederation, 103; on Constitutional Convention, 105; on history in education, 164-65; on plan of education for Pennsylvania, 156-57, 160-61; on religion in education, 164; on education for republican government, 166, 167; on perfecting new forms of government, 95; proposes public libraries, 161; on Paine's *Age of Reason*, 133; inspires Paine's *Common Sense*, 74; becomes republican, 94; theology of, 139, 142; *Address to the Inhabitants of the British Settlements in America, upon Slave-Keeping, An*, 87; *Plan for the Establishment of Public Schools . . .in Pennsylvania, A*, 156-57

Science: in America, 66; Biddle on gradual advancement of, 49; and progress, 17; propagation of, 146-50
Separation of powers, 97; John Adams on, 97-100; Jefferson on, 100-102; in U.S. Constitution, 102, 107; in Northwest Ordinance, 102
Shays's Rebellion, 103
Slavery: campaigns for abolition of, 86-92
Small, William, 27-28
Smith, William (New York): on religious freedom in New York, 123
Smith, William (Philadelphia), 138; provost of Philadelphia Academy, 153; opposes Franklin, 153; observes Transit of Venus, 59
Social contract, 17-18; in American experience, 72-73; and Declaration of Independence, 17; Mason on, 96; Paine on, 78-79; and revolution, 17-18
Spectator, The. See Addison, Joseph
Steele, Richard. *See* Addison, Joseph
Sterne, Laurence: Jefferson on, 39; *Sentimental Journey, A*, 39

Taylor, John (of Caroline), 84; on use of religion for foul ends, 118
Turgot, Anne Robert Jacques: on American state constitutions, 97; on Franklin, 67

Unitarians, 126, 137-38; contrasted with Universalists, 141
Universalists, 138-41; contrasted with Unitarians, 141

Vermont: separates church and state, 123
Virginia: Anglican Church in, 119; separates church and state, 119-22; Declaration of Rights, 75, 76, 119, 120, 179n21; recodification of law of, 81-83; Presbyterian dissenters in, 119; Society for Promoting Useful Knowledge, 148
Virginia, University of: Jefferson founds, 157-60; plan of education for, 172
Virtue: in Enlightenment, 18, 44-48; in life of Franklin, 44-47; and survival of republic, 166-67, 170-71
Voltaire, François Marie Arouet de: has no influence on Jefferson, 40; believes in "jumar," 49

Warren, John: on virtue and survival of republican government, 170-71
Washington, George: 126, 142; on Ethan Allen, 129; presides at Constitutional Convention, 105; influenced by Paine's *Common Sense*, 19, 73; on political factions, 109; and Society of the Cincinnati, 85
Webster, Noah: on classics and utilitarian subjects in education, 163; on history in education, 165; on education for republican government, 166-67
Wedderburn, Alexander, 36, 150
Whitefield, George, 126, 152-53; in Great Awakening, 136-37; on religion in Franklin's proposed academy, 163
William and Mary, College of, 27-28, 155; influence of Deism on, 143
Winchester, Elhanan: Universalist views of, 139-40

Winthrop, John (Governor): *Model of Christian Charity, A,* 21

Winthrop, John (Professor), 57, 62; assists Chauncy in development of Universalist ideas, 139; on earthquakes as natural phenomena, 50, 61; supports Franklin's views on electricity, 61; elected professor at Harvard, 59-60; on role of science, 61; observes Transit of Venus, 60; *Lecture on Earthquakes,* 61; *Letter to the Publishers of the* Boston Gazette. . .*Containing an Answer to the Rev. Mr. Prince's Letter,* 61;

Two Lectures on Comets, 61

Wise, John: on democracy of Congregational churches, 69-70; *Vindication of the Government of the New-England Churches, A,* 70

Woolman, John, 87

Wythe, George, 81, 96, 142, 154; and Jefferson, 28; supports Jefferson on rights of Americans, 72

Yale College: influence of Deism on, 142-43

Young, Thomas: introduces Ethan Allen to Deism, 129